From Bondage to Blessing

*The Redemption, Restoration and
Release of God's Women*

Dee Alei

Sovereign World

Sovereign World Ltd
PO Box 777
Tonbridge
Kent TN11 0ZS
England

ISBN 1 85240 309 8

The publishers aim to produce books which will help to extend and build up the Kingdom of God. We do not necessarily agree with every view expressed by the author, or with every interpretation of Scripture expressed. We expect each reader to make his/her judgment in the light of their own understanding of God's Word and in an attitude of Christian love and fellowship.

Cover design by CCD, www.ccdgroup.co.uk
Typeset by CRB Associates, Reepham, Norfolk.
Printed in the United States of America.

Contents

About the Author

Dee Alei has worked in team ministry alongside her husband, Dave, for the past 11 years. She is an ordained minister, a pastor, counselor and teacher of the Word who longs to see individuals equipped and released to fulfill the plan and destiny God has for their lives. With a special place in her heart for the broken and the hurting, Dee endeavors to bring encouragement and vision to those who feel hopeless and disqualified. She is involved with an apostolic work in the northeast of England and currently resides there with Dave and their two children, Lauren and Justin. In *From Bondage to Blessing*, Dee writes with a prophetic anointing that brings fresh insight and an impartation of life to the study of women's roles in the Church. Her fervent prayer is that the entire Body of Christ might *arise* and step into that place of intimacy and authority that the Lord purposed for His Church from before the foundation of the world.

website: www.alei-lifeline.com

Acknowledgements

In every undertaking, the end result is often an amalgamation of the insight, impartation and involvement of many people. I would like to take this opportunity to acknowledge the contribution of those who helped make this book a reality:

☐ To my husband Dave, and to Lauren and Justin, I say a big thank you for encouraging me in this endeavor and for sacrificing time with me as I plodded away researching and writing. Dave, thanks for your priceless input and unfailing love and support. I am truly honored to be your teammate!

☐ To Fuchsia Pickett, thank you for your impartation into my life and for demonstrating to me what it really means to be a woman of God. Your life is a testimony of how God's grace and power can bring change to the Body of Christ through a humble, yielded woman.

☐ To Tim Pettingale, CEO at Sovereign World, thanks for combining enthusiasm and warmth with professionalism and integrity. It has been a blessing to work with you on this project.

☐ To Dee and Wendell Seitz, who allowed me to "hide out" at their Texas farm to finish the manuscript – what servant hearts you have! I'm not sure I'd be finished yet without your help!

☐ To the LWCC gang from Los Alamos, thank you for your love, friendship, support and grace as I first stepped into

pastoring and began the process of learning what it is all
about. Thanks for teaching me the reality of how this is
all supposed to work, giving me a vision of what the Body
of Christ can be.

☐ To the students of the NRMTC and members of Lifeline
Christian Fellowship in England, I extend thanks to one
and all for your continued encouragement and blessing. I
pray this book will facilitate the release of greater vision,
strengthening and freedom as the Lord works in our midst.

☐ Finally, to Jesus – my love, my friend, my Lord – thank you
for Your unconditional love, for picking me up and dusting
me off when I slip and miss the mark, and for Your
faithfulness to complete the work You have begun in my
life. This book is dedicated to You and to Your precious
Body. May we increasingly discover and embrace Your
mind and heart in these last days.

Foreword

Seldom does a professor, teacher or instructor witness one of their students *become* in person, "the truth" they have pursued. Dee Alei has devoted herself to the pursuit of what God's Word really teaches about His eternal purposes for women and their role in establishing His Kingdom. As her search uncovered the truth, the revelation of God's Word became a reality to her. In this book she peels away the layers of prejudice created by religion, custom, tradition, and denominationalism, all of which have only brought bondage and confusion to the Body of Christ. I believe this book accurately reveals God's mind, heart, will and purposes for women.

I have read, studied, searched and listened to many share and teach on the subject of women in ministry, but I have not found anyone who has exceeded Dee Alei's writings in addressing the issue, enabling us to find the truth about women direct from the heart of God.

Dr. Fuchsia Pickett

Chapter 1

A Symphony of Discordant Notes

"Even things without life, whether flute or harp,
when they make a sound, unless they make a distinction in
the sounds, how will it be known what is piped or played?
For if the trumpet makes an uncertain sound,
who will prepare for battle?"
(1 Corinthians 14:7–8)

I vividly remember my first introduction to the confusion surrounding the issue of women in positions of ministry or authority in the Church. My husband Dave and I had been pastoring a local church for several years as licensed ministers and were both submitting applications for ordination to one of the networks functioning as a covering for us. Included with our applications were to be several letters of recommendation from other church leaders and pastors with whom we had worked. We decided to ask a local denominational pastor who had known us for a number of years. He was perfectly willing to write a letter of recommendation for both of us. However, his comments took us by surprise! He told us that while his denomination allowed women to function in church leadership, they "didn't believe in" ordaining them. In other words, women could do the work, but they couldn't be *officially recognized* as doing the work. Dave and I looked at each other and wondered, "What sort of double talk is this?" not realizing that in the coming years we would find the disparity even worse than we imagined.

The issue heats up in the Church

The gender issue, or "the woman question" as it is often called, has become more prominent in the Church in recent years due to particular developments within western culture which arose in the 1960s and 70s. The advance of the women's liberation movement and the dramatic increase in numbers of women seeking involvement in ministry were *catalysts* which initiated a new uncertainty in theological circles. As a result, theologians, church leaders and saints within the Body of Christ were prompted to question in a fresh way the theology behind traditional views of gender roles and the place of women in the Church. Although these developments have initially created much controversy and confusion within the Church, I believe they can challenge us to a place of greater openness, honesty and objectivity in our interpretation of the Scriptures. Let's look at them more closely.

Women's lib

When radical feminism began to raise its strident voice, it muddied the real issues that we face in the Church. "What does the Bible really say? What is God's heart and mind on women in leadership, and what are His eternal purposes for women?" are the questions Christians needed to be asking. The loudest voices in the feminist movement were often those who were the most hurt, and they spoke angrily out of that hurt. Many determined that the movement was merely a great deal of emotionalism and rhetoric spewed out by angry, bitter, man-hating women. This was not just the male viewpoint either. As a young woman watching with interest from the sidelines, I have to confess this was my conclusion as well! To a great degree it was probably true. But, sadly, such assessments began to color our perception of *anyone* who questioned the "traditional" interpretation of the Scriptures regarding authority, headship and women's roles, or who presented evidence contrary to this traditional interpretation.

The radical feminist movement adapted much of its philosophy from humanistic sources, Greek mythology, hedonism, fertility cults and goddess worship.[1] For this reason, many Christians began to view *any* defense of women in ministry as a feminist challenge to biblical authority, even if those raising the questions were scholars or leaders equally as committed to biblical authority.

Those who, in recent years, have presented evidence that questions the accuracy of the traditional interpretation of Scripture regarding women have been labeled as feminists or accused of giving in to their influence. Because most people are unaware of the wealth of scholarship available which *predates* the feminist movement (from as early as the seventeenth century [2]), they assume that such ideas are "new" and a product of this secular movement. The result has been that many in the modern Church have never bothered to prayerfully consider the validity of such studies or the weight of the evidence presented.

In some cases, the Church has gone *beyond* ignoring those who would raise questions to actually attacking them. For example, the April 1989 issue of *Christianity Today* ran a news story about possible heresy charges facing a Lutheran pastor and professor for his article addressing the role of women in the early Church and possible sexism in the Church today.[3] He was quoted as saying that his intent in writing the article was to "strip away the sexism of the church and get back to the root of how Jesus and the apostles treated women." He continued, "It is my opinion that we are wearing cultural blinders. I wanted to ask the church, 'Do the beliefs we hold reflect the biblical message? And can we divorce ourselves from the centuries of conditioning, set our blinders aside for a minute and look at how our Lord considered the role of women?'." For asking these kinds of questions, this church leader faced formal heresy charges!

Increased numbers of women seeking ministry involvement

The second significant development that has caused the issue of women in ministry to come to the forefront in recent years is that of the changing complexion of the clergy. More and more women are seeking to answer the call of God that they feel is upon their lives. As one Foursquare minister was quoted as saying in a 1996 issue of *Charisma* magazine,

"We are not women who wish to displace men. We are women who simply and humbly ask that we be given room to be obedient to the Lord who called us." [4]

The *Atlanta Journal and Constitution* ran a prominently placed article in August 1989, looking at the flood of women into ministerial training institutions. They showed that between 1976 and 1987, the percentage of women in America's theological schools had doubled. In looking at some of the Atlanta area seminaries, they found that some had extremely high ratios of women studying for the ministry. At Columbia seminary, for example, it was revealed that 42% of the student body was female. They concluded, "in a majority of Protestant denominations, tomorrow's minister is much more likely than ever to be a woman." [5]

This phenomenon has caused the Body of Christ to examine over the past decade the question of women in ministry as never before. Reflecting this flurry of concern, the Council on Biblical Manhood and Womanhood, for example, spent countless dollars running a two-page ad in a 1989 issue of *Christianity Today*. They were seeking support for their "Danvers Statement", which basically affirmed what has been considered the traditional view of women in ministry. [6] As an example of more recent interest and concern, Strang Communications in the United States, publisher of several popular Christian magazines, has featured articles on the woman issue every year since 1995. [7] In recent years, Strang has offered a new magazine called *Spirit Led Woman* to meet the billowing cry among women for validation and greater equipping for ministry.

Even among evangelicals – confusion reigns

With an increased determination within the Body of Christ to re-examine what the Bible has to say about women in ministry, the sound emerging from the evangelical community, in particular, has been one of discordant notes. In other words ... noise!

This lack of harmony has created a great degree of uncertainty and confusion among the many tenderhearted saints who comprise our churches. Is any wonder? Some have been taught that women should not speak in church. Others have been taught that women may pray, even "prophesy" in the church, but may not "teach". Then, of course, there is the common position that women may teach; they just should not teach men ... or they may teach men, but not from behind a pulpit. Or they may preach and teach, but women should hold no "positions of authority" within the church. Some circles even allow women to hold such positions of authority on the mission field (acceptable) but not in the local church (unacceptable). Other groups, such as the denomination with which our pastor friend was affiliated, allow women the liberty to preach, teach or hold positions of authority within the church, but refuse to ordain them. Interestingly enough, *all* of those who hold these differing points of view regarding women in ministry *claim to base their conclusions and teaching on Scripture.* No wonder the saints are confused!

Even Evangelicals with the same commitment to inerrancy of the Scriptures, using similar guidelines for interpretation, frequently arrive at opposing conclusions. Robert K. Johnston, Dean of North Park Theological Seminary in Chicago in the 1980s, pointedly illustrates this fact.

His example reveals contradictory findings by those with similar commitments to biblical authority on a denominational level. These differing conclusions are exhibited by position papers drawn up by the Christian Reformed Church (CRC) and the Evangelical Covenant Church in the mid-80s. The study initiated by the CRC resulted in a report stating that men should exercise primary leadership and direction-setting in the home, church and society in general based upon a "creational norm" recognized in both the Old and New Testament. Their ruling was that women should not be ordained as elders, ministers or evangelists, though it would be permissible to allow them to serve as deacons.

The Board of the Ministry of the Evangelical Covenant Church, however, initiated a similar study, which produced a verdict opposite to that of the Christian Reformed Church. In looking at such things as the book of Genesis, Jesus' actions, the role of women in the early church, Pauline teachings, biblical concepts of authority, and the theology of the priesthood of the believer, they concluded that there is a "legitimate and theological basis for women in ordained ministry".[8]

Why the current state of affairs?

How have we arrived at this confusing place? Let's look at some factors that have contributed to the current state of affairs within the Church regarding our understanding of the role of women and their qualifications for leadership and ministry.

Historically – loss of truth to the Church

By the close of the first century, Christianity had spanned three generations. We can see through a study of the later epistles and the book of Revelation that secular thinking and false teaching were already making inroads into the Church. To get an idea of just how things may have changed by the end of the first century, take a look at the Methodism of today contrasted with the Methodism that existed at the beginning of the twentieth century. There is a noticeable difference!

The deterioration of the spiritual Church, which had been birthed in revelation and supernatural power, actually began by the second century. This deterioration was *significant*, however, after the Roman Emperor Constantine's Edict of Toleration was issued in A.D. 313. At that time, an end was put to the persecution that had so marked the period from A.D. 100 onward. Seventy years later, the emperor Theodosius took things a step further and established Christianity as the state religion of the Roman Empire. All Roman subjects were forced to accept Christianity in order to maintain citizenship, hold office or conduct business.[9] As one Church history text states, "The ceasing of persecution was a blessing, but the establishment of Christianity as the state religion became a curse."[10] Another notes that it was at this point that the military spirit of Imperial Rome entered the Church, causing it to "nose dive into a millennium of dead works, formalism, and slavery to man-made religion."[11] Pagan customs and symbolism began to infiltrate the Church. The old heathen feasts became church festivals. The worship of the images of saints and martyrs began to appear in churches. The adoration and worship of the Virgin Mary was substituted for worship of Venus, Diana and the other goddesses. The "elder" evolved from a preacher into a priest.[12] Spirituality died and selfish ambition took its place. It has been noted that candles, incense, garlands, holy days, and elaborate priestly robes were also brought into the Church at this time.[13]

After about A.D. 500 the deterioration accelerated as the Church entered that period of its history that we call "the Dark Ages". One church historian declares that at this point, the result was no longer Christianity, but "a more or less corrupt *hierarchy* controlling the nations of Europe, making the Church mainly a political machine."[14] One result of the development of this hierarchical institution and ecclesiastical structure was the gradual obstruction of women from leadership and official ministry within the Church.[15] During this time, *many* of the truths that had been foundational to the life and practice of the early Church were lost.

God began a restoration of these lost truths to the Church when He brought a revelation of justification by faith, the authority of Scripture, and the priesthood of the believer to Martin Luther's heart. The result was the Protestant Reformation. However, as Susan Hyatt points out, "How to interject the biblical principle of the priesthood of all believers into a society and ecclesiastical system that rejected the principle of biblical equality of women was problematic."[16] The Reformation did not change church practice to any great degree, but it was a start! What the Lord began through the Reformation, He has continued in the centuries that followed. He has gradually brought an unveiling and restoration of many lost truths back to the Church. These include an understanding of holiness, divine healing, the baptism of the Holy Spirit, and the gifts of the Spirit. It also includes a restored revelation of the spiritual and functional equality of women within the Body of Christ. As we shall see later, the first century church operated out of this revelation. Women participated in leadership as part of early church practice. God has been in a process of restoring this truth to the Church since the time of the Reformation and the process continues today.

The myth of certainty

Another reason the confusion surrounding women's roles in the Church exists is because a great deal of tradition, inference and conjecture has been taught in the Church as cold, hard fact. J.I. Packer, a well-respected evangelical theologian, has concluded that the Scriptures only establish three things with certainty regarding women: (1) men and women are equal before God; (2) man is the "head of the woman" (or at least of his wife), though what this actually means is unclear and (3) Christian spouses are to model the redeeming love/ responsive love relationship of Christ and His Church. Other things beyond these, he says, are a matter of "rival possibilities".[17] Robert Johnston quotes Packer as saying, "It is the way of Evangelicals to expect absolute certainty from Scripture on everything and to admire firm stances on secondary and disputed matters as signs of moral courage. But in some areas, such expectations are not warranted by the evidence, and such stances reveal only a mind insufficiently trained to distinguish certainties from uncertain possibilities."[18]

This brings to mind something my doctor once told me when he couldn't find an explanation for some curious neurological symptoms I had been experiencing. After lengthy testing, he finally arrived at the diagnosis of a fairly common disorder. I questioned him, though, because I could tell he was not completely satisfied. "Excuse me, Doctor," I said, "but it sounds to me like you have arrived at this diagnosis because you don't know what else to make of it!" His response to me was to reveal that we often think of medicine as an exact science. "But, it's not," he said and concluded with a big grin, "More often than not, we doctors are flying by the seat of our pants." How true this can be in the realm of theology as well!

The myth of objective exegesis

Exegesis is the art of interpretation of the Scriptures. It is helpful to realize that there is no such thing as "objective exegesis". It is a myth! Because (like medicine) biblical interpretation is not an exact science, the facts available will often suggest, at least on the surface, different possibilities. There can actually be a great deal of subjective reasoning involved. Whether we like it or not, our understanding of the Scriptures is influenced and affected by our theological perspective, training and experience. It is also influenced by the problem of sin that hinders our objectivity, receptivity to new perspectives, and willingness to allow God to change our mindsets. As one theologian has put it, "All interpretation is socially located, individually skewed, and ecclesiastically and theologically conditioned."[19] While Evangelicals, in particular, like to hide behind a facade of impartiality, it is important that we recognize the difficulty in any of us being completely objective!

We can quite easily approach biblical texts with some sort of preconception in mind, reading into the Scriptures from our mindsets and biases. This is one reason why each of us is admonished to *"be transformed by the renewing of your mind, that you may prove what the will of God is . . . "* (Romans 12:2). We need God's thinking on the matter and that can only come as we invite Him to renew our minds and submit ourselves to that process.

The effects

The effects of embracing a theology that subtly devalues women and questions their calling as legitimate members of the Body of Christ has been devastating. The more oppressive teachings and attitudes regarding the place of women in the Church have greatly wounded many women filling our church pews and chairs. Several of the speakers at the 1984 Evangelical Colloquium on Women and the Bible spoke at length about the grieving, anguish and agony which they had personally experienced. The message these women have received is that they are not fully human, inferior to their brothers, flawed, disqualified by Eve's sin, and deluded or disobedient because they think they have a call of God on their lives.[20] Patricia Gundry in her book, *Neither Slave Nor Free*, talked about the feelings of isolation, hurt, fear and anger, and about the self-doubts and the desperation of women who are searching for answers.[21]

Moving towards healing and restoration

Although we do not want to downplay the reality of the pain and anguish women have experienced in feeling like second class citizens in the Body of Christ, it is important to identify our real enemy. People are not the enemy! The Bible identifies Satan as the one who comes to kill, steal and destroy (John 10:10). In a nutshell, he wants to neutralize us, whether it be through lies and deception, or through unforgiveness and bitterness. Whatever hook he can find to trip us up and render the Body of Christ less effective, he will exploit it.

In Ephesians 6:12, the apostle Paul reminds us that our battle is not against flesh and blood but against a hidden hierarchy of evil. As we recognize that our battle is a spiritual one, we can be set free from the victim mentality to become overcomers through Christ who strengthens us and gives us His authority. We do not have authority over people, to change their thinking, their attitudes or their hearts, but we *do* have authority over the kingdom of darkness. We further have authority over our own hearts and the choices we face on a daily basis. We can *choose* to walk in forgiveness and let go of the victim mentality. We can pray and stand in the gap for the Church and church leaders. We can share what we have to offer with joy and confidence, secure in the knowledge of where we stand with God. We can become agents of change, ministers of reconciliation, women who foster unity and bring blessing to the Body of Christ. We can find that fulfillment which has eluded so many of us in the past.

As Bishop Barbara Amos has declared, "There are people hurting and dying out there, and God has called me to help them. So I'm going to fulfill my ministry, and then people can evaluate it and call it whatever they like." Rather than focusing on any alienation or rejection she might have experienced, Bishop Amos is using her influence to educate and bring change in the Body of Christ.[22]

Summary

A great deal of confusion has surrounded the gender issue in the Church. In recent years the chaos has intensified as the feminist movement came on the scene and as the Church world experienced a dramatic increase in the number of women seeking to be involved in ministry. Even among Evangelicals with identical commitments to biblical authority, bewilderment has been characteristic as one group after another has reached conflicting conclusions. One reason for this is the fact that biblical interpretation is not an exact science. There are many variables, and often we try to arrive at simplistic conclusions without taking into account all of the factors. Another reason we find such a wide array of positions regarding certain Scriptures is the fact that objective exegesis is a myth. Despite our assertions to the contrary, our training, experience, theological perspectives, mindsets and sin influence the process of biblical interpretation to some degree.

Satan is the author of confusion. He is also the author of deception and misunderstanding which drains life from the Body of Christ and robs us of the talents, abilities and spiritual gifts that women have to offer. In the midst of all this, God is continuing to bring a restoration of the truth that He set in motion with the Protestant Reformation. Developments over the past twenty to thirty years have exposed an underlying mindset that has pervaded the world of the Church and brought it out in plain sight where we are forced to examine it. God can only bring revelation where we see our need, confess our sin and seek His cleansing.

Biblical interpretation has never taken place in a vacuum. For this reason, there is a very real need to submit our hearts and minds to God, and allow our thinking to be transformed by the renewing of our minds (Romans 12:1–2). As we move ahead and onward, we must also allow God the opportunity to transform our hearts. We must allow Him to help us learn to use spiritual weapons for what is really a spiritual battle, recognizing that we wrestle not against flesh and blood but against a hidden hierarchy of evil.

It is time for God's women to come under His covering, under the shadow of His wings, to find healing from their hurts. It is time for God's women to release any anger or bitterness from the misunderstandings, accusation, isolation, rejection, alienation and ungodly control that they may have experienced in the past. It is a new day! As we step out from under the shadow and captivity of these things, we can become the women of God and the spiritual force He has created us to be. We can become modern day Esthers, world changers, who fulfill the purpose and destiny that the Lord has designed for each one of us.

Chapter 1 notes

[1] Richard N. Longenecker, "Authority, Hierarchy and Leadership Patterns in the Bible" in *Women, Authority and the Bible*, Alvera Mickelsen, Ed. (InterVarsity Christian Fellowship, 1986), p. 84.

[2] David M. Scholer, "1 Timothy 2:9–15 and the Place of Women in the Church's Ministry", Ibid., p. 216–217.

[3] *Christianity Today* (April 21, 1989), p. 43.

[4] "Pentecostals Urged to End Bias Against Women Ministers", *Charisma & Christian Life* (December 1996), p. 16.

[5] *Atlanta Journal & Constitution* (August 1989).

[6] *Christianity Today* (January 13, 1989).

[7] Randall Parr, "The Woman Question", *Ministries Today* (Sept/Oct 1995), p. 45–50.

"Pentecostals Urged to End Bias Against Women Ministers", *Charisma & Christian Life* (December 1996), p. 16.

Valerie G. Lowe, "The Lady is a Warrior", *Charisma & Christian Life* (March 1997), p. 26–32.

Barbara Amos, "The Woman Question", *Ministries Today* (May/June 1997), p. 44–47.

Cindy Jacobs, "Women of God Arise", *Charisma & Christian Life* (May 1998), p. 76–78.

Larry Keefauver, "Empower the Women"; Cindy Jacobs, "Women on the Frontlines of Ministry", *Ministries Today* (May/June 1998), pp. 9; 28–33.

Fuchsia Pickett, "Male and Female Created to Co-Labor with God", *Spirit Led Woman* (June/July 1999).

[8] Robert K. Johnston, "Biblical Authority and Interpretation: The Test Case of Women's Role in the Church and Home Updated" in *Women, Authority and the Bible*, Alvera Mickelsen, Ed. (InterVarsity Christian Fellowship, 1986), p. 33–34.

[9] Bill Hamon, *The Eternal Church* (Christian International, 1981), p. 89.

[10] Jesse Lyman Hurlbut, *The Story of the Christian Church* (Zondervan, Grand Rapids, original copyright 1918, current 1970), p. 62.

[11] Bill Hamon, *The Eternal Church*, (Christian International, 1981), p. 89–90.

[12] Jesse Lyman Hurlbut, *The Story of the Christian Church* (Zondervan, Grand Rapids, original copyright 1918, current 1970), p. 62.

[13] Bill Hamon, *The Eternal Church* (Christian International, 1981), p. 93.

[14] Jesse Lyman Hurlbut, *The Story of the Christian Church* (Zondervan, Grand Rapids, original copyright 1918, current 1970), p. 63.

[15] Ruth A. Tucker and Walter Liefeld, *Daughters of the Church* (Zondervan, Grand Rapids, 1987), pp. 122, 133, 136.

[16] Susan C. Hyatt, *In the Spirit We're Equal* (Hyatt Press, Dallas, 1998) p. 65–66.

[17] Robert K. Johnston, "Biblical Authority and Interpretation: The Test Case of Women's Role in the Church and the Home Updated" in *Women, Authority and the Bible*, Alvera Mickelsen, Ed. (InterVarsity Christian Fellowship, 1986), p. 39.

[18] Ibid.

[19] David M. Scholer, "1 Timothy 2:9–15 and the Place of Women in the Church's Ministry", Ibid., p. 215.

[20] Patricia Gundry, "Why We're Here" and Gretchen Gaebelein Hull, "Response", Ibid., pp. 10–21, 22–27.

[21] Patricia Gundry, *Neither Slave Nor Free* (Harper and Row, San Francisco, 1987), pp. 1–7.

[22] Valerie G. Lowe, "The Lady is a Warrior", *Charisma & Christian Life* (March 1997), pp. 26–32.

Chapter 2

The Search for Truth

"Be diligent to present yourself approved to God,
a worker who does not need to be ashamed,
rightly dividing the word of truth."
(2 Timothy 2:15)

We are rapidly entering a time and a season where we, as instruments in the Creator's symphony, can no longer afford the indistinction of sound which has characterized the Church in the past. The end of the age is upon us. Everything is accelerating, as all of creation groans in anticipation of the return of the King of kings. There is a lost and dying world before us, waiting for a touch from the hand of the Master which will bring life, love and liberty. As one woman minister has said regarding this issue of women in ministry, "We are, in a sense, watching the house burn down while arguing about which fire truck to use."[1] Another woman minister has put it this way, "There is enough kingdom building for all of us to do: Let's get on with it."[2]

Part of "getting on with it" is taking the time and making the effort to ascertain what God is really saying. A clear understanding of God's Word brings confidence. God's women *need* that kind of confidence in order to arise and fulfill their destiny.

We must move beyond merely asking, "What does the Bible say?" We must also be willing to commit ourselves to study, being diligent to present ourselves approved to God, rightly dividing or handling with skill and accuracy the word of truth (2 Timothy 2:15). That involves a willingness to weed out the contamination of tradition, prejudice or culture from our understanding of the Word. It means being diligent *to seek*:

> *"Yes, if you cry out for discernment,*
> *And lift up your voice for understanding,*
> *If you seek her as silver,*
> *And search for her as for hidden treasures;*
> *Then you will understand the fear of the* LORD,
> *And find the knowledge of God.*
> *For the* LORD *gives wisdom;*
> *From His mouth come knowledge and understanding."*
>
> (Proverbs 2:3–6)

"Getting on with it" necessitates seeking a revelation of Jesus, who is the Truth (John 14:6) and the living Word (John 1:1–4, 14). He told the Pharisees,

> *"You search the Scriptures because you think that in them you have eternal life; and it is these that bear witness of Me; and you are unwilling to come to Me that you may have life."*
>
> (John 5:39–40)

Jesus emphatically declared to the religious leaders of the day that knowing the Scriptures was not enough. We must come to Him for life. The apostle Paul said something similar to the church at Corinth. He wrote, "... *for the letter kills, but the Spirit gives life"* (2 Corinthians 3:6). Theologian J.I. Packer identifies legalism as part of the problem in the woman issue, what he calls "anxious observance to the letter of the law in disregard of the Spirit." He says this legalism steals fullness of life, is relationally repressive, intrinsically harmful and antihuman! [3]

God, thankfully, is a rewarder of those who diligently seek Him (Hebrews 11:6). He promises that if we seek Him with all of our hearts, we will find Him (Jeremiah 29:13). If we seek to move beyond the letter to the life of the Spirit, then we must allow the Holy Spirit to be our teacher. He is the one who brought the divine inspiration for the Scriptures to men in the first place, and should be our primary teacher in understanding them. Jesus called the Holy Spirit the *"Spirit of truth"* and said *"He will testify of Me"* (John 15:26). He revealed that, *"when the*

Spirit of truth has come, He will guide you into all truth" (John 16:13). Of course, this is not automatic! Dr. Fuchsia Pickett, a well-known Bible teacher with over 50 years experience in ministry, has suggested that until we come into a proper relationship with the Holy Spirit, we cannot operate with a true understanding of God's divine order for mankind. Neither can we expect illumination of the Word of God that brings understanding of His purposes.[4]

Seeking God's mind and heart

First and foremost, we must seek to know God and understand His mind and heart. How can we understand what the real Author of the Scriptures meant if we don't have an understanding of His eternal plan and purposes, His ways, or how He thinks and feels?

I remember getting a letter from Dave before our marriage when we were dating long-distance. In those days I was clingy and insecure, always needing reassurance of how he felt about me. It was just more than he could take. One day, I got a letter from him, which looked to all appearances like what we call a "Dear John" letter. I showed it to my brother, George, who did not know Dave at all, and asked him what he thought Dave was trying to say. He told me to forget the man! He gently dropped the bombshell that it was obvious Dave was severing our relationship. I accepted George's interpretation of the letter for a few days, but my intimate knowledge of Dave's thoughts and feelings finally brought me to a different and, obviously, more accurate conclusion. Knowing him in a deeply personal way made all the difference in the world. Through this experience, I learned the value of intimate relationship when attempting to come to an understanding of the heart and meaning behind someone's words. How true this is of our attempts to understand difficult and confusing passages of Scripture. *Knowing God intimately makes all the difference in the world!*

Seeking God's message in His Word

We must look at the original language of the Scriptures to discover God's intended message. "Losing something in the translation" has become a cliché we often employ in humorous situations when someone doesn't get the joke, but it is more than a cliché. It is a reality! We can't base our theology and practice solely on the English words ascribed by the translators. Sometimes difficulties or errors in translation can lead to serious misunderstandings. I worked with a well-known Christian ministry for a few years helping to facilitate, among other duties, the publishing of their material in other languages. They had previously published one book in Spanish. In the course of my job, I began to hear stories from Spanish pastors about the horrendous misunderstandings which were occurring among their congregations as a result of the faulty translation of this book. The translators were sincere and skilled in their understanding of the language. But there were nuances and regional differences that they did not understand. For example, "speaking boldly" was actually rendered "speaking dirty words" in their translation. You can imagine the furor this caused in Christian circles! Translators have provided only the first step. We must recognize the limitations and do our utmost to overcome them.

Let's look at a simple example of how translation and interpretation might affect our understanding of God's Word. There are three Greek words that can be translated as "love" in English. They are *eros, phileo* and *agape*. Using very simple definitions, *eros* refers to erotic sensation or lust; *phileo* refers to brotherly love or friendship; and *agape* refers to divine, supernatural, perfect love, the source of which is God. Now, let's look at Romans 13:8: *"love one another"*. What did the Author of the Scriptures mean? If I only look at the English word "love", then my understanding of love shapes my interpretation of what God is saying. If the only love I have ever known is erotic love, then I might understand this verse to condone sexual relationships. Surely not! But what *is* Paul saying here? How can we know for sure? By going back to the original language. Did the Holy Spirit direct the apostle Paul to use the word *eros*, the word *phileo*, or the word *agape*? One of the easiest resources to use in searching this out is a concordance. Looking up the word "love" in a Strong's Condordance, we find that the number corresponding to our particular scripture is 25. We then look up number 25 in the Greek dictionary at the back of the concordance and find the specific word used in this passage. In this case, Paul used *agapao*, a verb form of the noun *agape*. So we know that God is directing us to love one another with a supernatural, divine love which comes from Him working through us. This is something we might never have known had we stopped with a superficial look at the English translation of this verse!

There are numerous Greek and Hebrew resources available to those who have limited knowledge of these languages. In addition to concordances, there are more in-depth and thorough resources such as lexicons, word study guides, expository dictionaries, encyclopedias, and commentaries. Further, different translations will often bring out different shades of meaning from the original language. I usually check 4 or 5 different translations before I go on to further study and analysis of a verse or passage. All of these resources are helpful in discovering the real message that the Lord intended to communicate to us.

Seeking the whole counsel of God

In ministering together, Dave and I listen very carefully to one another's sermons to provide encouragement and affirmation, as well as to bring attention later (and privately) to anything that was not clear. In the early days, I would sometimes listen to Dave preaching and think, "If someone only hears this one sermon, they will have a skewed impression of what he really believes!" Invariably, this would happen when he was trying to bring balance to some attitude or way of thinking by heavily emphasizing the *other* side of things. We began to realize that if visitors to our church tried to understand Dave's theology based on just one morning's message, they would almost certainly arrive at a completely erroneous conclusion. Does this sound familiar?

My point is that we communicate *fully* only within the context of many communications. We rarely share every nuance of our thoughts on a matter in one reference or one conversation . . . or sermon. But rather, as people come to know us and hear us share what we think and feel over a period of time, they begin to understand what we actually think and where we really stand.

It is no different with God. It is critical, I think, that we look at the progressive revelation of His mind, heart and will throughout the *whole* of the Scriptures to fully understand what He thinks, feels and desires for all of His children. As David Scholer, a Baptist Dean of Seminary and Professor of New Testament, has explained, understanding difficult passages of Scripture requires that we look carefully at the immediate context of the paragraph, the context of the entire letter or book, and the context of the entire Word of God, as it speaks to that particular subject.[5] I would put it this way: If our theology does not fit the *principles* found throughout the Scriptures, then our theology needs adjustment! Catherine and Richard Kroeger speak of a valuable lesson learned from one theology professor. They discovered, "...that the Bible, if it is truly the Word of God, will hold up to intense scrutiny; that we can dissect it, shake it in a test tube, grind it fine, and analyze it carefully. If we find apparent contradictions, this is an invitation to further study."[6]

It's imperative that we be willing to scrutinize, dissect, shake, grind and analyze the Word of God. We must be willing to seek the whole counsel of God, not being satisfied with one or two portions of Scripture which seem to confirm our own theology. Bear in mind that throughout history, slavery and racism have been justified by a selective study of the Bible! Those on both sides of the issue of women in ministry have made similar mistakes, contributing fuel to the fire of accusation and misunderstanding in the Church. Anyone can develop a proof-text to support his or her own particular position. We need to make a commitment to go beyond proving our point and examine the entire context of the Scriptures. As Marianne Meye Thompson, a professor of New Testament at Fuller Theological Seminary has said,

"Both those who favor women in ministry and those who oppose women in ministry can find suitable proof texts and suitable rationalizations to explain those texts. But if our discussion is ever going to move beyond proof texting ... I suggest that the starting point ... lies in the God who gives gifts for ministry and in the God who is no respecter of persons."[7]

A contributing factor to the differences in Scripture interpretation is ambiguity. Some of the apostle Paul's teaching, in
particular, may appear confusing and contradictory at first
glance. Further, he sometimes used ambiguous expressions that
seem to make no sense. However, there is a basic rule of
interpretation that we can apply in these situations which is
helpful. David Scholer describes this axiom, "Clearer texts
should interpret less clear or ambiguous texts (i.e. the ambiguous ones should be 'read through' those which more clearly
seem to express the heart and mind of God)..." He notes that
those who use 1 Timothy 2:11–12 to restrict women in ministry, for example, usually assume it is a clear text through which
other New Testament passages should be read. He suggests,
however, along with F.F. Bruce, that this verse should be read
through or understood in relation to Galatians 3:28, not vice-
versa.[8] Galatians 3:28 explains, *"...there is neither male nor
female; for you are all one in Christ Jesus."*

Why did Paul not spell out more clearly what the roles of
women should be in the Church? Perhaps the first century
Church did not share our preoccupation with organizational
structure and traditions. Perhaps they were too busy spreading
the gospel and reveling in their newfound love relationship
with the Lord to be concerned about such things. Maybe they
looked at roles and functions in the Body of Christ from a
perspective that was fresher and closer to the heart of God than
our own. There is evidence, as we shall see later, that roles and
functions in the newly emerging Church were determined by
spiritual gifts and anointing, not gender, status or ecclesiastical
position.

There is another factor that contributes to the confusion. We
must realize that the writings of Paul, while inspired by the
Holy Spirit, are in the form of personal letters to various
churches and individuals. He frequently did not spell out the
situations he was expounding upon because the churches to
whom the letters were directed were familiar with the issues and
circumstances. In some of these passages, it is left up to us to try
to ascertain, through cultural and historical studies, exactly
what he might be addressing. These types of studies can also
aid us in better interpreting and understanding the Scriptures
by providing a backdrop and a wider context within which to

place specific verses. They also help us to identify the underlying biblical principles and apply what seem to be culturally specific passages to our own lives. As Davis and Johnson point out, the goal is "to accept biblical teaching as authoritative but to translate it into appropriate contemporary cultural expression."[9]

Seeking historical validation

A specific application of the use of historical and cultural studies to aid biblical interpretation is that of examining the historical accounts sprinkled throughout the Old and New Testaments. If, for example, God had never used a single woman in leadership or in a position of authority throughout the Scriptures, it would lend credibility to the traditional interpretations of several confusing New Testament passages. However, there are numerous women leaders mentioned in both testaments. Examining whom God used and how He worked through them to accomplish His purposes helps us to come to a proper understanding of His mind and heart. The Kroegers share how one fundamentalist leader, in scouring the Scriptures, came to the startling conclusion that one hundred passages in the Bible "affirm women in roles of leadership", and fewer than half a dozen appear in opposition.[10]

Early Church practice further helps us to understand the revelation of the heart and mind of God as understood by the church leaders of that day. They are the ones who co-labored with God to write the very passages that are confusing to us. For example, we can observe that women were as visible in the apostle Paul's ministry as they were in the ministry of Jesus. When we realize that Paul's practice was, in fact, diametrically opposed to what we have traditionally thought and taught he was saying, then we are forced to admit there must be something skewed in our initial interpretation!

Finally, it is also important to look at Church practice throughout history and the fruit that has resulted. As we see God's hand of blessing on the Sunday School movement and the missionary movement of the 19th century, both of which involved huge numbers of teaching women, it should cause us to reanalyze our thinking. Would God have so abundantly blessed these movements if, at their very core, there were practices that were contrary to His commands?

Summary

It is a time for renewed seeking, as the end of the age is upon us, and we are confronted with a lost and dying world. Release from the captivity of confusion and disunity which has characterized the Church's understanding of women in leadership will come as we study to show ourselves approved to God, cry out for discernment, and seek for truth.

The Bible says, *"And you shall know the truth and the truth shall set you free"* (John 8:32). However, the truth is more than a body of facts and information. The truth is a Person. Jesus said, *"I am the way, the truth, and the life"* (John 14:6, emphasis added). It is as we seek to know Him and understand His mind and heart, His message, and His whole counsel, that we will come to know the Truth that sets us free.

Studying to show ourselves approved to God is a necessity if we want to understand His mind, His heart and His message. This depth of understanding involves being willing to move beyond a superficial study of the Scriptures to dig, scrutinize, and analyze. It involves being willing to utilize the many resources available to believers to look at the original languages and compare translations. Examining confusing Scripture verses in light of their context, within their passages, their specific books, and the Scriptures as a whole, is also essential for accurate interpretation. Reading ambiguous passages of Scripture "through" the clear ones further helps in our effort to ascertain what God is saying. Cultural and historical studies also aid in this endeavor by providing a backdrop and a larger context in which to place difficult passages. These studies additionally help us to identify the underlying biblical principles and apply what seem to be culturally specific passages to our own lives.

Chapter 2 notes

[1] "Pentecostals Urged to End Bias Against Women Ministers", *Charisma & Christian Life* (December 1996), p. 16.

[2] Susan Finck-Lockhart, "An Open Letter", *The Priscilla Papers* Volume 10, Number 2, Spring 1996 (CBE, St. Paul, MN), p. 5.

[3] J.I. Packer, "Understanding the Differences" in *Women, Authority and the Bible*, Alvera Mickelsen, Ed. (InterVarsity Christian Fellowship, 1986), p. 298.

[4] Fuchsia Pickett, "Male and Female Created to Co-Labor with God", *Spirit-Led Woman* (June/July 1999).

[5] David M. Scholer, "1 Timothy 2:9–15 and the Place of Women in the Church's Ministry" in *Women, Authority and the Bible*, Alvera Mickelsen, Ed. (InterVarsity Christian Fellowship, 1986), pp. 193–219.

[6] Richard C. Kroeger and Catherine C. Kroeger, *I Suffer Not a Woman – Rethinking 1 Timothy 2:11–15 in Light of Ancient Evidence* (Baker Book House, Grand Rapids, 1992), pp. 30–31.

[7] Marianne Meye Thompson, "Response" in *Women Authority and the Bible*, Alvera Mickelsen, Ed. (InterVarsity Christian Fellowship, 1986), p. 94.

[8] David M. Scholer, "1 Timothy 2:9–15 and the Place of Women in the Church's Ministry", Ibid., pp. 212–213.

[9] James T. Davis and Donna D. Johnson, *Redefining the Role of Women in the Church* (Christian International Ministries Network, 1997) p. 33.

[10] Richard C. Kroeger and Catherine C. Kroeger, *I Suffer Not a Woman – Rethinking 1 Timothy 2:11–15 in Light of Ancient Evidence* (Baker Book House, Grand Rapids, 1992), p. 33.

Chapter 3

Genesis: The Father's Heart

"The counsel of the LORD stands forever,
The plans of His heart to all generations."
(Psalm 33:11)

The book of Genesis, which literally means "beginning", is considered the seedbed of the entire Bible. Every biblical truth can be found in seed form in Genesis. For this reason, it is important to look at the Father's mind, heart and purposes revealed in the book of Genesis as we go back to the creation of woman.

Genesis chapter 1

"Then God said, 'Let Us make man in Our image, according to Our likeness; let them have dominion over the fish of the sea, over the birds of the air, and over the cattle, over all the earth and over every creeping thing that creeps on the earth.' So God created man in His own image; in the image of God He created him; male and female He created them. Then God blessed them, and God said to them, 'Be fruitful and multiply; fill the earth and subdue it; have dominion over the fish of the sea, over the birds of the air, and over every living thing that moves on the earth'."
(Genesis 1:26–28)

In God's image

The first thing we see from this account is that mankind was created in the image and likeness of God. Most scholars agree that the likeness was spiritual, intellectual, emotional and moral. Others refer to a likeness in authority, since God gave *'adam* (Hebrew *'adam* here meaning 'human being' or 'mankind') delegated authority. Mankind's creation in the image and likeness of God does not refer to physical likeness or likeness in those divine attributes such as omnipotence, omnipresence or omniscience. Man is not God. As Matthew Henry so eloquently stated, man is God's image "only as the shadow in the glass, or the king's impress upon the coin." [1] Mankind in God's image and likeness means the pattern and features are recognizable, but the life, depth and scope of the original are not quite there.

Female in God's image

Secondly, we see that man (Hebrew *'adam* – 'human being' or 'mankind') was initially both male and female. This means that the female part of *'adam* was also made in the image and likeness of God. Contrary to popular belief, God is not male. Nor is He female, as the goddess cults would have us believe. Rather, God is Spirit (John 4:24). Tucker and Liefeld note that pagan deities were always in the image of mankind, either masculine or feminine. God, however, is infinitely greater and "transcends human masculinity and femininity." [2] Spencer points out that the New Testament writers were always careful to describe Jesus as *anthropos* (generic human – a Greek word corresponding to *'adam* in the Hebrew [3]) rather than as *aner* (male). She concludes, "Although God became a male, God primarily became a human." [4] Her statement is supported by the understanding of the early Christians as expressed in the Nicene Creed (A.D. 325). [5]

A study of the Bible will show us that God possesses certain characteristics which we (not He) have classified as female. For example, God called Himself El Shaddai (Genesis 17:1). According to rabbinical understanding, this name portrays God as our sufficiency. [6] Dakes identifies El Shaddai as meaning "strong, breasted one." He notes the name reveals God as "Strong Nourisher, Strength-giver, Satisfier, and all Bountiful, the Supplier of the needs of His people." He goes on to say that God revealed Himself in El Shaddai as "Life-Giver" to Abraham and Sarah. [7] We see that El Shaddai can have the connotation of life-giving, nourishing and nurturing – attributes we usually attribute to women. Women actually have this attribute because *God* has this attribute. It is all part of being in His image and likeness!

In the book of Isaiah, God revealed the "feminine" side of His nature when He promised the remnant of Judah, *"As one whom his mother comforts, so will I comfort you"* (Isaiah 66:13). Other Old Testament passages which reveal this "feminine" side of God include: Numbers 11:12, Deuteronomy 32:18, Jeremiah 31:20, Isaiah 42:13–14 and 46:3–4. Jesus, in His lament over Jerusalem, also portrayed Himself in a way we would describe as distinctly feminine. He sadly told them, *"How often I wanted to gather your children together, as a hen gathers her chicks under her wings, but you were not willing!"* (Matthew 23:37). Matthew Henry, in his commentary on Isaiah, draws upon the female imagery of God revealed in Scripture. He wrote,

> "The word of God, the covenant of grace (especially the promises of that covenant), the ordinances of God, and all the opportunities of attending on him and conversing with him, are the breasts, which the church calls and counts as the breasts of her consolations, where her comforts are laid up, and whence by faith and prayer they are drawn. *With her therefore we must suck from these breasts, by an application of the promises of God to ourselves...*"[8]
>
> (emphasis added)

Leonard Swidler interestingly points out that "all through this Hebrew writing [of the Old Testament] the divine spirit, Ruach, is feminine in gender, with the adjectives and verbs following in form."[9]

It is important to emphasize that we are not attempting to portray God as female! Rather, we are recognizing that females, made in God's image and likeness, exhibit unique aspects of God's character.

Unity of male and female in 'Adam

The third item of note in Genesis 1:26–28 concerns the awareness that male and female together reveal the fullness of God's image. Theologians disagree on whether this passage refers to *'adam* as being male and female in one person or whether it refers to the two individuals after the later creation of the woman. Modern scholars who take the latter view tend to use disparaging terms such as androgynous and hermaphrodite to describe a male-female Adam. However, this was the traditional understanding in Hebrew thought, and it certainly fits the facts available better than any other interpretation:

1. We see what we would consider both male and female characteristics in God's revelation of Himself.

2. How would God take the woman *out* of *'adam* (Genesis 2:21–22) if she were not *in* *'adam* to begin with?

3. It also explains why men and women complement each other and why God ordained that when man and woman join together in marriage, they once again become "one flesh" (Genesis 2:24).

Within the larger context of the Body of Christ, we find that each gender offers something unique in terms of vision, perspective, discernment, awareness of needs, etc. to bring *completion* to the expression of God's mind and heart in the earth.

Joint dominion

Lastly, regardless of whether *'adam* was male and female in one person or two, we find that both male and female were given joint dominion over the earth. According to Lawrence O. Richards, and substantiated by numerous other scholars, the ideal of full equality as persons is clearly taught in Genesis 1:26–28.[10] The picture exhibited in Genesis chapter 1 is that of male and female sharing in power, authority and dignity as God's representatives on the earth. This was God's purpose for men and women before the fall. Because Jesus came to bring restoration and liberty from the penalty and results of sin brought on by the fall, we can accept that equal dominion is *still* God's purpose for men and women today.

Psalm 8, which reveals the glory of God in creation, substantiates that even after the fall, mankind (meaning men and women) was ordained to have dominion and authority over the *natural* realm. The Hebrew word used is *'enosh*. It ascribes no particular gender, and means mortal humankind in all their

weakness and frailty. It is often used as an alternative term for
'*adam*.[11] Psalm 149 similarly describes the *spiritual* authority
and dominion given to God's people. It concludes, *"This honor
have all his saints"* (emphasis added). Even after the fall, God's
design was that both men and women would share in natural as
well as spiritual rulership and authority.

Genesis chapter 2

> *"And the LORD God formed man of the dust of the ground, and
> breathed into his nostrils the breath of life; and man became of
> living being ... And the LORD God said, 'It is not good that man
> should be alone; I will make him a helper comparable to him' ...
> And the LORD God caused a deep sleep to fall on Adam, and he
> slept; and He took one of his ribs, and closed up the flesh in its
> place. Then the rib which the LORD God had taken from the man
> He made into a woman, and He brought her to the man. And
> Adam said,*
>
>> *'This is now bone of my bones*
>> *And flesh of my flesh;*
>> *She shall be called Woman,*
>> *Because she was taken out of Man.'*
>
> *Therefore a man shall leave his father and mother and be joined
> to his wife, and they shall become one flesh."*
> (Genesis 2:7, 18, 21–24)

Genesis 2 is important to look at because so many throughout
history have read into it their own ideas of subordination and
submission of woman to man. It has also been used to establish
woman's inferiority to man because of what is called her
"secondary creation" (the argument being that woman was
created second, and is therefore inferior). We need to read it
with fresh eyes, setting aside bias from tradition or prior
teaching, and look for God's heart and purposes as we look at
the original language.

The source of woman is God
First of all, God formed '*adam* (mankind, both male and female)
out of the dust of the ground, breathing His life into him,

making him a living being. In one of his famous sermons entitled "Triune Salvation", John G. Lake forcefully asserted, "God breathed into him [*'adam*] His own self, His own being ... that heavenly materiality of which God consists. He injected or breathed Himself into the man, and the man then became a composition of the heavenly substance or materiality, and earth or the substance of the earth." [12] A study of the original language lends credence to Lake's assertions. Kay Rhodes, in studying the Hebrew in this passage, has concluded that the translation could literally read, "The covenant-keeping, creative God formed A-dam (God's blood) out of tiny particles of Himself and breathed into him all that God was and man became all that He is – the exact likeness of God". [13] Without the breath of God, mankind was just dust. As He breathed the breath of life into *'adam*, He became mankind's source. This is true for both men and women. In Him we live and move and have our being (Acts 17:28), regardless of gender. Susan Hyatt remarks that an important biblical principle is established here: that man and woman are made of the same substance. She is "bone of his bone and flesh of his flesh." She is also filled with the same life and nature of God. This dispels the pagan idea that woman is made of a substance inferior to that of the man. [14]

'Ezer Kenegdo – *powerful help*

Secondly, God said it was not good for *'adam* (mankind) to be alone. He therefore decided to make a *"a help meet for him"* (Genesis 2:18, KJV), *"a helper suitable for or corresponding to him"* (NAS), *"a helper comparable to him"* (NKJV). The Hebrew here contains the words *'ezer kenegdo*, which imply a helper *of his like*, fit for him. Brown, Driver, and Briggs describe it as a help *corresponding* to him, one that is equal and adequate to himself. [15] John Garr, who has pioneered research and teaching on the Hebrew roots of the Christian faith, concurs, defining it as "a helper over against or in front of him." He goes on to point out that the implication of the phrase is that woman was intended to be a power equal to the man. [16] Aida B. Spencer, in her study *Beyond the Curse*, says the Septuagint translators were careful to preserve this idea of equality by using the Greek word *kata*, followed by the direct object. As she points out, this signifies horizontal rather than perpendicular direction in the

relationship.[17] She notes that it can mean one who is "in front
of" and "opposite to" (as in a mirror image), and that the
passage contains the preposition *neged*, which means "in front
of". The same word in noun form signifies "one in front" and
was used to describe David and Solomon's roles as rulers over
Israel. She goes on to say, "If Eve had been created in an inferior
position, the writer should have used a term to mean 'after' or
'behind'."[18]

As we will later see, the understanding that the woman was
inferior or subordinate to the man was a product of pagan
Hellenism in the pre-Christ era. Hellenistic influence has been
preserved in much of the culture of the Middle East. My
husband's grandfather was Palestinian. Had his family
embraced the culture more fully, his grandmother would have
been expected to walk two or three paces behind his grandfather to signify her subservience and inferiority as a woman. As
it was, she was often expected to work while he played
pinochle. Spencer's study lends tremendous support to the
verdict that such a mindset is the product of human thinking
and tradition, rather than the heart of God.

Spencer concludes that Genesis 2, "which some suppose to
teach a hierarchy of male and female, grammatically reveals
that here is no subordination of the helper to Adam."[19]
Swartley came to similar conclusions, arguing that exegetically,
there is no foundation for subordination of woman to man
here, explicit or implicit.[20]

In fact, it is my opinion that both Spencer and Swartley have
understated the case! While *'ezer* (the helper in verse 18) is often
construed to imply a secondary or inferior role, the Hebrew
actually means anything but that. It comes from the root *azar*
and means to surround, protect, aid, help, and succor. *It is used
predominantly (16 times) in the Old Testament to refer to God
Himself – the one who comes to our help in time of need.* Katherine
Bushnell, a Greek and Hebrew scholar of the early 20th century,
says the word implies for this reason superior, as opposed to
inferior, help.[21] Spencer quotes R. David Freeman in the *Biblical
Archaeology Review* as suggesting that "the term 'helper' etymo-
logically signifies 'a power (or strength) who can save. The word
comes from the two roots, one which means 'to rescue, to save'
and one meaning 'to be strong'."[22]

While this might not fit our typical concept of what women are like (or should be like), let me pose a question. Why are most intercessors women? Why do women seem to more easily flow into that position of standing in the gap on behalf of others, of spiritual warfare and of taking hold of the kingdom of heaven with a forceful perseverance that does not let go until the purposes of God are made manifest? Answer: Because God made them that way. He put in them the fierce protectiveness, the strength to rescue, the heart of compassion, and the patient determination which are exhibited by the God who comes to our rescue and who stands as High Priest, forever making intercession for us! Why should it surprise (or threaten) us that the helper God made for Adam was strong and powerful on his behalf?

Matthew Henry, in his quaint style, suggests that if Adam was the best and most excellent of all God's creation because he was created first, then there is a special honor upon the female because she was made after and out of Adam. He says, "If he is the head, she is the crown ... the man was dust refined, but the woman was dust double-refined, one removed further from the earth." [23] This is a direct reference to Proverbs 12:4 which describes an excellent wife as the "crown" of her husband. A different picture is presented here than the one proposed by those who argue that woman is inferior to man because of her secondary creation! John Bristow makes an excellent point:

> "It is interesting to note that no one has carried out this basis of ranking according to the order of creation to its logical conclusion: that cows are superior to man since cows were created before Adam ... " [24]

The rib myth exposed

Church tradition describes the woman as being made from Adam's rib. Even many modern day translations render the Hebrew in verse 21 as "rib" when it describes the separation of *'adam* into male and female. We think God took a little piece of man and with this little piece created a little woman. However, deeper study presents a different picture. Hyatt points out that this same word translated "rib" occurs 42 times in the Old Testament and this is the *only* place it is rendered "rib". It is usually translated as "side" or "sides". As Hyatt also notes, the Septuagint (the Greek translation of the Hebrew Scriptures written before the birth of Christ) affirms this meaning for verse 21.[25] The correct translation of this verse is meaningful in light of God's purpose and intent for women. God took a side of *'adam* to create the woman. Out of the whole, He created two complementary parts. Thus the Body of Christ, both male and female members, are designed to complement one another and be united as one in Christ, the last *'adam* (John 17:21).

Positional equality

There are some who have proposed that women are spiritually equal, but appointed by God to a subordinate role or position. They desire to affirm the value of women, but without rocking the boat or offending their own sensibilities, traditions, or mindsets. It is a concession of sorts to the value of women in God's eyes, but it remains unbiblical. What is biblical can only be determined by looking at the whole counsel of God throughout the Scriptures, and by straining our various interpretations and ideologies through the filter of God's purposes regarding woman when He made her. God's perspective was clearly revealed in the creation accounts of Genesis chapters 1 and 2, revealing not only spiritual equality for women, but positional equality as well. Dominion over the earth was given to *both* men and women in *'adam*. He created woman out of the side of *'adam*, that male and female might stand together as one. God provided for the male a female counterpart who was not only a mirror image of him, but one who would surround, protect and nurture him as well. It was not the manner or timing of woman's creation which has determined her subject status through the centuries. Rather, the low status of women has resulted from human sinfulness and a willingness to embrace the pagan philosophy of the Greeks, as we shall see in Chapter 6.

Genesis chapter 3

Chapter 3 of Genesis describes the serpent's clever deception and temptation of the woman in verses 1–5 and then continues,

"So when the woman saw that the tree was good for food, that it was pleasant to the eyes, and a tree desirable to make one wise, she took of its fruit and ate. She also gave to her husband with her, and he ate." (Genesis 3:6)

Do you see that Eve's husband was right there with her? They *both* ate, and they *both* sinned. Adam was equally responsible for the fall of mankind from grace.

Afterwards, God walked through the garden looking for them, calling for them out of His desire for fellowship and companionship. Man and woman had meanwhile retreated behind the bushes. They were overcome with shame over their nakedness, and fearful that their nakedness would be exposed. Fear drove them to a controlling desire to hide their nakedness from God and one another, so that their shame would not be seen! This shame–fear–control cycle, which began as sin entered the world, has become a prevalent pattern in mankind since the fall. It has also become an important dynamic in the relationship between fallen man and woman.

When God got them to confess their sin to Him, He responded with a curse upon the serpent (verse 14) and a curse upon the ground (verse 17). He did not, directly at least, curse the man or the woman.[26] To the woman God said,

"I will greatly multiply your sorrow and your conception;
In pain you shall bring forth children;
Your desire shall be for your husband,
And he shall rule over you." (Genesis 3:16)

To the man, Adam, God said,

"Cursed is the ground for your sake;
In toil you shall eat of it
All the days of your life.
Both thorns and thistles it shall bring forth for you,
And you shall eat the herb of the field.
In the sweat of your face you shall eat bread
Till you return to the ground,
For out of it you were taken;
For dust you are,
And to dust you shall return." (Genesis 3:17–19)

Did God curse Eve?

Those who have taken the position that these passages do not
reflect a curse of God upon the man or woman, see them
instead as a description of what the consequences of their sin
will be. Kathryn Bushnell, for example, points out that the
"shalls" in these verses are future tense, not imperative. She
says God is not commanding anything to happen, but rather
prophesying that these things will come to pass.[27] Swidler notes
that the simple future tense of the verbs is used, rendering
God's statement "not prescriptive, but descriptive" of what
would happen in the future.[28] Lawrence Richards agrees, stating
that "Genesis 3:16 contains God's announcement of one
impact of sin on human experience. The intended equality will
be distorted; dominion and subordination will mar relationships between the sexes."[29]

Personally, I think it is a moot point. While God may not
have directly cursed Adam and Eve, His words describe a curse
operating in their lives as the result of their sin. A curse is simply
a predisposition to failure. Deuteronomy chapters 11 and 27–30
detail the consequences of disobedience in terms of the principle of sowing and reaping. It is simple. If we sow disobedience,
we will reap cursing. God may be merely prophesying here that
these things will come to pass. But even if He is simply
describing the consequences of sin, there is an active element
of cursing involved in those consequences. For example,
Deuteronomy 28:20, describes the cursings of disobedience,
*"The LORD will send on you cursing, confusion, and rebuke in all
that you set your hand to do..."* Chester and Betsy Kylstra, in
their counseling manual *Restoring the Foundations*, have defined
these curses as the penalty exacted for violating the terms of the
covenant with God. They liken it to paying a fine for speeding as
a penalty for breaking the laws of the land.[30] While the fine may
merely be a consequence of disobedience, someone also has to
levy that fine and enforce the penalty that had been previously
established. Consequently, there is both a passive and an active
element to the penalty.

I see the point as inconsequential because even if God had
directly cursed Adam and Eve as punishment for their sin, the
penalty was paid in full at Calvary! The shed blood of Jesus

made that payment on our behalf. As the Kylstras point out, "Through His sacrifice on the Cross, we can by faith apply His blood to cover our sins, to pay the penalty, to stop the curse."[31] Galatians 3:10–13 explains that without Jesus, we *are* under a curse! The law of God brought a curse upon each of us because we can never fulfill it. We were liable in the legal sense for the curse of disobedience found in Deuteronomy chapters 11 and 27–30. Verse 13 of Galatians 3 tells us that Jesus redeemed (set us free, released us) from this curse by becoming a curse for us. Praise God!

Enmity and redemption

In verse 15 of chapter 3, the Lord makes an intriguing statement to the serpent, which sets the stage for the millenniums to come. He says,

> *"And I will put enmity*
> *Between you and the woman,*
> *And between your seed and her Seed;*
> *He shall bruise your head,*
> *And you shall bruise His heel."*

This is a Messianic prophecy with which some of us may be familiar. But let me call your attention to the first part of this prophecy: *"I will put enmity between you and the woman."* Enmity is hatred between enemies. The Lord says here that He is allowing hatred between Satan and women to be set in place. From the time of the fall onwards, Satan would blow the hot breath of his fiery hatred upon all women because of the Seed of redemption carried by the woman, a Seed which would one day crush His head. Also, he would hate the woman because the woman is a type of the Church, the Bride of Christ who is to be the executor of God's written judgement on the enemy and his kingdom (Psalm 149). Satan would release the fullness of his fury upon women in every way imaginable – through misunderstanding, accusation, betrayal, suppression, oppression, captivity, slavery, abuse, even death. Yet here also, the promised redemption in Christ Jesus majestically overshadows the prophetic declaration of the pain and suffering to come! This promise has enabled God's women to march humbly yet steadfastly through the centuries as servants of God, proclaiming, *"I will . . . and if I perish, I perish!"* (Esther 4:16).

Summary

Genesis, the book of beginnings, reveals a great deal concerning the purposes of God for women. It reveals that woman was made in the image and likeness of God, and like man, has her source in God. Because male/female *'adam* was created in God's image, then woman was taken out of man, she retained certain unique characteristics of God which the male does not have. This "feminine" side to God's nature is unveiled in both the Old and New Testaments. As a result of the separation of *'adam* into male and female, it takes both genders contributing their unique strengths and giftings to fully reflect the image of God within the Body of Christ.

Genesis also reveals that *'adam*, both male and female, was given joint dominion over the earth. It paints a picture of male and female sharing in power, authority and dignity as God's ambassadors in the earth. Passages from the Psalms confirm this as God's intent. While woman was given to man as a helper, the Hebrew indicates one who is an equal in terms of adequacy and perfect in terms of fit together. The Hebrew even suggests a powerful helper, identifying one who is strong and powerful on behalf of another. The same word is used predominantly in the Old Testament to refer to God Himself as our helper in time of need. In every respect, the accounts of creation demonstrate positional as well as spiritual equality for men and women.

Chapter 3 of Genesis details the fall of mankind from grace into sin, revealing that both Adam and Eve ate. Both were disobedient. Both sinned. Here we see the cycle of shame–fear–control beginning to dominate their lives upon the entrance of sin into the world. This cycle also began to mar their relationship with one another, as we shall see in later chapters. In verse 15, the Lord prophetically declared that an enmity between Satan and the woman, as carrier of the divine Seed, was set in place. Yet there is a promise of redemption in Christ Jesus which overshadows God's prediction of the pain and suffering to come.

This chapter of Genesis also reveals the effects or curse of sin in operation in the lives of the man and the woman. But this curse was broken as Jesus paid the penalty for their sin and ours with His blood! Legally, the blood of Jesus redeemed *both* man and woman. He has restored us to a place of freedom from the penalty of sin and given each of us the ability to fulfill the purposes He had for us in the beginning.

Chapter 3 notes

[1] Matthew Henry, *A Commentary on the Whole Bible Volume One* (Fleming H. Revell Company, New York), p. 10.

[2] Ruth A. Tucker and Walter Liefeld, *Daughters of the Church* (Zondervan Publishing House, Grand Rapids, 1987) p. 450.

[3] The New International Dictionary of New Testament Theology Volume Two, Colin Brown, Ed. (Zondervan, Grand Rapids, 1975), pp. 562, 564.

[4] Aida Besacon Spencer, *Beyond the Curse* (Hendrickson, Peabody MA, 1985), p. 22.

[5] Leonard Swidler, *Biblical Affirmations of Woman* (The Westminster Press, Philadelphia, 1979), p. 281.

[6] *Theological Wordbook of the Old Testament Volume Two*, R. Laird Harris, Ed. (Moody Press, Chicago, 1980), p. 907.

[7] *Dake's Annotated Reference Bible* (Dake Bible Sales, Lawrenceville GA, 1961, 1963), p. 14.

[8] Matthew Henry, *A Commentary on the Whole Bible Volume Four* (Fleming H. Revell Company, New York), p. 392.

[9] Leonard Swidler, *Biblical Affirmations of Woman* (The Westminster Press, Philadelphia, 1979), p. 50.

[10] Lawrence O. Richards, *The Word Bible Handbook* (Word Books, Waco, 1982), p. 33.

[11] *The Spirit-Filled Life Bible*, Jack Hayford, General Ed. (Thomas Nelson, Nashville, 1991), p. 714.

[12] John G. Lake, *John G. Lake – His Life, His Sermon, His Boldness of Faith* (Kenneth Copeland Publications, Fort Worth, 1994), p. 4.

[13] Kay D. Rhodes, *Let My Women Go* (Kay D. Rhodes, Rock Hill SC, 1994), p. 10.

[14] Susan C. Hyatt, *In the Spirit We're Equal* (Hyatt Press, Dallas, 1998), p. 234.

[15] Francis Brown, S.R. Driver and Charles Briggs, *Hebrew and Greek Lexicon of the Old Testament* (trans. Edward Robinson, Clarendon, Oxford, 1907), p. 617.

[16] John D. Garr, "The Biblical Woman", *Restore!* (Winter 1999), p. 7.

[17] Aida Besancon Spencer, *Beyond the Curse* (Hendrickson, Peabody MA, 1985), p. 25.

[18] Ibid., p. 24.

[19] Ibid., p. 25.

[20] Willard M. Swartley, "Response" in *Women, Authority and the Bible*, Alvera Mickelsen, Ed. (InterVarsity Press, Downers Grove IL, 1986), p. 85.

[21] Katherine C. Bushnell, *God's Word to Women* (1923, reprinted by Ray Munson, N. Collins NY), par. 34.

[22] Aida Besancon Spencer, *Beyond the Curse* (Hendrickson, Peabody MA, 1985), p. 27.

[23] Matthew Henry, *A Commentary on the Whole Bible Volume One* (Fleming H. Revell Company, New York), p. 19.

[24] John Temple Bristow, *What Paul Really Said About Women* (HarperCollins, San Franciso, 1988), p. 17.

[25] Susan C. Hyatt, *In the Spirit We're Equal* (Hyatt Press, Dallas, 1998), p. 235.

[26] *The Spirit-Filled Life Bible*, Jack Hayford, General Ed. (Thomas Nelson, Nashville, 1991), p. 9.

[27] Katherine C. Bushnell, *God's Word to Women* (1923; reprinted by Ray Munson, N. Collins, NY), par. 74.

[28] Leonard Swidler, *Biblical Affirmations of Woman* (The Westminster Press, Philadelphia, 1979), p. 80.

[29] Lawrence O. Richards, *The Word Bible Handbook* (Word Books, Waco, 1982), p. 33.

[30] Chester and Betsy Kylstra, *Restoring the Foundations* (Proclaiming His Word, Santa Rosa Beach FL, 1994,1996), p. 53.

[31] Ibid.

Chapter 4

Genesis 3:16 – A Source of Confusion

"I will greatly multiply your sorrow and your conception;
In pain you shall bring forth children;
Your desire shall be for your husband,
and he shall rule over you."
(Genesis 3:16)

A few years ago, I was reading a book on church leadership when the author shocked me with an assertion that I had never heard before! He stated that women were disqualified from leadership and listed Eve's sin in the garden and the subsequent curse put upon her as the primary reason. Recent scholarship has focused a great deal of attention on the meaning of Genesis 3:16 because of this sort of reasoning. For centuries Eve has been blamed for the fall of man and this alleged curse has been used to justify the oppression of women. As we shall see in this chapter, the focus on Eve's sin and the supposed curse suggests the pursuit of a scapegoat. Secondly, we will look at possible mistranslations of Genesis 3:16 and how they have contributed to the use of this passage to disqualify women from positions of leadership within the Church.

Eve as a scapegoat for the fall of man

As pointed out in the previous chapter, Adam was there with Eve and they both ate of the forbidden fruit (Genesis 3:6). Both disobeyed God, and both sinned. Though Eve sinned as a result of Satan's deception, Adam apparently sinned with knowledge according to 1 Timothy 2:14. It seems that He knew what was happening, yet made a conscious choice to go along with it anyway. Which is really worse – deception or willful disobedience?

It does not appear to me that God assigned greater judgement on one than the other. The apostle Paul, in his epistle to the Romans and first letter to the Corinthian church, assigns responsibility for sin and death to Adam (Romans 5:12–19; 1 Corinthians 15:21–22). However, it is the Greek counterpart of the Hebrew *'adam.* As we have seen previously, *'adam* was used in Genesis 1 and 2 to refer to mankind, both male and female. In these passages Paul uses the gender generic word *anthropos* rather than any specific words for male or female. Both suffered the consequence or curse of sin, as we read in Genesis 3:16. Charles Trombley, however, argues that God puts the responsibility and judgement for the fall of man on Adam's shoulders, referring to a use of the Greek masculine gender in Romans 5:12. His conclusion? "By implicating Adam as the originator of sin, he [Paul] eliminated the grounds for subjugating women as part of Eve's curse." [1] The Kroegers agree with Trombley's assessment that God put responsibility for the fall from grace on Adam. They write, "By our reckoning, Paul ascribes the guilt to Adam nine different times in these passages [Romans 5 and 1 Corinthians 15]." [2] Ironically, however, Eve has been blamed for the fall of man since the pre-Christ era. Katherine Bushnell has traced the teaching that God cursed Eve, and through Eve all women, to the Babylonian Talmud. [3] The Talmud is merely rabbinical commentary that became tradition. The blame it assigned to Eve has been used as justification for the subjection of women to men, and is a major source of the false teaching that this suppression of women is ordained of God as punishment for Eve's sin.

Blame-shifting started with Adam

Note that the blame-shifting started with fallen Adam. He said to God, *"The woman whom You gave to be with me, she gave me of the tree, and I ate"* (Genesis 3:12). It is clear that Adam laid the blame for the fall on Eve's doorstep. He tried to shift all the responsibility over to Eve despite the fact that he chose to sin by his own free will, with full knowledge of what he was doing and the consequences of his actions. Although we want to be careful not to read more into the Scripture than is there, Adam's words further suggest that he was not only blaming the woman but God. He sounds as if he were saying, "That woman *you* brought into my life was responsible for all of this" – implying that since God gave her to Adam, He is responsible as well. Blame-shifting came in with the fall and is part of the fallen, carnal nature. It comes to the forefront whenever mankind yields to that nature. Job asked, *"If I have covered my transgressions as Adam, by hiding my iniquity in my bosom ...?"* (Job 31:33–34). What better way to cover and hide sin than to assign it to someone else! In recognizing the dynamics of this attempt to shift the blame, it becomes clearer that Eve was used by fallen Adam to sidestep taking responsibility for his sin and facing his own sense of inadequacy. To be fair, however, he undoubtedly had a great deal of help from the kingdom of darkness. Satan and his minions are always working to stir up strife and division, operating under the maxim, "divide and conquer." Further, Satan had every reason to hate the woman through whom would come the Divine Seed, the Savior, who would ultimately defeat him. Some have speculated that it is really this enmity between Satan and the woman which is behind the domination and abuse of women through the centuries, as well as the attempts to blame her for all the sin in the world.

The blame for the fall put upon Eve has been given credibility by a number of possible mistranslations of Genesis 3:16. The verse is divided into two major parts, which we will look at separately.

"I will greatly multiply your sorrow and your conception" (Genesis 3:16a)

Many translators read this passage as a curse that God put upon the woman of increased infirmity, suffering and grief during pregnancy and childbirth. However, the Hebrew scholar Katherine Bushnell challenged this translation in the early part of this century based on her close examination of the Hebrew. She concluded that a more correct translation would be, *"A snare hath increased thy sorrow and thy sighing."*[4] Modern scholars Trombley [5] and Davis and Johnson [6] acknowledge the validity of Bushnell's translation.

"Your desire shall be for your husband and he shall rule over you" (Genesis 3:16b)

There are three primary "traditional" (and erroneous) interpretations of what God is saying in the second part of Genesis 3:16:

1. Eve was a temptress who constituted a moral threat to Adam. God intervened and caused the woman to lust after her husband to the extent that she became putty in his hands. God's intervention enabled him to take his rightful place in dominion over her. This was the rabbinical interpretation, as evidenced in the Ten Curses of Eve and other parts of the Babylonian Talmud.

2. Eve would desire to rule over her husband and subjugate him as the result of sin. Therefore God intervened and gave the husband a divine assignment to have dominion over her instead.

3. Eve's desire for her husband and the subjugation of her will to his was part of the "curse" which God put on Eve for her sin, a curse carried by all women after her.

One will often hear some variation or combination of these interpretations as well. If we take these traditional interpretations at face value, this passage reads like an edict, command or pronouncement of divine judgement upon Eve for her sin. We shall see, however, that the original language does not agree with *any* of the above interpretations!

Rather, the Hebrew presents a picture of God stating what will happen – either in the sense of a warning to the woman or as a prophetic declaration regarding the natural progression of sin and its diseased effects on the relationship between man and woman. As Davis and Johnson remark, "Genesis 3 describes and predicts the inevitable results of banishment from God's presence. As man and woman were alienated from God they were, at the same time alienated from each other." [7] Dr. Fuchsia Pickett asserts that in this statement, "God was not revealing His divine order for the woman; He was telling us how a *fallen* man and woman were going to relate to each other." [8] First of all, to complete the thought that they assumed God was trying to make, the translators inserted the words "shall be". The NKJV, for example, shows these words in italics, which means they were not part of the original text.

Next, "desire" in this verse is the Hebrew word *teshuqa*, a word used only three times in the Old Testament: Genesis 3:16 (regarding Eve and Adam), Genesis 4:7 (in relation to sin and Cain), Song of Solomon 7:10 (regarding the King and the Shulamite as representative of Christ and His Church). Bushnell points out that the word does not imply anything like sensual desire or lust. The root, *shuq*, is a verb meaning literally "to run". *Teshuqa* bears the connotation "to run repeatedly" or "to run back and forth", giving us a picture of "turning".[9] It also implies no idea of inferiority or subordination as the traditional interpretation would indicate. If that were the case, its usage in Song of Solomon 7:10 would imply that Christ is inferior or subordinate to His church.

The Septuagint, the Greek translation of the Old Testament completed around 300 B.C., also renders the meaning of *teshuqa* as "turning." It uses the Greek word *apostrophe* as a synonym for the Hebrew word *teshuqa*. *Apostrophe* means turning, towards something and away from something; in other words reversing direction. The Septuagint is considered the best translation of the Old Testament, as it was written at a time when ancient Hebrew was better known and understood, and before the language had undergone the linguistic changes which have taken place over the past two thousand years. Bushnell points out that, in fact, all of the most ancient versions of the Scriptures present the idea of turning for *teshuqa*.[10]

Where did the idea of sensual desire, with its subtle implication of dependence and inferiority, come from? It came from the Babylonian Talmud, that compilation of rabbinical thought and Jewish oral tradition. The Talmud portrays Eve as a temptress to be eternally punished by God, enslaved now to lust for her husband, enabling the man to fend off her threat to his superior moral position and properly rule over her.

Some scholars, even in recognizing that *teshuqa* does not mean sensual desire, have still been influenced by the rabbinical mindset that woman is an evil temptress, in league with Satan to destroy man if she is not held in check. The Spirit-Filled Life

Bible, for example, notes that Genesis 3:16 is a "difficult" passage in the Hebrew, but goes on to offer this conclusion: "Most likely the expression carries the idea that, remembering their joint-rule in the Garden, she would desire to dominate her husband. *He shall rule over you* asserts the *divine assignment* of the husband's servant–leader role" (emphasis added).[11] While the editors go on to qualify this traditional statement, the fact that they made it at all reveals a prior mindset that the husband has been given a divine assignment to keep woman in her place. As Davis and Johnson point out, western religious art has, through the centuries, depicted Eve as one who was Satan's accomplice in overthrowing Adam. They note, in fact, that medieval art often portrayed the serpent in the garden as female or portrayed Satan as a mirror image of Eve.[12] All this has contributed to the idea that man must protect himself by dominating and suppressing woman, and actually has biblical sanction to do so. However, self-protection is another characteristic of the carnal nature, which never has God's sanction.

To return to the concept of turning implicated in the use of the Hebrew word *teshuqa*, there is necessarily a turning from something towards something else. What or who was Eve turning from when she turned to her husband in her fallen, sinful state? The obvious answer is God Himself. Therein lies the key to understanding this passage! We find the principle in the New Testament that when we yield to someone or something other than God and allow it to have power over us, we then become enslaved (Galatians 4:9 and 2 Peter 2:18–22). When Eve turned her focus from God to her husband, she gave him power to rule over and enslave her. Hence, God was explaining what the consequences of her turning would be (*"he shall rule over you"*). Today, we call this condition "codependence". When we turn our focus from God to someone else or some other thing, we slip into idolatry.

Kay Rhodes has considered both the translation of Genesis 3:16 favored by Bushnell, Trombley, Davis and Johnson, and the real meaning of *teshuqa*. She concludes that, "God is merely warning Adam (female) that if she turns away from God to her husband, it will become a great snare for her. This snare will be provided by the subtle serpent who now rules Adam (male)".[13] This ties in with something the Lord revealed to my husband

Dave a few years ago: When we are completely submitted to God and give Him control of our lives, we have dominion over the devil (see James 4:7). However, when we take control ourselves or yield our members to somebody or something else through our worship or idolatry, it gives the devil dominion over us!

In Genesis 3:16 we see how the operation of sin and the dominion of darkness began to alienate man and woman from each other. Eve, out of shame, fear, and self-centeredness, turned from God and began to look to the man, Adam, for gratification of her needs. She began to look to him as her *source* of comfort, provision, protection, and fellowship. Jane Hansen, the International President of Women's Aglow, admits that even now this is very much the case.

> "In spite of living in this age of enlightenment, with few exceptions, a woman still gets married having unspoken expectations that the man she has chosen will meet all her needs for security, purpose, worth and identity. We may laugh at the 'prince on the white horse', but it is evident it is a fairy tale deeply embedded in the heart of nearly every young woman." [14]

She also comments, "You have only to look around you to see how women, even Christian women, set their desire on men. They have turned to them to gain their approval, to be found acceptable, worthy, admired and chosen." [15] It is idolatry, pure and simple!

Idolatry gave man control over the woman. That is how it works. If we worship money, it enslaves us. If we seek or serve fame, that desire controls us. If we go after financial security, putting our trust in it rather than in the Lord, then financial security begins to rule our lives and our decisions. As Eve put her faith and trust in the man, Adam, to meet all her needs, it opened the door for a plague of problems in man-woman relationships. Out of his own shame, fear and self-centeredness, man began use the power woman had inadvertently given him over her to dominate her and thus feel better about himself. He began to see her as less than himself and an object provided for his pleasure, comfort and use. Woman, in turn, experienced disappointment, hurt and resentment when she felt used, and when the man did not meet her needs and live up to her expectations. As a result, walls of isolation developed between the two genders. Each began to hide from the other behind these new "fig leaves", assert their independence from one another, and subscribe to a burgeoning attitude of "I don't need you!"

What a mess sin gets us into! Thankfully, we are washed, cleansed and set free from the *power* of sin by the blood of Jesus. The dysfunction of sin need not continue to mar our relationships with one another. Whatever the results of the fall, whether it was divinely imposed curses or merely a reaping of what was sown, we have also been redeemed from the *penalty* or judgement of this sin. It is ridiculous to try to use Genesis 3:16 as proof that man is supposed to rule over and dominate woman because of Eve's role in the fall from grace.

Bristow sums up the absurdity of using the traditional interpretations of this passage as a basis for the subjugation of women. He says, "If this kind of marital relationship, far from being divinely ordered, is the product of sin and God's curse, then it is to be avoided rather than commended. It is characteristic of marriage outside of God's grace. To prescribe that kind of relationship is to advocate living under the penalty of sin imposed upon Adam and Eve, as if Christ brought nothing new to marriage relationship." [16] Certainly, we could make the same argument regarding church relationships. *All* Christian men and women have been redeemed from the results of the fall and have been set free to work together in harmony to fulfill God's original design as presented in the book of Genesis before the fall occurred.

Summary

Genesis 3:16 has often been used to justify the oppression of women. In the Church, it has been used to disqualify women from leadership positions. The traditional interpretations of this passage portray the woman as an evil temptress, a male-dominating controller, and/or the one who is cursed and forced to submit to the man as part of the punishment for her role in the fall. These interpretations are based on a faulty assumption.

They assume that Eve was to blame for the fall because Satan deceived her. Such a conclusion completely ignores Adam's role in the fall, his sin, and the assignment of responsibility by the apostle Paul to both the man and the woman (in the use of the word *anthropos* in his letters to the Roman and Corinthian churches). The teaching that Eve was to blame for the fall and uniquely cursed as a result was traced to the rabbis of the pre-Christian era. We also saw that blame-shifting started with fallen Adam. This blame-shifting has been given justification by possible mistranslations of Genesis 3:16, and in particular a misunderstanding of the Hebrew word *teshuqa*. The word implies no ideas of inferiority or subordination as the traditional interpretations indicate, but rather means to run back and forth, giving a picture of "turning". *Teshuqa* presents a picture of Eve turning from God to her husband and the natural consequence of that idolatry, that Adam would rule over her. The spiritual principle found in 2 Peter 2:18–22 and Galatians 4:9 reveals that yielding to something (or someone) other than God, gives it (or them) power over us. Genesis 3:16 does not pronounce divine judgement or punishment upon Eve for her sin. This passage stands as a prophetic declaration of what the consequence of sin would be for both Eve *and* Adam. Eve would experience captivity through codependency and dictatorship, bringing much pain and sorrow. The verse provides insight into the suffering ahead, offering a brief glimpse into why man and woman will need the redemption of a Savior in the generations to come.

Chapter 4 notes

[1] Charles Trombley, *Who Said Women Can't Teach?* (Bridge Publishing, South Plainfield NJ, 1985), p. 33.

[2] Richard C. Kroeger and Catherine C. Kroeger, *I Suffer Not a Woman – Rethinking 1 Timothy 2:11–15 in Light of Ancient Evidence* (Baker Book House, Grand Rapids, 1992), p. 20.

[3] Katherine C. Bushnell, *God's Word to Women* (1923, reprinted by Ray Munson, N. Collins NY), par. 102.

[4] Ibid., par. 15.

[5] Charles Trombley, *Who Said Women Can't Teach?* (Bridge Publishing, South Plainfield NJ, 1985), p. 108.

[6] James T. Davis and Donna D. Johnson, *Redefining the Role of Women in the Church* (Christian International Ministries Network, Santa Rosa Beach, FL, 1997), p. 44.

[7] Ibid., pp. 27–28.

[8] Fuchsia Pickett, "Male and Female Created to Co-Labor With God", *Spirit Led Woman* (June/July 1999).

[9] Katherine C. Bushnell, *God's Word to Women* (1923, reprinted by Ray Munson, N. Collins NY), par. 16.

[10] Ibid., par. 16.

[11] *The Spirit-filled Life Bible,* Jack Hayford, General Ed. (Thomas Nelson, Nashville TN, 1991), p. 9.

[12] James T. Davis and Donna D. Johnson, *Redefining the Role of Women in the Church* (Christian International Ministries Network, Santa Rosa Beach, FL, 1997), p. 27.

[13] Kay D. Rhodes, *Let My Women Go* (Kay D. Rhodes, Rock Hill SC, 1994), p. 52.

[14] Jane Hansen, *Fashioned for Intimacy* (Regal Books/Gospel Light, Ventura CA 1997), p. 70.

[15] Ibid., p. 69.

[16] John Temple Bristow, *What Paul Really Said About Women* (HarperCollins, San Francisco, 1988), p. 18.

Chapter 5

Affirmation of Women in the Old Testament

"Charm is deceptive, and beauty is fleeting;
but a woman who fears the LORD is to be praised.
Give her the reward she has earned,
and let her works bring her praise at the city gate."
(Proverbs 31:30–31 NIV)

As we have seen in earlier chapters, God created Adam and Eve with joint dominion and positional equality. But from the time of the fall onward, a gradual decline in the status of women ensued, as both men and women began to operate out of the shame, fear and self-centeredness that are so much a part of the carnal nature. Because of sin, the relationship deteriorated from the mutual honor and submission that existed before the fall, to an unhealthy relationship where woman began to serve man instead of God. The man in turn, began to see her as an object for his own pleasure and convenience, someone to be put up with rather than loved and cherished as his own body. In the codependent relationship, he began to use the authority she gave him over her to control and dominate.

We have biblical proof of Eve's turning from God to serve Adam. By 1100 B.C., record exists of women referring to themselves, whether literally or figuratively, as "slaves" of both their husbands and other male authority figures. We see this in the relationship of Hannah and Eli the Priest (1 Samuel 1:16, 18), Ruth and Boaz (Ruth 3:9), Abigail and the soldier David (1 Samuel 25:24), and in the husband–wife relationship of Bathsheba and David (1 Kings 1:17). The Hebrew in each of these cases speaks of a servant, slave or maid – someone who is controlled by another and lives to do their bidding. God, however, has taken great care to affirm the value of women. The Father has more than once intervened in order to save us from ourselves and our poor choices. God sought to liberate woman from the snare into which she had fallen, invoking a plan which culminated in the Cross and in restoration of joint dominion, positional authority and freedom from the curse of sin.

God's mind and heart expressed in the Old Testament

Many of us have been taught that God's dealings with women under the old covenant were repressive and set men into a place of superiority over women. Study shows us this is not true! As Lorry Lutz has concluded, "The Old Testament honours women, and nowhere does it teach their inferiority or culpability." [1]

Divine directives

The Scriptures mention God's directive for man to "cleave" to his wife four times: in Genesis 2, Matthew 19, Mark 10 and Ephesians 5. The Hebrew *dabaq*, "to cleave", implies more than sexual union. It denotes a relationship of intimacy, transparency, and nurture. *Dabaq* means "to cling to, stick to, join oneself to." The Lord intended for man to join himself to His wife, and to open himself to her as a part of himself.

The Lord's repeated injunction to the Israelites was that they were to *honor, respect and obey* both father *and mother* (Exodus 20:12; Leviticus 20:9; Deuteronomy 21:18–19; 27:16; Leviticus 19:3; Proverbs 15:20; 30:17). There was no time limit put on this charge, rather it was to continue throughout their lifetime. Adult men, therefore, were required to submit to at least one woman. But more importantly, the Father's heart to see women respected and honored is revealed through these passages.

Sarah and Abraham

In studying Genesis chapter 21, we see that God treated Sarah with respect and honor. He told Abraham (circa 2500 B.C.),

"Whatever Sarah has said to you, listen to her voice" (Genesis 21:12). He explained that Sarah was correctly discerning His plan concerning Hagar and Ishmael and indicated that Abraham was to submit to her.

God not only changed Abraham's name (from Abram), but He also changed Sarah's (from Sarai). He treated them equally, adding an "h" sound to both names. Some have said this "h" sound represents God breathing upon and into Abram's life. If that is the case, He was careful to breathe into Sarai's life as well! The Lord prophesied to Sarah as well as Abraham, declaring in Genesis 17:16 (NIV) that Sarah would be *"the mother of nations"* and that *"kings of peoples will come from her."* We hear so much about the promises made to Abraham, but rarely about the similar promises made to Sarah! I never realized that the Lord had made the same promises to both of them until I recently studied this passage again in depth.

We find greater equality in Abraham and Sarah's relationship than is often taught. For one thing, when God appeared to Abraham at the oaks of Mamre (Genesis 18), He asked Sarah's whereabouts. And although she was present only from behind the tent door, as was the custom of the time, God knew she was there and brought her into the conversation at the end saying, *"No, but you did laugh!"* (Genesis 18:15). Sarah also seemed to have a great deal of input in the decision-making. Going into Hagar was her idea (maybe not such a good one either) and *"Abram heeded the voice of Sarai"* (Genesis 16:2).

Interestingly enough, both names Sarai and Sarah are from the same Hebrew root *sar*, which means "a prince, ruler, leader or chief". Katherine Bushnell quotes a Professor Robertson Smith who points out that the stem of the word "Israel" is from the same root *sar* as Sarai and Sarah. He points out that her name (not Abraham's) was handed down to the children as their family name in the word "Israel".[2] It is important to note that it was the Lord who gave this name to Jacob (Genesis 32:28), making a public statement that He affirmed the value and dignity of women.

Protection and provision

We find that God included women, protected women and provided for women throughout the historical record of the

Old Testament. We've heard the negative, but let's look at the positive:

* God made His covenant with *all* Israel, including women and children (Deuteronomy 5:1–3).

* God provided for the happiness of new wives, calling the husband to lay down his life and his own agendas to serve her and focus *solely* on their relationship for the first year of their marriage (Deuteronomy 24:5).

* God commanded Moses to make provision for daughters to inherit in certain cases (Numbers 27:1–8; 36:2–9; Joshua 17:3–6). Job, after he received a greater revelation of God's mind and heart through his suffering, provided for his daughters to inherit as well as his sons (Job 42:15).

* God took a special interest in making provision for widows, so they would not be abandoned or abused (Deuteronomy 25:5–9; Exodus 22:22–24; Psalm 68:5–6; Malachi 3:5).

* God made sure that women captives (prisoners of war) were treated fairly, forbidding them to be sold as slaves and commanding that they must be set free if the Israelites did not care to keep them (Deuteronomy 21:10–14).

* Fathers were absolutely forbidden to prostitute their daughters (Leviticus 19:29).

* While impoverished Hebrew parents sold their daughters as slaves or servants, we find that girls were not singled out – they also sold their sons into servitude as well. While this was not an ideal situation, God made provision for *both* male and female Hebrew servants to be set free after six years (Deuteronomy 15:12–18). Also, *both* male and female slaves were allowed to stay and become bondservants by choice at the end of the six years if they so desired (Deuteronomy 15:16–17). The exception involved a girl sold to be a bride. In this case the Lord made other provision for her (Exodus 21:7–11).

Hagar: an example of God's heart to lift up women

The account of Hagar is an example of the special interest that God takes in women. Hagar was carrying Abraham's child, and was contemptuous of Sarah because of her barrenness. Sarah responded to the hurt by hurting Hagar back and treating her so harshly that she ran away into the desert. There God met Hagar and let her know that He understood what she was going through. For this reason, she called Him *"You-Are-the-God-Who-Sees"* (Genesis 16:13). God convinced her to return and submit to Sarah, assuring Hagar that He had a plan. Many years later, after Isaac was born, Sarah once again got upset with the whole situation, this time because she saw Ishmael mocking them at the party to celebrate Isaac's weaning (Genesis 21:9). So Hagar and the boy were sent away into the wilderness. After all the food and water was gone and she resigned herself to perishing, God met her again. He comforted her, encouraged her and then supernaturally sustained her and the boy in the Wilderness of Paran. Whatever Hagar's mistakes, God had His eye on her and was there to uplift her, provide for her, sustain her, encourage her and even use supernatural means to ensure that she fulfilled her destiny!

Social conditions in ancient Israel

Prior to 500 B.C., we find that women had much more liberty than many suppose. Women in ancient Israel operated in more freedom than the Hebrew women of later generations before Christ. Will Varner, former Dean of the Institute for Biblical Studies, writes from a Messianic Jewish perspective. Regarding women in ancient Judaism, he says, " ... there was more freedom for women than has been taught. In the centuries following the close of the Old Testament, however, the rabbis instituted practices that went beyond the biblical norms and resulted in much greater restrictions on women's privileges. These rabbinical strictures were not inspired by God." [3] More will be said, however, about the changes that occurred during the Intertestamental period in Chapter 6.

Matthews and Benjamin, in the *Social World of Ancient Israel 1250–587 BCE*, looked at the Hebrew household and the role of women in the domestic sphere. They discuss at length the "mother of the household" in ancient Israel. They conclude that:

- The mother of the household "had significant power and authority over decision-making and problem solving for both land and children."

- "Although the power and authority of the mother of the household were distinct from the power and authority of the father of the household, they were not necessarily inferior to his."

- "Not every man became the father of a household ... in some cases, the status of the mother of the household was equal to or greater than the status of many men in the village."

- In the context of the household, her authority was absolute and "in the world of ancient Israel, a man's home was his wife's castle. She had the domestic authority which he did not." [4]

As some scholars have pointed out, a distinction seemed to be made between public and private spheres of life in ancient Israel. Generally, the man was dominant in one sphere (the visible, public one) and the woman dominant in the other (the hidden, private one). [5]

Women in the public sphere

Even though the authority of women was normally within the private sphere in ancient Israel, we see exceptions to this historically. Hebrew women *were* given authority in the public sphere as well. The Lord at times placed women in official, public positions of leadership.

Varner, in studying the role of women in ancient Judaism, concluded, "women were able to serve at the door of the Tabernacle (Exodus 38:8), take a Nazirite vow (Numbers 6:2), hear the Word of God (Nehemiah 8:2–3), engage in music ministry (Exodus 15:20–21; 1 Chronicles 25:6), and sometimes even prophesy (Exodus 15:21; Judges 4:6–7)." [6] In an unpublished research paper which was designed to bring some preliminary observations to a further look at the role of women during the Second Temple Period, J. Julius Scott notes that "informal sources portray some specific women as occupying specific positions that many would consider impossible. For example, inscriptional evidence describe some individuals as *archisynagogus, elder,* and even *mother of the synagogue,* at times without reference to their husbands – they seem to have held these positions on their own!"[7]

Regarding the women who served and had a place in the Tabernacle services, both Exodus 38:8 and 1 Samuel 2:22 mention these women. The King James Version says they "assembled", but the Hebrew actually has a military connotation meaning to fight, to wage war or to serve as a soldier. The assembling is as army troops! *In the Hebrew,* Psalm 68:11 uses the same word and presents the same picture of women warriors. The NASB version is one of the few which directly brings out the gender in this verse. In the Spirit-Filled Life Bible, for example, one must turn to a Kingdom Dynamics note under Romans 16:1 to discover the Hebrew in Psalm 68:11 is actually speaking of a company of women.

We must be reminded that in joining with Barak at his request, Deborah functioned as a military leader as well as a political and spiritual leader. I've heard it taught that God only allowed Deborah in these positions of leadership because there were no qualified men available. Baloney! God is perfectly capable of raising up whoever He wants to put in leadership. God says in His Word, *"By me kings reign, and rulers decree justice. By me princes rule, and nobles, all the judges of the earth"* (Proverbs 8:15–16, emphasis added) and *"I commanded judges to be over my people Israel"* (2 Samuel 7:11). Is God's declaration only true in circumstances where the person in authority is a man?

Here are a few specific examples of how the Lord sanctioned women in positions of leadership or authority in the Old Testament period, operating in the public sphere in a way which may be surprising:

1. **Miriam** – She was a recognized prophetess (Exodus 15:20) who led the women in public praise after God's deliverance at the Red Sea (Exodus 15: 20–21). She was considered one of the leaders of Israel, along with her brothers Moses and Aaron (Micah 6:4).

2. **Deborah** – As mentioned previously, she was a prophetess as well as judge and military leader who joined with Barak in directing the defeat of the Canaanite army (Judges 4:4–5:31). Because of her courage and submission to God, the nation enjoyed peace for 40 years. Most translations

render Judges 4:4 as Deborah "a prophetess, the wife of Lapidoth". However, according to Kathryn Riss, a student of the Hebrew language, the word translated "wife" here equally means "woman". She goes on to note that Lapidoth is not a recognized man's name. "Rather, she says, it is the ordinary feminine plural for the word 'fire'."[8] Deborah was well known as a woman full of fire.

3. **Huldah** – She was a recognized prophetess whose advice was sought by the high priest and the head scribe of Judah in 2 Kings 22:12–20. Interestingly enough, her advice was sought rather than that of Jeremiah, who was prophesying in Jerusalem at the same time! The result of her involvement was that revival came to the nation.

4. **The "Host of Women"** – Psalm 68:11 speaks of a host of women who proclaimed God's Word. Some translations simply use "company" or "host" without specifying gender, however, there is often a footnote explaining that the Hebrew refers to women. The New American Standard Bible reads, *"The LORD gives the command; the women who proclaim the good tidings are a great host."* The Hebrew word for "host" is the word *tsaba'*. It is a military word denoting an army or an assembly of army troops or warriors. As mentioned earlier, this is the *same* word used to describe the women who assembled and served at the door of the Tabernacle (Exodus 38:8; 1 Samuel 2:22).

5. **The Wise Woman of 2 Samuel 20** – Sheba, son of Bicri, had incited people to desert King David and follow him instead. So David sent his emissary, Joab, and troops after Sheba. He ran from them and hid himself in a city called Abel Beth Macaah. As they were battering the city wall to bring it down and continue their search for Sheba, a "wise woman" put her head over the wall and asked to speak to Joab. She recognized that they would destroy the city to find him (verse 19). After ascertaining the details of the situation, the woman spoke for the entire city and said, *"His head will be thrown to you over the wall"* (verse 21). Then, the account tells us, she went to all the people and convinced them this was the best course of action. Not only did they listen to her, but they also followed her

advice and obeyed her. Her wisdom and influence saved her city from destruction.

6. **Salome Alexander** – Ruler of Judea from 76–67 B.C. She was supportive of the Pharisees, the cutting edge church leaders of her day. It is said they "blossomed" under her rule. Rabbinical tradition remembers the nine years of her reign as "a miniature golden age."[9]

Summary

Despite the curse of sin affecting man–woman relationships, God continually affirmed the value of women and made provision for them throughout the record of the Old Testament. The biblical record shows that God called the men of ancient Israel to treat women fairly, to mutually submit, and to listen to their wives. It also shows that God put women in positions of political and spiritual leadership. Contrary to popular belief, the Lord did not place women in these positions because there were no qualified men available. This is an argument often used by traditionalists to explain how Deborah came to be a judge of Israel. Proverbs 8:15–16 and 2 Samuel 7:11 refute this notion, however. God placed exactly who He desired in positions of leadership to fulfill His will and purposes.

In studying the culture of ancient Israel we find that women actually had more freedom and authority than what is generally assumed. In the domestic realm, the mother of the household wielded significant power and authority. Women were also given authority in the public sphere, as archeological and inscriptional evidence has shown. Even as late as the Second Temple period women functioned as elders, mothers of the synagogue, and even synagogue rulers. However, as we shall see in the next chapter, the freedom and authority held by women in ancient Israel was gradually withdrawn as Hebrew culture was increasingly affected by Greek thought and Hellenism.

Chapter 5 notes

1 Lorry Lutz, *Women As Risk-Takers for God* (World Evangelical Fellowship in assoc. with Paternoster Publishing, Carlisle, Cumbria, 1997), p. 27.

2 Katherine C. Bushnell, *God's Word to Women* (1923; reprinted by Ray Munson, N. Collins, NY), par. 278.

3 Will Varner, "Jesus and the Role of Women, *Israel My Glory* (August/September 1996), pp. 17, 20.

4 Victor H. Matthews and Don C. Benjamin, *Social World of Ancient Israel 1250–587 BCE* (Hendrickson Publishers, Peabody, MA, 1993), pp. 23–25.

5 Richard N. Longenecker, "Authority, Hierarchy and Leadership Patterns in the Bible" in *Women, Authority and the Bible*, Alvera Mickelsen, Ed. (InterVarsity Christian Fellowship, 1986), p. 67.

6 Will Varner, "Jesus and the Role of Women", *Israel My Glory* August/September 1996), p. 17.

7 J. Julius Scott, unpublished paper Wheaton College Graduate School, "Women in Second Temple Judaism: Some Preliminary Observations".

8 Kathryn Riss, "Women Prophets" in *God's Word to Women* web page, 1998.

9 F.F. Bruce, *Paul – Apostle of the Heart Set Free* (William B. Eerdmans Publishing Co., originally published by Paternoster Press Ltd., Exeter, 1977), p. 48.

Chapter 6

The Deteriorating Status of Women As Sin Has Multiplied

"For the wages of sin is death . . . "
(Romans 6:23)

Sinful patterns began to operate in the lives of Adam and Eve after the fall, working spiritual death into all aspects of their lives. Indeed, these patterns became intrinsically woven into the fabric of the carnal human nature. Dysfunction characterized by fear, mistrust, competition, blame, deception, selfishness, stubbornness and domination became a part of the human condition and the relationship between men and women. The enemy's strategy was to separate man, male and female, not only from God, but also from one another! God's plan to establish them in joint dominion and authority over the earth, to be interdependent, cleaving to and helping one another, seemed to be successfully blocked. As time marched on, the sin operating to isolate, divide and separate men and women from one another progressed to unbelievable proportions. According to one authority on repeated patterns of sin and curses:

> "Generational influences multiply ... a curse becomes magnified as it is relived in each succeeding family. Sin begets sin. There is a law of increasing returns with each generation." [1]

Certainly, we see this pattern in the historical record of the Bible. By the time Noah came along, sin had multiplied so greatly that,

> *"the* LORD *saw that the wickedness of man was great in the
> earth, and that every intent of the thoughts of his heart was
> only evil continually. And the* LORD *was sorry that He had made
> man on the earth, and He was grieved in His heart."*
>   (Genesis 6:5–6)

Noah, however, found favor with God. The Lord identified
Noah as a man of justice and integrity (v. 9). When He decided
to wipe out the human race and start all over again, He
preserved the life of Noah and his family to be those who would
once again replenish the earth. Within a matter of generations,
however, mankind was expressing his sinfulness again by
exalting himself, trying to make a name for himself and
endeavoring to save himself through his own efforts at the
Tower of Babel (Genesis 11:1–9).

The entire Old Testament is a record of the downward
spiral of mankind, the nation of Israel in particular, into the
labyrinth of sin. It is a testimony of the generational legacy that
became part of our earthly inheritance at the fall, revealing
clearly our need for redemption and for a Savior.

In this chapter, we shall see how the position of women grew
increasingly worse as sin multiplied. We shall trace the thread
of oppression through Greek culture to its influence on the
rabbis of the pre-Christian era, on the Church Fathers and,
ultimately, on the church leaders of the modern day. We shall
also look at how the status of women worldwide has been
affected by the progression and multiplication of sin in human
relationships.

Old Testament examples

We see scriptural evidence of the worsening plight of women as
sin propagated greater sin. The following examples from the
Old Testament reveal the growing alienation between men
women, resulting in degradation and abuse of women.

1. **Genesis 19:8** – When Lot's home was surrounded by the
    men of Sodom who wanted to have sexual relations with
    the angels who were staying with him, Lot offered them his
    virgin daughters.

2. **Genesis 38:24** – Judah operated by a double standard – He was ready to have his daughter-in-law Tamar burned because she had prostituted herself, even though he had himself visited a prostitute (whom he later found out was Tamar in disguise). Once his own sin was exposed, he graciously did not follow through with the order to have her burned!

3. **Judges 19:22–20:5** – When a travelling Levite was surrounded by the men of Benjamin who wanted his host to throw him out to them so they could have homosexual relations with him, the host pleaded with the men to take his virgin daughter and the Levite's wife instead. When the men would not listen, the host threw out the Levite's wife anyway and the men of Benjamin gang-raped and abused her throughout the night. She died the next morning.

4. **2 Samuel 16:20–22** – Absalom publicly raped the ten women whom king David had left in charge of the household in Jerusalem to assert his right over David's kingdom.

The Bible does not condone these acts. It merely records that they happened. However, all Scripture is profitable to us – *"for doctrine, for reproof, for correction, for instruction in righteousness"* (2 Timothy 3:16). Do you think it is possible that these things were recorded so that we might see how horribly far we have fallen and repent?

Greek philosophers' views on women

As early as the 9th century B.C., the Greek bias towards women was evident. The story of Pandora's Box (circa 800 B.C.) was a Greek myth that promoted the idea that women were responsible for the evil in the world. It is Katherine Bushnell's contention that the rabbis, influenced by this Greek tale and its underlying philosophy, began to conform the story of Eve to that of Pandora.[2] Pythagoras (580 B.C.) similarly taught that Adam would have remained happy and immortal if there had been no Eve.[3] We see a melding of this Greek myth with Judaism in the apocryphal book Ecclesiasticus (also called Sirach). Susan Hyatt marks this as the first recorded reference to Eve being evil and responsible for all the evil in the world, like Pandora.[4] Ecclesiasticus was written about 250 B.C., during the Intertestamentary period.

The foremost Greek philosophers who influenced ideas about women for centuries to come were Socrates, Plato and Aristotle. Plato was teaching about the time that the scribes (who would later become rabbis) were being raised up under the leadership of Ezra after the Babylonian captivity.

Plato (428–347 B.C.) studied under and was a disciple of Socrates, who is said to have "immortalized the Athenian disdain for women."[5] Although Socrates thought that everyone should perform the responsibilities of citizenship, he did not believe in equality. Socrates expressed his view of male superiority by saying things like, "Do you know anything at all practiced among mankind in which in all these respects the male sex is not far better than the female?" He also said that being born a woman was divine punishment since women are halfway between a man and an animal.[6] Another disciple of Socrates', Xenophon, is quoted as saying that the ideal woman was one who "might see as little as possible, hear as little as possible, and ask as little as possible."[7] Aristotle, a disciple of Plato's said the "inequality" between male and female "is permanent" and used the same analogy to describe the husband/wife relationship as he used to describe a master/slave relationship.[8] He described females as deformed males and believed they were inferior to men in their ability to reason.[9] Aristotle's bias towards women is illustrated in his study of bees. He unquestioningly assumed that since swarms of bees followed one leader bee, this leader must be a male. Centuries later, of course, it was discovered that this "king bee" was really a queen bee![10]

Respectable Greek wives were forced to lead secluded lives. They could take no part in public affairs, could make no appearances at meals or social occasions, had limited social contact and communication, and received no education. Only the courtesans or high class prostitutes were allowed more freedom. Pericles, the principle ruler of Athens was quoted as saying that the duty of an Athenian mother was to live a life so retired that her name would never have to be mentioned by men for any reason.[11] In other words, a woman's duty was to be a non-person! Greek Stoic philosophers developed the conviction that women were just a temptation and distracted men from higher pursuits. They taught that sexual intercourse was justified only for the purpose of procreation. As John Bristow writes, "In subsequent centuries, the essence of that appeal was felt within the Christian Church ... the finest and most devout men and women would forego sexual intimacy and marriage for the sake of higher spiritual goals." [12] It was through these Greek philosophers that women came to be seen as the source of sin.

The influence of Greek philosophy on Judaism

Greek philosophy continued to be a pervading force in shaping cultural norms and perspectives well into later centuries. There was a tremendous Hellenization of Jewish thought after Alexander the Great's conquest of Judea in the fourth century B.C. J. Julius Scott, in researching the Second Temple Period, noticed that the view of women in Judaism appeared to have degenerated considerably. He goes on to say, "Clearly something happened between the testaments that affected the perception and status of women." He identifies this "something" as the coming of Hellenistic culture. [13] Indeed, Longenecker identifies the third and fourth centuries B.C. as the time in which "an ominous note arose within Judaism, which widened the traditional division between men and women and provided a twisted rationale for male chauvinistic attitudes." [14] The effect of sin on men–women relationships was now given sanction and justification through pagan philosophy! Bushnell claims the Jews were fascinated with Greek culture, leading them to try to reconcile the biblical worldview with the paganism of the Greeks. There were political advantages that supported this process of Hellenization. [15] Edersheim likewise notes the reconciliation of Greek philosophy with Jewish thought during the apocryphal period. He concludes, "Thus, the theology of the Old Testament would find a rational basis in the ontology of Plato, and its ethics in the moral philosophy of the Stoics." [16] We may see evidence of this in 1 Maccabees 1:11–15 (NJB):

> "It was then that there emerged from Israel a set of renegades who led many people astray. 'Come,' they said

'let us reach an understanding with the pagans surrounding us, for since we separated ourselves from them many misfortunes have overtaken us.' This proposal proved acceptable, and a number of the people eagerly approached the king, who authorised them to practise the pagan observances. So they built a gymnasium in Jerusalem, such as the pagans have, disguised their circumcision, and abandoned the holy covenant, submitting to the heathen rule as willing slaves of impiety.''

Bristow agrees that the influence of Greek thought on Judaism was both subtle and far-reaching, citing the obvious influence of this philosophy upon the monastic Essenes, thought to be producers of the Dead Sea Scrolls (between 200 B.C. and A.D. 68) and Philo's attempt to marry the teachings of the Old Testament with the teachings of the Greeks.[17] Philo taught that the proper relationship of a woman to her husband was "to serve as a slave", using the argument that women are more easily deceived than men. He also taught that the only purpose for marriage is procreation [18] and that the creation of woman was the "beginning of all evils." [19] As mentioned previously, Jesus ben Sirach authored an apocryphal book written in the second century B.C. which illustrates the far reaching effect of Hellenism on rabbinical thinking. He wrote, "Woman is the origin of sin and it is through her that we all die." [20] Here we find blame on Eve and women in general for all the sin in the world.

Influence on rabbinical teaching

Rabbinical commentary found in the Jewish oral law also reveals clear influence from the Greek philosophers. The different Talmuds are rabbinical commentaries on the Mishna, which is itself a commentary on the Torah (the Law of Moses). These commentaries became what is known as the Jewish "oral law", rabbinical traditions which were passed down from one generation to the next.

Jesus made it clear in Matthew 5 that rabbinical teaching on the law of God missed the spirit of the law and was bereft of an understanding of the heart and mind of God. When the men brought the woman caught in adultery to Jesus in John 8:3–12 and urged Him to condemn her to stoning according to the oral law, He exposed the double standard of this oral law and the men left ashamed and convicted by God. The rabbinical teaching condemned only the woman and not the man – in opposition to Leviticus 20:10. When the Pharisees rebuked Jesus for not subscribing to this oral law (Mark 7:3, 5), He in turn rebuked them for following it. He quoted the prophet Isaiah and told them that Isaiah was talking about *them* when he prophesied,

> *"This people honors Me with their lips,*
> *But their heart is far from Me.*
> *And in vain they worship Me,*
> *Teaching as doctrines the commandments of men."*
>
> (Mark 7:6–7)

He also told them that they preferred their traditions over the commandments of God (verse 9) and that they made the Word of God of no effect through their tradition (verse 13). Will Varner, a scholar familiar with the Hebrew culture, has written, "These rabbinical strictures were not inspired by God and often reflect a wrong attitude towards women..." In fact, he goes so far as to say the oral law "certainly went far beyond what the Old Testament taught" and should not be identified as biblical.[21]

Trombley lists "Ten Curses of Eve" from Genesis 3:16 which are found in this tradition, having been excerpted from a Talmudic commentary on the book of Genesis. Looking at just a few of these curses, we find that the rabbis advocated conception only at the husband's choice and discretion; the concept that childbirth was a punishment on women for Eve's sin; the husband would rule over the wife since she was his property, the wrapping of woman like a mourner, and confinement to the house.[22] The mindset of the rabbis regarding women is clearly revealed in these "Ten Curses".

Bristow notes that the rabbis were often called "the bruised and bleeding ones" because they would shut their eyes whenever they saw a woman on the street and run into walls and houses![23] He also notes that they used the tenth commandment (Deuteronomy 5:21) to validate their view of women as property of their husbands. But he shows how the rabbis took this commandment out of context of the Ten Commandments as a whole to arrive at their erroneous conclusion. He asks, "How could dedicated scholars of Hebrew Scripture make this kind of blunder in interpretation?" He suggests that perhaps it was because they approached the Scriptures with a fundamental belief in the inferiority of women (a belief, he says, which had its origin outside of Scripture) and then imposed that belief on the Scriptures. In other words, they read *into* the Scriptures, rather than reading *out of* the Scriptures.[24] Fuchsia Pickett asserts that in her fifty plus years of ministry, she has found that many Christians today tend to do the same thing. She has discovered that people quite often "study their Bibles through the eyes of their own prejudices, customs and traditions."[25]

We also see the rabbinical prejudice and distaste towards women in other parts of the oral law. A few examples are in order, not for shock value, but to gain a feel for what was thought and taught. We must remember that *"out of the abundance of the heart, the mouth speaks"* (Matthew 12:34):

- "When a boy comes into the world, peace comes ... when a girl comes into the world, nothing comes."[26]
- "Rather should the words of the Torah be burned than entrusted to a woman ... Whoever teaches his daughter the Torah is like one who teaches her obscenity."[27]
- "All women are nymphomaniacs."[28]
- "A woman is a pitcher full of filth with its mouth full of blood, yet all run after her."[29]
- "He that talks much with women brings evil upon himself..."[30]
- "All we can expect of them [women] is that they bring up our children and keep us from sin"[31]
- A husband could divorce his wife and not return her dowry if she "goes out with her hair unbound ... or speaks to any man."[32]

Rabbinical interpretation of Scripture regarding women was at least partially rooted in the philosophy of the Greeks. It is also important to emphasize that rabbinical interpretation, with its inherent bias, greatly influenced attitudes towards women over the following centuries. Some have noted the similarities between comments made by the rabbis and comments made by the early Church Fathers.[33] These similarities can even be found in some teachings of the modern day Church. One rabbi who did not agree with the Aristotelian view of women, however, was Gamaliel.[34] He provides a noteworthy exception, since he is the rabbi under whom the apostle Paul studied! Later we shall see that Paul, despite what we have thought and taught, was likewise at variance with the Greek attitude towards women.

The influence of Greek philosophy on Christianity

In the preface to his book, *What Paul Really Said About Women*, John Bristow maintains that Greek philosophy has infused Christian theology, and boldly proclaims that "this same Greek philosophy is often preached from Christian pulpits, innocently assumed to be biblical theology."[35] A popular encyclopedia similarly states, "Platonic ideas have had a crucial role in the development of Christian theology", noting that early Church Fathers such as Origen, Augustine, and Clement of Alexandria were "exponents of a Platonic perspective."[36] How can this be? Could a pagan philosophy developed centuries before Christ really be influencing Christian doctrine and practice today? One scholar has put it this way: "The shadow of Plato is 2,300 years long, and has not faded. His thoughts have perhaps had more effect upon the way Westerners think and act than any single mortal man in history."[37] The Greek philosophers thus laid a lasting philosophical foundation for the premise that women are inferior to men. We can actually trace the thread of it from Socrates, Plato, Aristotle and the Stoic philosophers through Judaism and its influence upon the rabbis, to the early Church Fathers and its influence upon them. The writings of these men formulated the thinking of successive generations, becoming almost as authoritative for the Church as the Bible itself!

Origen (A.D. 185–254) was a student of Clement of Alexandria and became his successor as head of the catechetical school of Alexandria. He became Bishop of Alexandria in

A.D. 247. While a strong Christian leader, Origen was also influenced greatly by Gnosticism and Greek philosophy. Some sources identify him as a follower of Plato who endeavored to combine this philosophy with that of Christianity.[38] He saw women as earthly, fleshly and evil. He claimed God would never stoop to look at anything feminine and wrote, "It is not proper for a woman to speak in church, however admirable or holy what she says may be, merely because it comes from female lips."[39] He also said, "What is seen with the eyes of the creator is masculine, and not feminine, for God does not stoop to look upon what is feminine and of the flesh."[40]

Tertullian (A.D. 160–230), called the Father of Latin Theology, was also a Roman lawyer schooled in Stoic philosophy. We see the Stoic influence in his words, "woman ... do you not know that you are (each) an Eve? The sentence of God on this sex of yours lives in this age: the guilt must of necessity live too. *You* are the devil's gateway: *you* are the unsealer of that (forbidden) tree: *you* are the first deserter of the divine law: *you* are she who persuaded him whom the devil was not valiant enough to attack. *You* destroyed so easily God's image in man. On account of *your* desert – that is, death – even the Son of God had to die."[41] He blamed Eve for the fall of mankind, for sin and even for the death of Jesus Christ – then laid the guilt of it upon every woman who has ever lived!

Iranaeus (A.D. 125–165) was, in the earlier years of his ministry, a well known theological teacher and writer. He was one of the foremost representatives of the school of Asia Minor. Later, he moved to France and became Bishop of Lyons, where he served for about 25 years before being martyred. Iranaeus was another Church Father who placed blame for the fall squarely on Eve's shoulders alone. He wrote that by Eve's disobedience, she was the "cause of death both for herself and the whole human race."[42]

Clement of Alexandria (A.D. 150–215) was a founder of the famous Alexandrian school of theology. He taught, "Man is stronger and purer since he is uncastrated and has a beard. Women are weak, passive, castrated and immature...".[43] Clement didn't blame women for killing Jesus as did Tertullian. He simply used hairiness as a criterion for superiority! He is also quoted as saying that men should "turn away from the sight of women. For it is a sin not only to touch but to look."[44] Doesn't this sound like something straight out of the Talmud or the Mishna?

Epiphamus (A.D. 315–403) became Bishop of Cyprus and later Salamis. He wrote, "For the female sex is easily seduced, weak and without much understanding. The devil seeks to vomit out this disorder through women..."[45]

John Chrysostom (A.D. 345–407), nicknamed "the golden mouth" because of his eloquence, became the Bishop of Constantinople in A.D. 398. A man of apparent contradictions, he encouraged the work of deaconesses and yet he made statements that indicate an underlying bias towards women. For example, he said, "God maintained the order of each sex by dividing the business of human life into two parts and assigned the more necessary and beneficial aspects to the man and the less important, inferior matters to the woman."[46] He also compared going to a woman for instruction to that of going to the "irrational animals of the lower kind" such as the ant in Proverbs 6:6.[47] He further insisted that "there is one excuse for marriage, namely, avoiding fornication."[48]

Ambrose (A.D. 340–397), Bishop of Milan, is credited with the baptism of Augustine. He wrote, "Thus woman is inferior to man, she is part of him, she is under his command. Sin began with her, she must wear this sign, the veil."[49]

Jerome (A.D. 340–420) was known as one of the foremost scholars of the western Church during his time. He was responsible for producing the Latin translation of the Bible called the Vulgate. The Vulgate was the basis for the King James Version of the Bible produced in the 17th century. Jerome seemed to share the low view of women characterized by the other Church Fathers. He said, "Woman is a temple built over a sewer." He further commented that women, especially those who assumed leadership roles in religion, were "miserable, sin-ridden wenches." He felt that if a woman wanted to serve Christ, "she will cease to be a woman and will be called a man."[50]

Augustine (A.D. 354–430), Bishop of Hippo, probably had the greatest influence of all the early Church Fathers on modern Christianity. John Calvin and Martin Luther, leaders of the 16th century Reformation and fathers of the Protestant Movement, were both close students of Augustine. Manichaeism, a Persian dualistic philosophy that incorporated some Gnostic elements, heavily influenced him and his teachings. He was also influenced by Neoplatonism.[51] Augustine believed that women were not created in God's image – only men were, and that the Gnostic concept of evil flesh was embodied in woman whereas the concept of pure spirit was embodied in the husband. As a result, he believed women had no spiritual authority, disqualifying them from teaching or being witnesses for Christ.[52] It is important to note that the Lord did not seem to share Augustine's viewpoint! He chose women to be witnesses of Christ's resurrection, with the responsibility to share the good news with the rest of His disciples. Also, Augustine's statements conflict with the practice of the Church at that time, as it is historical record that women were ordained as abbesses who ruled and taught both men and women until about the 8th century.[53] They also functioned as teaching deacons through at least part of the third century.[54]

The rise of institutionalism

By time of Augustine's death, the Church birthed in Pentecost had undergone a complete transformation. It had changed from a thriving, living organism, sustained by the power of God, rooted in His love as expressed through relationship and community, with a decentralized base of control ... to a cold, dead institution, bereft of life and power, with liturgy as a substitute for relationship, and dominated by a hierarchical structure of control. As a result, lay ministry by both men and women began to disappear. It was replaced by the professional minister who was qualified by education, title and position rather than by gifting or anointing. It was replaced by people ordained of men rather than of God.

I was delighted one day in December 1997 to find a remark on the Internet credited to David (formerly Paul) Yonggi Cho, made during a church growth conference in Helsinki. He said, "If you want to build an organization, work with men. If you want to build Jesus' Church, work with women." While I was initially taken aback that such a prominent figure would make such a bold (and perhaps unpopular) statement, I could instantly see evidence of the truth of his statement in Church history. When women were an active part of the early Church, as we will see in more detail in later chapters, the Church was living and growing. But when the philosophy of the Greeks, with their disdain for women and conviction of their inferiority, finally impacted Christian doctrine and practice, the Church became an organization and an institution with a great deal of structure and no life.

During the sixth century, the Church entered what is known as the Dark Ages. As the infusion of paganism and Greek philosophy into Christian theology choked out biblical truth, the life and freedom Jesus came to bring was lost. In A.D. 567, for example, the Council of Tours blamed women for luring men into sin and compared them to serpents who "make themselves more alluring by shedding their skin."[55] Christian women were back in bondage again, held in chains by the tenets of a pagan philosophy cloaked in religious jargon.

Thomas Aquinas and pagan philosophy

In the later years of the Dark Ages, Thomas Aquinas (1225–1274) was instrumental in securing the melding of Christian beliefs with Greek philosophy.[56] He was a Dominican monk appointed by the Pope as an authoritative teacher of Roman theology. As Bristow has summarized,

> "Aquinas did more than any other to systematize Christian beliefs and to harmonize them with Greek philosophy. In this monumental task, Aquinas interpreted the writings of St. Paul through the mind of Aristotle, and the Greek deprecation of women became solidly infused within Christian theology. Since that time, both Catholics and Protestants have tended to read Paul's words through the eyes of pagan philosophers who lived 5 centuries before the apostle!"[57]

What was the fruit of this "harmonization" of Christianity with Greek philosophy? Susan Hyatt identifies one poisonous fruit as a result of this unholy matrimony. She calls attention to the fact that the Medieval Church sanctioned the beating of wives based on the "headship" supposedly espoused by 1 Corinthians 11:3 and on their concept of woman's sinfulness.

She continues on to explain that in the 13th century, "the Laws and Customs of Beauvais advised men to beat their wives 'only within reason' since an excessive number of women were dying of marital chastisement."[58]

As sin multiplied: domination of women a cultural norm

Multiplication of sin and man's domination of woman has stretched through the centuries to impact the world, inflicting great pain and suffering on women. These tragic patterns continue today. Lorry Lutz cites figures that are astounding. She notes that approximately one quarter of the world's women are violently abused in their own homes. Statistics reveal that in Papua New Guinea 60% of women are violently abused, in Thailand 50%, in Korea 60%, and in Pakistan a whopping 80%. She also notes that in 1996, almost 2 million girls around the world were forced to undergo genital "circumcision", a mutilation process that is said to "make girls more desirable for marriage, ensure virginity, and keep them from sexual wrongdoing." Nigeria, Ethiopia, Egypt, Sudan and Kenya are apparently the worst offenders.[59] As Jane Hansen points out, "The fact that sex will be excruciating for them the rest of their lives is of no consequence."[60]

Hyatt cites a *Time International* special report, which revealed that the international sex trade sold no less than *30 million* girls between 1991 and 1993.[61] Further, in Bosnia, 20,000 women have been raped "as part of Serbian ethnic cleansing."[62]

Buddhism, Hinduism and Islam all teach that women are inferior to men and a source of disdain. A Sri Lankan proverb says, "She is born a woman because she committed a thousand sins in the previous world."[63] Sri Lanka is a predominantly Buddhist nation. In Hinduism, women are of less value than a cow. "Her husband is her god," writes Lutz, "and serving him is the only way to gain merit." She quotes the Indian government's Department of Women and Child Development as saying, "In a culture that idolizes sons and dreads the birth of a daughter, to be born female comes perilously close to being born less than human."[64]

Islam likewise devalues women. The majority of female genital mutilation cases seem to occur among Muslims. Also, the highest incidences of violent abuse against women seem to occur among Muslims. Here is just one example. As early as 1998, a petition was circulating on the internet regarding the sub-human treatment of women in Afghanistan since the Taliban took power in 1996. This petition was to be submitted to the U.S. government, asking for intervention in the plight of women in that country. The petition compared the treatment of women to the treatment of Jews in pre-Holocaust Poland. As the petition explained, "Homes where a woman is present must have their windows painted so that she can never be seen by outsiders. They must wear silent shoes so that they are never heard. Women live in fear of their lives for the slightest misbehavior ... It is at the point where the term 'human rights violations' has become an understatement. Husbands have the power of life and death over their women relatives, especially their wives, but an angry mob has just as much right to stone or beat a woman, often to death, for exposing an inch of flesh or offending them in the slightest way." [65] This sort of treatment is just the natural progression of the Islamic mindset that looks upon women as property and valuable for four reasons: her money, her family, her looks or her religion.[66] Interestingly enough, according to Abdiyah Akbar Abdul-Haqq, an evangelist whose family converted from Islam, the prophet Muhammed was greatly influenced in his development of Islamic doctrine and practice by Christian and Jewish thinking of that time (6th–7th century AD).[67]

Even more recently, the Egyptian rape law has come to the forefront of the news. Men can be sentenced to death if convicted of rape, but there is a loophole. If the perpetrator, or one of the perpetrators in the case of gang rape, marries the victim, then all are set free! The shame and stigma of rape falls on the young girl or woman in this Muslim society. Often she is killed to restore honor to her family. As an alternative, she is often forced to marry the rapist. Supporters of this law say it is in the best interest of women – they need not be killed (for being the victim) and they have perhaps their only opportunity for marriage (to their attacker). Says one women's counselor in Egypt, "It is not enough that she was [emotionally] slaughtered by the rape. By marrying the rapist, she has the opportunity to be slaughtered again ... " Thankfully, Egyptian President Hosni Mubarak issued a decree to end this loophole. As of April 1999, the decree was awaiting legislative approval.[68]

Summary

While God had a plan for joint dominion and authority, for mutual honor and submission, for unity and intimacy, Satan had a plan to block it and bring separation, enmity and hurt between the sexes. What came in seed form at the time of the fall, blossomed into sheer ugliness with the multiplication of sin from one generation to the next.

The Old Testament records the downward spiral of the nation of Israel into sin, revealing clearly mankind's need for redemption. This downward spiral was revealed in many ways, one being the way in which men in the Old Testament often treated women. There are a number of examples of women offered for men's sexual pleasure and abuse, of double standards, of public humiliation and victimization of women. The Bible does not condone these things. It merely records the fact that they happened.

Satan's seed fell upon fertile ground in the hearts of the Greek philosophers who lived centuries before Christ. Most influential among these were Socrates, Plato and Aristotle. The bias, loathing and disdain they had for women were evident in their remarks and teachings. Greek philosophy became a force which pervaded and shaped cultural norms throughout the coming centuries. There is clear evidence that the Greek view of women had a penetrating influence upon rabbinical thought. The rabbis identified woman as the source of sin, blaming Eve for the fall of mankind. Ultimately, the thread of oppression promoted by the Athenian mindset worked its way through Judaism into the thinking and attitudes of the early Church Fathers. However, the early Church Fathers were *directly* affected by the Athenian mindset as well, since many of them were schooled in Greek philosophy and advocates of the Platonic perspective. Finally, the philosophy of the Greeks wound its way into western thought and the Church teachings of our modern day. Sin was, in effect, given justification within the Church by a pagan philosophy, which has subtly shaped interpretation of the Scriptures. God's heart and original plan and purpose for women were lost as the Scriptures have been interpreted out of a mindset that sees women as inferior, sinful, weak, and disqualified.

The multiplication of sin through the centuries has also led to the establishment of domination and abuse of women as a cultural norm in many eastern cultures. Buddhism, Hinduism and Islam all teach that women are inferior to men and a source of disdain. Shame, abuse and captivity are the logical conclusion of a sinful mindset that sees women as objects or possessions rather than people with an inherent value, dignity and worth. Jesus came to restore that worth and to bring a re-expression of the Father's heart towards women, as we shall see in the next chapter.

Chapter 6 notes

[1] Dan LeLaCheur, *Generational Legacy* (Family Survival, Inc., Eugene OR, 1994), p. 49.

[2] Katherine C. Bushnell, *God's Word to Women* (1923, reprinted by Ray Munson, N. Collins NY), par. 118.

[3] Lorry Lutz, *Women as Risk-Takers for God* (World Evangelical Fellowship in assoc. with Paternoster Publishing, Carlisle, Cumbria, 1997), p. 29.

[4] Susan C. Hyatt, *In the Spirit We're Equal* (Hyatt Press, Dallas, 1998), p. 238.

[5] John Temple Bristow, *What Paul Really Said About Women* (Harper Collins, San Francisco, 1988), p. 3.

[6] Ibid., pp. 4–5.

[7] Ibid., p. 5.

[8] Ibid., p. 6.

[9] Ibid., p. 111.

[10] Ibid., p. 5

[11] Ibid., pp. 6–7.

[12] Ibid., p. 8.

[13] J. Julius Scott Jr., unpublished paper Wheaton College Graduate School, "Women in Second Temple Judaism: Some Preliminary Observations".

[14] Richard N. Longenecker, "Authority, Hierarchy and Leadership Patterns in the Bible in *Women, Authority and the Bible*, Alvera Mickelsen, Ed. (InterVarsity Christian Fellowship, 1986), p. 69.

[15] Katherine C. Bushnell, *God's Word to Women* (1923, reprinted by Ray Munson, N. Collins NY), par. 86.

[16] Alfred Edersheim, *The Life and Times of Jesus the Messiah* (McDonald Publishing, McLean, VA, no date, originally published 1883), pp. 31–32.

[17] John Temple Bristow, *What Paul Really Said About Women* (HarperCollins, San Francisco, 1988), p. 24.

[18] Richard N. Longenecker, "Authority, Hierarchy and Leadership Patterns in the Bible" in *Women, Authority and the Bible*, Alvera Mickelsen, Ed. (InterVarsity Christian Fellowship, 1986), p. 70.

[19] Elaine Pagels, *Adam, Eve and the Serpent* (George, Weidenfeld and Nicolson, Ltd., London, 1988), p. 64.

[20] Sirach 25:24.

[21] Will Varner, "Jesus and the Role of Women", *Israel My Glory* (August/ September 1996), p. 20.

[22] Charles Trombley, *Who Said Women Can't Teach?* (Bridge Publishing, South Plainfield NJ, 1985), p. 30.

[23] John Temple Bristow, *What Paul Really Said About Women* (HarperCollins, San Francisco, 1988), p. 20.

[24] Ibid., pp. 22–25.

[25] Fuchsia Pickett, "Male and Female Created To Co-Labor with God", *Spirit-Led Woman* (June/July 1999).

[26] Babylonian Talmud, Niddah 31b.

[27] Babylonian Talmud, Kiddushin 70a.

[28] Babylonian Talmud, Ned 20a.

[29] Babylonian Talmud, Shabbath 152a.

[30] Mish Aboth 1:5.

[31] Bab Yebamoth 63a.

[32] Ketuboth 7:6.

[33] Ruth A. Tucker and Walter Liefeld, *Daughters of the Church* (Zondervan Publishing House, Grand Rapids, 1987), pp. 89–90.

[34] John Temple Bristow, *What Paul Really Said About Women* (HarperCollins, San Francisco, 1988), p. 27.

[35] Ibid., p. xii.

[36] Microsoft (R) Encarta, "Plato", Copyright (c) 1994 Microsoft Corporation. Copyright (c) 1994 Funk & Wagnalls Corporation.

[37] Christian Overman, *Assumptions That Affect Our Lives* (Micah 6:8, Chatsworth CA, 1996), p. 150.

[38] Microsoft (R) Encarta, "Origen", Copyright (c) 1994 Microsoft Corporation. Copyright (c) 1994 Funk & Wagnalls Corporation.

[39] Charles Trombley, *Who Said Women Can't Teach?* (Bridge Publishing, South Plainfield NJ, 1985), p. 203.

[40] Leonard Swidler, *Biblical Affirmations of Woman* (The Westminster Press, Philadelphia, 1979), p. 342.

[41] John Temple Bristow, *What Paul Really Said About Women,* (HarperCollins, San Francisco, 1988), p. 28.

[42] Ruth A. Tucker and Walter Liefeld, *Daughters of the Church* (Zondervan Publishing House, Grand Rapids, 1987), p. 95.

[43] Charles Trombley, *Who Said Women Can't Teach* (Bridge Publishing, South Plainfield NJ, 1985), p. 202.

[44] Ruth A. Tucker and Walter Liefeld, *Daughters of the Church* (Zondervan Publishing House, 1987), p. 97.

[45] Leonard Swidler, *Biblical Affirmations of Woman* (The Westminster Press, Philadelphia, 1979), p. 343.

[46] Ruth A. Tucker and Walter Liefeld, *Daughters of the Church*, (Zondervan Publishing House, Grand Rapids, 1987), p. 124.

[47] Ibid., p. 125.

[48] Ibid., p. 126.

[49] Charles Trombley, *Who Said Women Can't Teach* (Bridge Publishing, South Plainfield NJ, 1985), p. 205.

[50] Susan C. Hyatt, *In the Spirit We're Equal* (Hyatt Press, Dallas, 1998), pp. 55–56.

[51] Microsoft (R) Encarta, "Augustine, Saint", Copyright (c) 1994 Microsoft Corporation. Copyright (c) 1994 Funk & Wagnalls Corporation.

[52] Charles Trombley, *Who Said Women Can't Teach* (Bridge Publishing, South Plainfield NJ, 1985), p. 206.

[53] Ruth A. Tucker and Walter Liefeld, *Daughters of the Church*, (Zondervan Publishing House, 1987), p. 135.

[54] Leonard Swidler, *Biblical Affirmations of Woman* (The Westminster Press, Philadelphia, 1979), p. 313.

[55] Susan C. Hyatt, *In the Spirit We're Equal* (Hyatt Press, Dallas, 1998), p. 58.

[56] John Temple Bristow, *What Paul Really Said About Women* (HarperCollins, San Francisco, 1988), p. 29.

[57] Susan C. Hyatt, *In the Spirit We're Equal* (Hyatt Press, Dallas, 1998), p. 59.

[58] Ruth A. Tucker and Walter Liefeld, *Daughters of the Church* (Zondervan Publishing House, Grand Rapids, 1987), p. 131.

[59] Lorry Lutz, *Women as Risk-Takers for God* (World Evangelical Fellowship in assoc. with Paternoster Publishing, Carlisle, Cumbria, 1997), p. 33.

[60] Jane Hansen, *Fashioned for Intimacy* (Regal Books/Gospel Light, Ventura CA, 1997), p. 65.

[61] Susan C. Hyatt, *In the Spirit We're Equal* (Hyatt Press, Dallas, 1998), pp. 5–6.

[62] Ibid., p. 6.

[63] Lorry Lutz, *Women as Risk-Takers for God* (World Evangelical Fellowship in assoc. with Paternoster Publishing, Carlisle, Cumbria, 1997), p. 34.

[64] Ibid., p. 34.

[65] Melissa Buckheit, Brandeis University, *Petition: The Taliban's War on Women* (Email petition circulated, 1998).

[66] Anne Cooper, *Ishmael My Brother* (STL Books/Operation Mobilisation, Kent, England, 1985), p. 113.

[67] Abdiyah Akbar Abdul-Haqq, *Sharing Your Faith with a Muslim* (Bethany Fellowship, Minneapolis MN, 1980) pp. 13–15.

[68] Tarek el-Tablawy (Associated Press), "Marrying Victim No Longer Option for Egyptian Rapists" (*Washington Times* April 19–25, 1999), p. 25.

Chapter 7

The Son: Re-expressing the Father's Heart Towards Women

"This people honors Me with their lips,
But their heart is far from Me.
And in vain they worship Me,
Teaching as doctrines the commandments of men."
(Mark 7:6–7)

Ruth Tucker and Walter Liefeld open the first chapter of their book, *Daughters of the Church,* with a story out of the gospel of Luke. It is about two contrasting figures who appear at the opening of the Christian era: an old man, Zechariah, and a teenage girl named Mary. They point out that Luke artistically looks at one then the other, contrasting Zechariah's doubt with Mary's faith. Then they make this stunning statement, "The new era, about to be proclaimed in the gospel of Jesus Christ, begins with the faith of a woman." [1] Jesus ushered in this new era with a complete departure from the traditions of the time and the commandments of the rabbis concerning women. He was radical. He was infuriating. He paid no attention to the oral law of the rabbis. Instead He listened only to His Father, doing and saying only what the Father told Him to do and say (John 5:19; 8:19,28–29). His attitude towards women was very different from that of His day. While many argue that Jesus preserved the status quo and traditional view of women in failing to force a total break with Greek and Hebrew norms, they fail to acknowledge the radical departures that He did take from such norms. While they might argue that He did not go far enough, it is clear that He went a very long way towards changing the status of women in just three short years. We find a parallel in the way Jesus handled the "Gentile question". We know from the Old Testament, even as far back as the Abrahamic Covenant, that God purposed His kingdom to include Gentiles or non-Jews. Yet Jesus did not fully address this issue. The gospel was not preached to the Gentiles until after His death and resurrection (Acts 10:45–11:1).

Practical reasons why women could not be among the twelve

Some traditionalist Church leaders today suggest that women are disqualified from leadership on the basis of gender because Jesus did not choose any women to be one of His twelve disciples. While Jesus had a number of women disciples as we shall see later, this question about why no women were among the twelve needs to be studiously examined.

The first and foremost reason is that scholars recognize His choosing of the twelve was a symbolic act to represent the twelve tribes of Israel.[2] He chose twelve men to represent these twelve tribes (ruled by patriarchy) in order to make a statement that Israel was entering into a new day and a new covenant with the Lord. Tucker and Liefeld note that this is why a successor to Judas had to be chosen and why this group would never be accepted among the Jews if one of them was a woman.[3] Secondly, there are a number of practical considerations that would have prohibited a woman from travelling with Jesus and the twelve. This was an intimate group who talked, ate, slept and used the toilet together. Having traveled with a U.S. Forest Service fire crew in my younger years, fighting forest fires across Arizona and California, I can testify to the extreme practical difficulties of a woman travelling intimately with a group of men. My experience was in modern times when it was considered fairly acceptable, and with modern conveniences!

Third, although Jesus promoted women as both witnesses and disciples, establishing a woman as one of the twelve would have been a strategic blunder, given the serious prejudice and disdain for women in that day. The twelve were intended to be "official" witnesses of the resurrection of Jesus (Acts 1:15–26) and to be the foundation for the emerging Christian Church (Acts 1:2–3; Ephesians 2:20). From a purely practical standpoint, a woman would have been a hindrance to the fulfillment of God's plan because in the culture of the time, women were not considered valid witnesses legally and would not have been accepted as religious teachers or leaders. A foundation had to be laid first. Spencer, in noting that the barrier between Jew and Gentile was not broken until after Jesus' death and resurrection, deftly exposes the weakness of the popular argument which casts women as disqualified from spiritual leadership because the twelve disciples were all men. She says, "If Jesus' choice of 12 male disciples signifies that females should not be leaders in the Church, then, consistently His choice also signifies that Gentiles should not be leaders in the Church."[4] One must conceed she makes an excellent point!

How Jesus affirmed women

Jesus called Himself the "Son of Man", the Greek *anthropos* meaning humankind, male and female. In doing so, He established Himself as the coming Messiah, Savior and Redeemer for all human beings – male or female. During His three years of ministry on earth, He challenged the cultural and religious norms of the day and modeled something completely different. He laid a foundation for the liberty of women from the consequences of the fall which would be built upon after the new covenant was sealed in His blood.

Jesus intended His teachings for both men and women

The four gospel accounts show us that Jesus frequently used women as examples in His parables and teaching stories. This was unusual for His culture.[5] He taught using numerous parallel examples of both a man and a woman. For example, in Luke 15 Jesus first spoke of the parable of the lost sheep in which a man figures as the central character. Then He tells the parable of the lost coin, to illustrate the same truth, using a woman as the central character. This balance reveals Jesus' heart to give equal importance and place to men and women. It also shows that, unlike other rabbis, His teaching was intended for both men and women. He was careful to use situations and characters in

His parables that both groups could relate to and thereby understand the spiritual truth He was illustrating. The enormity of this is not clear until we recognize the fact that women were not normally allowed to be taught the Scriptures or to receive religious teaching or training under a rabbi. They were not considered worthy of it. He revealed in no uncertain terms that *His* teaching was for both men and women. It is also important to note that His depictions of women were *always* positive. He sometimes presented men in a negative light in His parables and teachings – as harsh, cruel, unmerciful, arrogant, etc. (for example: Luke 12:13–21; 18:9–14; Matthew 18:21–35; 21:33–44). However, He *never* presented women in a negative light. As Swidler notes, "This was in dramatic contrast to His predecessors and contemporaries"[6]

Jesus affirmed the value and dignity of women by healing them

Today, we think nothing of a woman being healed by God. But in that time and in that culture, a woman was considered to be inferior, unworthy, inconsequential and not important. The attitude was, "Why bother? It is only a woman." Yet Jesus flew in the face of the cultural attitudes towards women by responding to their cries for help and attending to their needs with love and compassion.

He healed Peter's mother-in-law who was sick in bed with fever (Mark 1:29–31). He healed Jairus' 12-year-old daughter by raising her from the dead (Mark 5:21–43). Of note here is that He ignored the laws concerning uncleanness by touching the corpse, which was considered unclean. On the way to heal Jairus' daughter, Jesus healed the woman with the issue of blood, again flaunting the laws about ritual uncleanness (Leviticus 15:19–30). According to the law, a woman with a discharge, whether menstrual or not, was considered unclean. Also, anyone or anything she touched was considered unclean. Jesus did not care and showed it publicly. He was more concerned with the woman than He was with the letter of the law. When He got the whole story from the woman who lay trembling at His feet, His response to her was simply, *"Daughter, your faith has made you well. Go in peace, and be healed of your affliction"* (Mark 5:34).

He also went out of His way to heal a woman on the Sabbath (a definite no-no), right in front of the leader of the synagogue! He was willing to risk the difficulties it brought for Him because He cared so much for the poor woman who had been bent over double for 18 years. This account is found in Luke 13:10–17. Several things are significant about this passage. First, He called to the woman, inviting her to come to Him. Men did not speak to women publicly, even their own wives.[7] Secondly, He risked a stir by healing her on the Sabbath. Thirdly, He called her a "Daughter of Abraham." This was an unusual expression. Men were called "Sons of Abraham" to show they were part of God's chosen people, but women were considered to have no part in the inheritance or covenant blessings of Abraham. By a subtle twist of words, Jesus made it clear that from God's perspective, women had an equal part in His covenant with Israel.[8]

Finally, Jesus healed the daughter of the Syrophoenician woman by delivering her from a demon (Matthew 15:21–28). This case was unique because Jesus actually stepped beyond the boundaries of His prescribed ministry ("I was not sent except to the lost sheep of the house of Israel") to heal a young woman, and at the request of another woman! Though the woman was a Gentile, and Jesus told her He was not sent to the Gentiles, her tenacity and faith caused Him to move on her behalf. Although Jesus could have rebuked this woman for being "pushy", He instead praised her "great faith" and granted her request.

Jesus put men and women on equal footing in marriage

"Some Pharisees came and tested him by asking, 'Is it lawful for a man to divorce his wife?' 'What did Moses command you?' he replied. They said, 'Moses permitted a man to write a certificate of divorce and send her away.' 'It was because your hearts were hard that Moses wrote you this law,' Jesus replied. 'But at the beginning of creation God "made them male and female". "For this reason a man will leave his father and mother and be united to his wife, and the two will become one flesh." So they are no longer two, but one. Therefore what God has joined together, let man not separate.' When they were in the house again, the disciples asked Jesus about this. He answered, 'Anyone who divorces his wife and marries another woman commits adultery

*against her. And if she divorces her husband and marries
another man, she commits adultery.'"*   (Mark 10:2–12, NIV)

To understand how powerful a statement Jesus was making
here, we must be reminded that divorce was allowed, but only
the man could initiate it. He could rid himself of his wife if she
displeased him in any way. According to Tucker and Liefeld,
some rabbis considered the size of the woman's bosom or bad
breath to be allowable considerations in a man's desire to
divorce.[9] She could also be divorced if she spoiled his dinner,
talked loudly or was not pretty enough.[10] She was considered a
"possession" of a man along with his oxen and home, per the
rabbis' interpretation of the Tenth Commandment (Deuteronomy 5:21).[11] Also, under Jewish law, a man was never
considered as having committed adultery against his wife. But
if the wife committed adultery, it was against her husband.[12] He
further had the right to send her away, but she could never
leave him.[13] In the above passage of Mark 10:2–12, Jesus brings
equality into marriage for the first time, giving the wife equal
rights and responsibilities that she did not have before. He did
this first by eliminating the idea of divorce completely, except
for unfaithfulness (Matthew 19:9). He then brought further
equality by introducing the concept that a man could commit
adultery against his wife. He introduced the idea that she was
not an object or possession to be used and abused, but another
valuable human being who could be sinned against. Finally, He
promoted equality by suggesting that the woman had the same
right to divorce her husband that the man had. He covered an
option that in reality did not exist at the time, just to affirm the
status of women.

Jesus encouraged women disciples

In the gospel accounts, we find recorded an amazing fact – Jesus
had women disciples who traveled with Him! Do you know I
was a Christian for over 20 years before I discovered this?

*"After this, Jesus traveled about from one town and village to
another, proclaiming the good news of the kingdom of God. The
Twelve were with him, and also some women who had been
cured of evil spirits and diseases: Mary (called Magdalene) from*

whom seven demons had come out; Joanna the wife of Cuza,
the manager of Herod's household; Susanna; and many others.
These women were helping to support them out of their own
means."   (Luke 8:1–3, NIV)

"Some women were watching from a distance. Among them
were Mary Magdalene, Mary the mother of James the younger
and of Joses, and Salome. In Galilee these women had followed
him and cared for his needs. Many other women who had come
up with him to Jerusalem were also there."
                                                 (Mark 15:40–41, NIV)

These women had left the shelter of their homes and families,
and left all convention behind to travel around with Jesus,
support Him financially, and minister to His needs. In a society
where a woman could be divorced for speaking to a man
publicly, this was unheard of! Further, Jesus allowed it! Swidler
reveals that variant renderings of Luke's gospel from the early
2nd century and from the 4th century speak of Him leading
women astray in chapter 23. He concludes that these renderings
"support the notion that Jesus was a feminist, was widely
known to be a feminist, was despised by many for being a
feminist, and was politically denounced as a feminist." He goes
on to say they suggest that Jesus' feminism was perceived as a
capital crime.[14] While I think it a bit much to suggest He
was crucified because He restored dignity, value and freedom
to women, it is possible that His revolutionary attitude towards
women contributed greatly to His plummeting popularity with
the religious leaders of the day!

In all three passages which speak of these women who
traveled with Jesus (Luke 8:1–2; Mark 15:40–41 and Matthew
27:55–56), the Greek *diakoneo* is used. This is the word from
which we get the word "deacon". Swidler cites three apocryphal
sources which corroborate that the early Christians thought of
and referred to these women as "disciples".[15] Tucker and Liefeld
ask the questions, "What does it mean that these women
'ministered' to Jesus? ... Could the women be called ministers?" They conclude that this might be overstating what was
meant by *diakoneo*.[16] But my own thoughts on this are thus:
"Ministry" in the biblical sense is service and our ulimate

ministry is to the Lord. If we are worthy to serve Him, certainly we are worthy to serve others!

These women disciples were faithful to Jesus to the very end. While the male disciples fled (Matthew 26:56; Mark 14:49–50), whether out of discouragement or fear remains a mystery, the women risked their lives to stay with Him. Luke 23:27 records that they met Him on the Via Dolorosa as He was carrying the cross. Matthew and Mark speak of their standing a distance away as He hung on the cross (Matthew 27:55; Mark 15:40). And John shares that several of them came up to the cross and spoke with Jesus before He died (John 19:25–27). As Tucker and Liefeld observe, "in spite of their grief, the fact that Jesus had been executed as a criminal, and the danger from the hostile crowds and officials that all the disciples felt, these women identified themselves as Jesus' followers..."[17] It is intriguing to note that by the time of Jesus' death, the women were accepted by the twelve as part of the larger group of disciples. Luke refers to them in 24:22 as "certain women of our company." They were definitely included!

Mary of Bethany was another woman who moved beyond the social norm of the time to conduct herself as a disciple in a way that was acceptable only for men. And Jesus clearly encouraged her in it! As Martha served, Mary sat at Jesus' feet and listened to His teaching. The picture presented is that of a disciple sitting at her Master's feet receiving instruction, not of worship as is commonly taught.[18] Even when Martha complained about it, Jesus applauded Mary's choice saying that she had chosen the better part (Luke 10:38–42). Mary related to Jesus in a special way that even His closest disciples could not. Unlike the men, she seemed to have a special sensitivity and understanding of His heart. John, Mark and Matthew each relate the story of Mary barging in on a dinner party in Bethany (again, a scandalous act) with an alabaster jar of costly anointing oil (John 12:1–8; Mark 14:3–9; Matthew 26:6–13). She began to anoint Jesus with it, pouring it on His head and anointing His feet, then wiping His feet with her unbound hair (another scandalous act!). Jesus did not resist her or rebuke her, though everyone else at the dinner table was probably in absolute shock. In fact, He commended her to the others for her beautiful act of worship and said that she would be honored for it in the years to come.

Earlier in Luke 7:36–50, another woman had come to Jesus with a flask of oil and done something similar. I've found that various commentaries and study Bibles sometimes confuse (in different ways) the four gospel accounts and the woman involved. However, it seems clear to me that John, Matthew and Mark all refer to the same event, even though there are some differences (as there always are with eyewitness accounts). All three accounts record the event as taking place a few days before Passover and in Bethany. The same words about the value of the spikenard are attributed to Judas or the disciples in each one. The account in Luke is quite different altogether, however. It appears to have occurred much earlier in the ministry of Jesus, before the 12 and the 70 were sent out. It occurred in the home of a Pharisee, not a leper. The woman in the Luke account is of a somewhat different background than Mary of Bethany and the discussion recorded is quite different.

> *"Then one of the Pharisees asked Him to eat with him. And He went to the Pharisee's house, and sat down to eat. And behold, a woman in the city who was a sinner, when she knew that Jesus sat at the table in the Pharisee's house, brought an alabaster flask of fragrant oil, and stood at His feet behind Him weeping; and she began to wash His feet with her tears, and wiped them with the hair of her head; and she kissed His feet and anointed them with the fragrant oil. Now when the Pharisee who had invited Him saw this, he spoke to himself, saying, 'This man, if He were a prophet, would know who and what manner of woman this is who is touching Him, for she is a sinner.' And Jesus answered and said to him, 'Simon, I have something to say to you.' So he said, 'Teacher, say it.' 'There was a certain creditor who had two debtors. One owed five hundred denarii, and the other fifty. And when they had nothing with which to repay, he freely forgave them both. Tell Me, therefore, which of them will love him more?' Simon answered and said, 'I suppose the one whom he forgave more.' And He said to him, 'You have rightly judged.' Then He turned to the woman and said to Simon, 'Do you see this woman? I*

entered your house; you gave Me no water for My feet, but she has washed My feet with her tears and wiped them with the hair of her head. You gave Me no kiss, but this woman has not ceased to kiss My feet since the time I came in. You did not anoint My head with oil, but this woman has anointed My feet with fragrant oil. Therefore I say to you, her sins, which are many, are forgiven, for she loved much. But to whom little is forgiven, the same loves little.' Then He said to her, 'Your sins are forgiven.' And those who sat at the table with Him began to say to themselves, 'Who is this who even forgives sins?' Then He said to the woman, 'Your faith has saved you. Go in peace.'"   (Luke 7:36–50)

This was a woman with a "bad name" (probably a prostitute). As with Mary, He did not resist or rebuke her for her actions. In fact, He spoke with her and let her touch Him and kiss Him – all in front of a Pharisee and his friends! If Jesus' disciples were scandalized when innocent Mary of Bethany did such a thing, this Pharisee and his friends were probably having apoplexy when Jesus let a prostitute unbind her hair, speak to Him and touch Him. He had no regard for their rabbinical laws, religious traditions, or attitude towards women. In fact, He chastised them for not honoring Him as she did. Rather than putting her down and ridiculing her with loathing as the religious leaders of the day would have done, He lifted her up as an example for them to follow. He not only treated her with compassion, but gave her honor, dignity and blessing.

Jesus revealed Himself to women and released them to share

In John 4:1–42 is recorded the account of Jesus and the woman at the well. This woman was a Samaritan who came to the well to draw water. Jesus was waiting there for His disciples while they were off getting food. Jesus again flaunted convention by striking up a conversation with a woman, and a Samaritan woman at that. Then He got a drink from her. That was equally shocking because as a Samaritan she was considered ritually unclean. But His interest and care for her overrode all traditions and custom. Next, He initiated a *theological* discussion with her! In this lengthy discussion, Jesus revealed Himself as the Messiah for the first time – to a woman. After His disciples arrived (in shock), she left her waterpots and took off into the city to tell everyone about Jesus. Verse 39 records that *"many of the Samaritans of that city believed in Him because of the word of the woman who testified..."* (emphasis added). The wording here in the Greek is almost identical to Jesus' words in the Greek in John 17:20, where Jesus prayed, *"I do not pray for these alone, but also for those who will believe in Me through their word."*[19] The Samaritan woman shared the good news, directing people to Jesus, and they believed in Him. This is evangelism. Thus, John 4 records the first evangelist in the New Testament, and it was a woman!

We also find that Jesus revealed Himself to Martha, the sister of Mary, in a way that He did not to the others. He uniquely revealed Himself to her as "the resurrection". As Swidler points out, "Jesus here revealed the central event, the central message, in the Gospel – the resurrection, His resurrection, His being the resurrection – to a woman!" He also notes that Martha made exactly the same public profession word for word (*in the original Greek*) of Jesus as the Messiah and Son of God in John 11:27 as Peter is recorded to have made in Matthew 16:16.[20] Much has been made in Church circles of Peter's divine revelation of who Jesus was, but few realize that a woman had exactly the same revelation, and spoke it in exactly the same words. This spoken revelation was a "prophetic word" in that it testified of Jesus (Revelation 19:10), and revealed the mind and heart of God.

Another woman who received a prophetic word concerning the identity of Jesus as the Messiah was Anna (Luke 2:36–38). She was a recognized prophetess and intercessor, a widow who lived in the temple, serving God *"with fasting and prayers night and day."* When Jesus was taken to the temple as a baby to be dedicated to the Lord according to Jewish law, the Holy Spirit sent a man called Simeon to the temple at the same time for a divine appointment (Luke 2:25–35). This was a devout man that the Lord had spoken to concerning the coming of the Messiah, and as he saw the child Jesus, he gave a prophetic word over Jesus revealing His identity. Just as he finished,

Anna walked in. She also was given a revelation of His true identity and echoed prophetically what Simeon had just said about Jesus as the Redeemer. Earlier we had mentioned how Jesus used parallel stories with both men and women as the central characters, to bring balance and equality of value and importance to women. Here, at the opening of the new age that dawned with the coming of the Messiah, the Father orchestrates the very same thing! A man and a woman *both* receive a revelation of Jesus' true identity and destiny, and *both* prophesy publicly over the baby as He is dedicated to the Lord. Also, the testimony of two or three witnesses was required to verify a fact (Deuteronomy 19:15; Matthew 18:16). The testimony of women, however, was not considered legally valid.[21] Their word did not count for anything. Yet here, the Father establishes women as valid witnesses contrary to the religious thinking and tradition of the time, by allowing a woman to be one of the two witnesses to the identity of His Son.

Finally, Jesus revealed Himself as the risen Lord first to Mary Magdalene and then gave her a commission to tell the others the good news of the resurrection (John 20:11–18). Separately, the whole group of women who came to the tomb were commissioned by an angel to tell the rest of the disciples the good news (Mark 16:1–8). Interestingly enough, both these accounts invoke the literal meaning of the Greek word *apostolos*, one which we call an "apostle". It means "a delegate, a messenger, or one sent forth with orders". A number of different sources mention that the early Church gave Mary Magdalene the title *Apostola Apostolorum*, meaning Apostle of the Apostles. One such source also sagely points out that these accounts must have their basis in fact because any story based on the word of a woman was highly unlikely to have been fabricated.[22] The Lord literally chose women as apostles! He also chose women to be the first witnesses to the resurrection. This again defied Jewish law and custom. As mentioned earlier, the testimony of a woman was not considered acceptable as a witness. This whole event, probably more than anything else, showed God's heart and intent to redeem women from their captivity and release them into a place of equality, dignity and importance in the kingdom of God.

Summary

Jesus continually broke with the traditions, religious law and attitudes of the time regarding women. He continually affirmed women, honoring them, encouraging them in their faith, giving them dignity, equality, value and lifting them up to the men as positive examples. Jesus showed compassion for the women's needs, even risking the hostility of the religious leaders on numerous occasions to receive their ministry to Him and to minister to them. He encouraged them as disciples, even allowing women to travel with Him (though not as intimately as the twelve). He revealed things about Himself to women, often before He revealed these same things to the men. Variant renderings of Luke's gospel suggest that one reason Jesus was executed was because His "feminist" tendencies were leading women astray.

The synoptic gospels not only reveal Jesus' unique attitude towards women and distinctive relationship with them, but also the emerging pattern of God's release of women into liberty and even into ministry. The *first* evangelist recorded in the New Testament was a woman with whom He struck up a theological discussion. The *first* to whom Jesus revealed Himself as "the resurrection" was a woman. The *first* at the tomb were the women and they were allowed to be the *first* witnesses to the resurrection. The *first* person He revealed Himself to as the risen Savior was a woman. He personally sent her as an apostle to the others to share this news.

Jesus' words and actions leave no doubt as to His position regarding women. He laid a sure foundation during the three years of His ministry on the earth for their release as valued witnesses, teachers and leaders in the emerging Christian Church.

Chapter 7 notes

[1] Ruth A. Tucker and Walter Liefeld, *Daughters of the Church* (Zondervan Publishing House, Grand Rapids, 1987), p. 19.

[2] Leonard Swidler, *Biblical Affirmations of Woman* (The Westminster Press, Philadelphia, 1979), p. 289.

[3] Ruth A. Tucker and Walter Liefeld, *Daughters of the Church* (Zondervan Publishing House, Grand Rapids, 1987), p. 47.

[4] Aida Besancon Spencer, *Beyond the Curse* (Hendrickson, Peabody MA, 1985), p. 45.

[5] Leonard Swidler, *Biblical Affirmations of Woman* (The Westminster Press, Philadelphia, 1979), p. 164.

[6] Ibid.

[7] John Temple Bristow, *What Paul Really Said About Women* (HarperCollins, San Francisco, 1988), p. 19.

[8] Leonard Swidler, *Biblical Affirmations of Woman* (The Westminster Press, Philadelphia, 1979), p. 182.

[9] Ruth A. Tucker and Walter Liefeld, *Daughters of the Church* (Zondervan Publishing House, Grand Rapids, 1987), p. 62.

[10] Lorna Simcox, "The Woman's Relationship to Her Home and Family", *Israel My Glory* (August/September 1996), p. 9.

[11] John Temple Bristow, *What Paul Really Said About Women* (HarperCollins, San Francisco, 1988), pp. 18–19.

[12] Leonard Swidler, *Biblical Affirmations of Woman* (The Westminster Press, Philadelphia, 1979), p. 175.

[13] Lorna Simcox, "The Woman's Relationship to Her Home and Family", *Israel My Glory* (August/September 1996), p. 9.

[14] Leonard Swidler, *Biblical Affirmations of Woman* (The Westminster Press, Philadelphia, 1979), pp. 276–277.

[15] Ibid., p. 195.

[16] Ruth A. Tucker and Walter Liefeld, *Daughters of the Church* (Zondervan Publishing House, Grand Rapids, 1987), p. 38.

[17] Ibid.

[18] Ibid., p. 26.

[19] Leonard Swidler, *Biblical Affirmations of Woman* (The Westminster Press, Philadelphia, 1979), p. 190.

[20] Ibid., p. 216.

[21] Ruth A. Tucker and Walter Liefeld, *Daughters of the Church* (Zondervan Publishing House, Grand Rapids, 1987), p. 26.

[22] Lynn Picknett and Clive Prince, *The Templar Revelation*, (Bantam Press, Great Britain, 1997), p. 79.

Chapter 8

Early Church Practice
Reveals New Revelation

*"There is neither Jew nor Greek, there is neither slave nor free,
there is neither male nor female;
for you are all one in Christ Jesus."*
(Galatians 3:28)

After the resurrection, the biblical account takes up forty days later with Jesus' ascension into heaven to be with the Father (Acts 1). Before ascending, however, He commanded the disciples to wait in Jerusalem for the promise of the Holy Spirit. They returned to Jerusalem and gathered together in the upper room to pray and wait on God. The interesting thing though, was that it wasn't just the eleven apostles who gathered there to pray as Jesus commanded. The group included these men, but also Jesus' natural family and "the women". The account does not list all the women individually, but we can make an educated guess that it was the same women disciples who traveled with Jesus, those mentioned in Luke 8, Mark 15 and Matthew 27.

This was a climactic moment in history for women. The veil of the temple was rent in two, the new covenant sealed with the blood of the Messiah, a new order was being birthed ... and women were invited to be included from the very beginning! As most scholars identify the day of Pentecost as the birthing of the Christian Church, we might consider the day when men and women first met together *"with one accord"* to pray and wait on God as the *conception* of the Church. From that point on, women were a valid and integral part of the early Church and its leadership. They were, that is, until paganism began to make its subtle infiltration into the teaching and practice of the Church several hundred years later.

A new church order

Jesus frequently exhorted that the kingdom of God was at hand and encouraged people to come to a place of repentance. Repentance in the Greek is the word *metanoia*, which means literally "a change in thinking." Jesus' primary message was, "Change the way you think!" Indeed, the kingdom of God can only be understood and apprehended through a change in mindset. Today, we hear a lot of talk about "new paradigms" and that "paradigm shifts" are needed to move with what the Lord is doing. But the men and woman of the early Church had some *real* paradigm shifts taking place, especially in relation to the role of women. Let's look *at three key shifts* in mindset that characterized the early Church.

First – anointing for every Christian

The Holy Spirit, along with His empowerment and giftings, was now for everyone, not just a select group. The group of 120 men and women disciples were still gathered together in the upper room when the Holy Spirit fell on the day of Pentecost (Acts 2:1–4). As people looked on in amazement and perplexity, Peter began an explanation of what was happening, referring back to a prophecy in Joel 2:28–32. The key points regarding women were that:

1. God was pouring out His Spirit on *all people*

2. Sons *and daughters* would prophesy

3. He would pour out His Spirit on both men *and women* who served Him (and they would prophesy).

The Greek verb used to denote "prophesy" here means "to speak or share by divine inspiration" and can incorporate Spirit-led praying, worshiping, preaching, teaching or foretelling of future events. We must remember that Revelation 19:10, *"for the testimony of Jesus is the spirit of prophecy,"* reveals that prophecy in the broadest sense of the word is merely that which testifies of Jesus.

We find evidence that the shift in mindset regarding women as valid recipients of the gifts of the Holy Spirit actually worked its way into church practice. Bristow notes that the apostle Paul referred to women praying and prophesying in "such a casual manner" (1 Corinthians 11:4–6) that it suggests public ministry by women in these areas were well established.[1] 1 Corinthians 14, specifically verse 31, makes it clear that *all* may prophesy and that we are to desire the gift of prophecy. Note, though, that the office of the prophet is a higher calling than the gift of prophecy, and not everyone who prophesies is a prophet. Justin Martyr's *Dialogue With Trypho* is one piece of historical evidence that both men and women were operating in the gifts of the Spirit in the early Church.[2]

Second – every Christian a priest

The priesthood – those who could minister to God and minister to the people – was no longer limited to the tribe of Levi but was opened up to *all* believers. The "priesthood of the believer" was established as the blood of Jesus was sprinkled upon the mercy seat for all who would believe in His Name. All the requirements of the priesthood were fulfilled through Jesus Christ: the need to be of special birth, the need to be washed, the special clothing, the anointing with oil, the access to the Holy of Holies. Because of His sacrifice, we can all walk before God as a holy and royal priesthood:

> *"You also, as living stones, are being built up a spiritual house, a **holy priesthood**, to offer up spiritual sacrifices acceptable to God through Jesus Christ ... But you are a chosen generation, a **royal priesthood**, a holy nation, His own special people, that you may proclaim the praises of Him who called you out of darkness into His marvelous light; who once were not a people but are now the people of God, who had not obtained mercy but now have obtained mercy."*
>
> (1 Peter 2:5, 9, 10, emphasis added)

> *" ... To him who loves us and has freed us from our sins by his blood, and **has made us to be a kingdom and priests to***

*serve **his** God and Father – to him be glory and power for ever and ever! Amen.''*   (Revelation 1:5–6 NIV, emphasis added)

*"And they sang a new song, saying: You are worthy to take the scroll, and to open its seals; for You were slain, and have redeemed us to God by Your blood out of every tribe and tongue and people and nation, **and have made us kings and priests to our God**; and we shall reign on the earth.''*

(Revelation 5:9–10, emphasis added)

In this new order of priests, no distinction is made between male and female. Further, believers were admonished in the early Church to teach and learn from one another without any reference to gender. For example, Ephesians 5:19 and Colossians 3:16 both encourage believers to speak to, teach and admonish one another with psalms, hymns and spiritual songs. 1 Corinthians 14:26 says *"Whenever you come together, **each** of you has a psalm, has a teaching, has a tongue, has a revelation, has an interpretation. Let all things be done for edification"* (emphasis added).

Jesus began this paradigm shift by selecting uneducated and untrained people to be the twelve who would represent the move of the twelve tribes into a new era. They became the leaders of a divine movement, laying a foundation for the leadership in this move to rest on God's calling and divine equipping rather than on worldly trappings, position, power, education or gender.

Priest of the home? Some church leaders are fond of saying that a husband is "priest of his home." This, however, is an unscriptural concept and a tradition of man. Nowhere in the Bible is a man called to be priest of his home. In discussing this concept, Dr. Fuchsia Pickett maintains there is more than semantics involved. She suggests that by using the term "priest", man is being given authority over women that God did not give him.[3] Susan Hyatt links this "priest of the home" tradition with the English feudal concepts which permeated the Church of England upon its inception. She says, " ... the home was to be seen as a little kingdom where the man was to rule as king of 'his castle' in the same way that the King of England was to rule the state. Furthermore, the home was also seen as a little church where the man was to rule as high priest in the same way that the King was to rule the Church of England." [4]

Third – the dividing walls are broken down in Christ
The dividing wall between Jew and Gentile, between slave and free, between men and women was broken down, bringing a new unity and oneness in Christ.

> *"For as many of you as were baptized into Christ have put on Christ. There is neither Jew nor Greek, there is neither slave nor free, there is **neither male nor female**; for you are all one in Christ Jesus. And if you are Christ's, then you are Abraham's seed, and heirs according to the promise."*
> (Galatians 3:27–29, emphasis added)

> *"For he himself is our peace, who **has made the two one and has destroyed the barrier, the dividing wall of hostility**, by abolishing in his flesh the law with its commandments and regulations. His purpose was to create in himself **one new man out of the two**, thus making peace, and in this one body to reconcile both of them to God through the cross, by which he put to death their hostility. He came and preached peace to you who were far away and peace to those who were near. For through him we both have access to the Father by one Spirit."*
> (Ephesians 2:14–18 NIV, emphasis added)

Tucker and Liefeld observe that the language of Galatians 3:28 "emphasizes the difference between the old age of the law and the new age of faith." [5] The context of the passage in Ephesians 2 is the hostility between Jew and Gentile. But as we put this passage in context with Galatians 3, we can see that it could equally apply to the enmity between men and women as well. The *spiritual principle* is the same – He desires to break down the dividing wall between us, absolve our differences, and under a new dispensation of grace make us one in Him as we clothe ourselves with Him. His purpose to *"create in himself one new man out of the two"* sounds very much like His intent to unite man and woman in *"one flesh"*. Here we see God's redemptive purposes played out to establish a family, a dwelling place for Himself built of living stones who will complement one another, to reveal Himself in fullness and display His glory in the earth!

Theology in practice – women in the first century Church

As we mentioned at the beginning of the chapter, the emerging Church was conceived as men and women disciples met together in Jerusalem to pray and wait on God for the promise of the Holy Spirit. The women were filled with the Spirit on the day of Pentecost as well as the men, and empowered to be witnesses for Jesus in all the earth as He foretold in Acts 1:8. From this point on, the biblical and historical record shows that they were an integral part of church life and leadership. Bristow advocates that "Jesus' example regarding women became the norm within the apostolic church." He offers Luke 24:22; Acts 1:14; 5:14; 8:3, 12; 9:1–2 and 22:4–5 as evidence.[6] Of special note are the passages that refer to Saul of Tarsus' persecution of Christian men and women. Saul violently pursued and dragged off both men and women to prison, making no distinction between the genders. The inference is that Christian women were visible, of importance or value to the spread of the faith, and considered just as much a threat to Judaism as the men.

The book of Acts makes mention of women quite frequently. Luke was careful to record how they played a part – whether positively or negatively. In Thessalonica, he recorded that a number of the leading women of the city were persuaded to follow Christianity and joined themselves with Paul and Silas (Acts 17:4). Again in Berea, it was reported that a number of Greek women of high standing were saved, as well as some men (Acts 17:12). In Antioch in Pisidia (Asia Minor), women also played a key role, but this time in resisting the gospel! The account in Acts 13:50 tells us that some Jews worked up the devout women of the upper classes and leading men of the city and persuaded them to turn against Paul and Barnabas and expel them from the territory.

Study of the New Testament brings to the forefront a number of women who figured prominently in the early Church. The very fact that these women believers are named specifically is an indication of their importance in the life of the Church.[7]

Lydia (Acts 16:14–15, 40)

Paul, Silas, Timothy and Luke found a meeting place in Philippi one Sabbath morning and shared the good news with the women there. That means they engaged in public conversation with a group of women, certainly not acting according to Jewish tradition at all. They were preaching to women! One of these women was Lydia. She was a businesswoman, a person of means and influence. She received what they had to say and had her whole household baptized with her. The first European convert to Christianity was a woman. She then convinced them to come and stay in her home. They did for a season, establishing their mission headquarters there. After the altercation with the girl with divination, Paul and Silas were thrown in prison. After a miraculous release in which the jailer was saved, they returned to Lydia's where they met with "the brethren" encouraged them and departed. F.F. Bruce, a well-known evangelical scholar, assessed that by the time they moved on, "they had gathered a promising young church together."[8] It certainly sounds as if a church was meeting in Lydia's home, whether or not she was the leader is not known. However, a good case can be made for her being the pastor. Since no husband or father was mentioned, it is probable that Lydia was head of her own household. Roman households were often large, and Lydia's would have been even larger due to the fact that she managed her own business and most businesses were home-based. Since her whole household was baptized with her, and she was most likely already head of the household, it is very probable that she also took on the role to lead them in becoming established in the faith. This is the role of a pastor.

Damaris (Acts 17:34)

Damaris is the only woman mentioned by name who was converted as a result of Paul's preaching on Mars Hill, also called the "Aeropagus" or "Hill of Ares" after the Greek God Mars (called Ares by the Romans). It was an open forum for philosophical debates and was located southwest of the Parthenon on the Acropolis. Damaris was an Athenian who apparently was there during Paul's debate with the Epicurian and Stoic philosophers. Paul's intellectual arguments concerning the existence of God must have struck a chord in her heart, for the Greek text tells us that Damaris and the others (one of whom was a member of the Aeropagus court) not only believed, but joined themselves to Paul "like glue'!

Chloe (1 Corinthians 1:11)

Paul, in writing to the Corinthian church, said that he had heard from some of "Chloe's people" that there were dissentions among them. F.F. Bruce thinks they were part of a house church.[9] Chloe's role is uncertain, but some scholars believer she may very well have been the leader.

Dorcas (Acts 9:36–42)

Dorcas was a woman "disciple" from Joppa who had died. Her name is given in both Aramaic (Tabitha) and Greek (Dorcas) in this passage, suggesting that the society in Joppa was bilingual and bicultural. She seems to have been highly esteemed and very loved. Her friends heard that Peter was close by in Lydda, so they sent for him. He sent everyone out of the room, then got down on his knees and prayed. Then he turned to her, called her by name and told her to get up. At this point, she opened her eyes. He helped her up and presented her alive to the rest of the group. Verse 42 tells us that word of this miracle spread through the city and many believed in the Lord as a result.

Priscilla (Acts 18:2–3, 28; Romans 16:3–5; 1 Corinthians 16:19; 2 Timothy 4:19)

Paul met Priscilla and her husband Aquila, both Jews, in Corinth after they had been forced to leave Rome by the Emperor Claudius (in A.D. 49). They, too, were tentmakers like Paul and he stayed with them while he was in Corinth. Then when he set sail for Syria, they both went with him. He left them in Ephesus while he went on to Caesarea and Antioch. While they were in Ephesus, another Jew came to Ephesus named Apollos (Acts 18:24). He was *"an eloquent man and mighty in the Scriptures"*. The account says he was fervent and bold, but lacking in his understanding (probably that of the new covenant and the ministry of the Holy Spirit) because he only knew about the baptism of repentance preached by John the Baptist.

He was already an educated, able teacher and minister. Priscilla and Aquila took him aside and *"explained to him the way of God more accurately"* (verse 26). In other words, they discipled him. Some believe that the order of the names here implies that it was Priscilla who took the lead in teaching Apollos.[10] Bristow notes that Chrysostom (one of the fourth century Church Fathers) wrote that "Priscilla was a teacher of Apollos, pastor of the church in Corinth after Paul left."[11] Certainly, Apollos went on to be a well known leader in church circles around Corinth, and was used mightily by God to disciple others, as we see from 1 Corinthians 1:12; 3:4–6, 22; 4:6; 16:12.

In Paul's letter to the Roman church, he mentioned Priscilla and Aquila as *"my fellow workers in Christ Jesus"* (Romans 16:3) and as those who had *"risked their own necks for my life."* Please note that he includes Priscilla as a fellow worker in Christ and as one who risked her own life for his! He gave his personal thanks and extended thanks to them both from all the Gentile churches. Then he asked the Romans to *"greet the church that is in their house."* This church in their house was mentioned again by Paul when he was writing to the Corinthian church and sending greetings from Aquila and Priscilla and their house church. They apparently knew Timothy as well, because Paul asked him to greet them for him in his second letter to Timothy, written from prison in Rome (2 Timothy 4:19). Here, he used the nickname "Prisca", revealing a deep familiarity and fondness for Priscilla.

The unique thing about this couple is that they stand out as the first husband–wife ministry team of the emerging Church. They are *always* mentioned together. Neither seems to have been given place or importance above the other, though Bruce comments that more often than not Priscilla's name was mentioned before that of her husband [4 out 6 times]. He speculates that she may have been the more impressive personality of the two.[12] However, the bottom line is that they were both recognized as able ministers of the gospel.

Eunice and Lois (2 Timothy 1:5)

Timothy was a young pastor being mentored by Paul. The letters to Timothy and Titus are often called "the Pastoral Epistles" by scholars. In his second letter to Timothy, Paul credited Timothy's grandmother Lois and mother Eunice with imparting to him their sincere, unhypocritical faith. In 2 Timothy 3:15, Paul speaks of how Timothy has known the Scriptures since he was a *brephos* (meaning embryo, fetus, newborn or baby). Remember any references to "the Scriptures" in the New Testament refer to the Old Testament, as the New Testament had not yet been written or canonized. Certainly, Eunice and Lois would be credited with this accomplishment as well, since Timothy would not have learned the Jewish Scriptures from his Greek father. Paul's implication is that the Lord mightily used these two women to train up this man of God, who would go on to be a significant figure in the early Church.

Euodia and Syntyche (Philippians 4:2–3)

In Paul's letter to the Philippian church, he implores Euodia and Syntyche to come into agreement and urges an unknown person to help them. He calls them *"these women who labored with me in the gospel"*. Swidler points out that the verb used is a strong one and says, "Clearly ... these women did not simply supply material support for Paul and the other men, but preached, taught and spread the gospel as vigorously as they." [13] Herb Hirt, Director of the Institute for Jewish Studies, points out that the verb Paul used implies the idea of "fighting together, as soldiers fighting side by side in battle." [14] Bristow suggests that the very fact that he named them (and was so concerned about their disagreement, I might add) indicates their importance within the Church. [15]

Nympha (Colossians 4:15)

In writing to the church at Colosse, Paul sends greetings to *"Nympha and the church that is in her house"* (NIV). Although the KJV and NKJV give the masculine form of the name, it is noted that the NU text (the most modern prominent Critical Text of the Greek New Testament) specifies the feminine form of the name. The NIV bases its translation on this text. Swidler asserts that Nympha was "unquestionably" a woman. [16] Many feel it very possible that she was also a pastor. If Nympha simply hosted this house church rather than pastoring it, why did Paul not also greet the pastor? And if he did not know the pastor, why would he have reason to know the hostess well enough to call her by name and send his greetings?

Mary and Junia (Romans 16:6–7)

At the beginning of Romans chapter 16, Paul lists a number of church leaders by name who are worthy of praise and greeting. In this list of 28 people, about one third of them are women! This is truly amazing, considering the status of women before Jesus came along. Also, Tucker and Liefeld comment upon this passage, "in the opinion of an increasing number of scholars, two of the highest offices or roles are ascribed to women: deacon (Phoebe) and apostle (if Junias is a woman, Junia)." [17]

One of the women whom Paul mentions in Romans 16 is Mary, *"who labored much for us."* There is no clue here as to how she helped the apostles, but the very fact that Paul knew her well enough to send greetings and to honor her with such a comment is important. If we look at his comment through modern day lenses, it doesn't look like much. But relative to the status that women had before Jesus came (inferior, disdained, loathed), it is significant that he said anything at all. John Chrysostom who was normally rather critical of women, wrote about Paul's greeting of Mary in this passage:

> "How is this? A woman is again honored and proclaimed victorious! Again are we men put to shame ... we are put to shame, in that we men are left so far behind them ... For the women of those days were more spirited than lions." [18]

It is very possible that this Mary is the mother of John Mark mentioned in Acts 12:12. Indications are that she was the pastor of a house church. When Peter was released from prison, he went straight to her house where he knew there would be a gathering of Christians. The International Standard Bible Encyclopedia acknowledges that Mary's house was obviously "a well-known center of Christian life and worship." [19]

In the next verse, Paul also asks that they greet Junia, who he says is *"of note among the apostles."* Strong's Concordance and KJV/NKJV versions identify this person as a woman. Other sources, like *The Spirit-Filled Life Bible*, sidestep any controversy and state, "It is impossible to tell whether this name refers to a

man or a woman."[20] Bristow believes that the confusion comes
in because the name actually occurs in the accusative form in
the Greek text as a recipient of the verb "greet", i.e. it occurs as
Junian. The International Standard Bible Encyclopedia
substantiates his assertion.[21] Bristow's opinion is that Junian is
the accusative form of the feminine name Junia.[22] Swidler
is much more adamant in presenting his case for Junia being a
woman. He states, "Some scholars, unwarrantedly, argue that
Junia is a contraction of a much less common male name; but
even the virulently misogynist fourth-century bishop of
Constantinople, John Chrysostom, noted: 'Oh, how great is
the devotion of this woman that she should be counted worthy
of the appellation of apostle!'" He notes that the earliest
commentator on the book of Romans, Origen of Alexandria
(c. 185–253) also understood Junia to be a woman, as did
Jerome.[23] Junia was apparently recognized as a woman until
the Middle Ages when a male Church hierarchy could not
fathom the idea of a woman apostle. From that point on, the
name appeared in masculine form in various manuscripts.[24]
Katherine Riss cites Bernadette Booten, a philologist, who
comments on the possibility of Junia being the masculine
Junias: "...It is unattested. To date, not a single reference in
ancient literature has been cited by any of the proponents of
the Junias hypothesis. My own search for an attestation has also
proved fruitless. This means that we do not have a single shred
of evidence that the name Junias ever existed."[25] It would
appear that those who argue that Junia was really a man, may
do so because of their inability to accept the fact that there
might have been a woman apostle. And yet, we have already
seen how the women disciples were sent as apostles (the Greek
meaning "a delegate, messenger, one sent forth with orders")
to the twelve as they were commissioned to go tell them the
good news. In the case of the group of women, an angel did
the commissioning (Matthew 28:5–8). However, in Mary
Magdalene's case, this commissioning was accomplished by
the risen Savior Himself (John 20:14–18).

Phoebe (Romans 16:1–2)

Phoebe is another women lauded and greeted in Romans 16 by
the Apostle Paul. Many scholars believe she was the one Paul

sent to carry his letter to the brethren in Rome.[26] Her name means "bright", from the Greek word *phos*. This is where we get the word phosphorus, an ingredient in matches. Of Phoebe he says,

> *"I commend to you Phoebe, a fellow-Christian who holds office in the congregation at Cenchreae. Give her, in the fellowship of Christ, a welcome worthy of God's people, and stand by her in any business in which she may need your help, for she has herself been a good friend to many, including myself."*
>
> (Romans 16:1–2 NEB)

Of note in this passage are two Greek words, *diakonos* and *prostatis*, which Paul uses to describe Phoebe.

1. **Diakonos.** The first is the word *diakonos*, a servant, minister or deacon. Most translations, because of a prior mindset that women should not hold office in the Church, translate this word "servant". The Jerusalem Bible translates it as "deaconess." Tucker and Liefeld point out that, "in the Pauline epistles, the noun form *diakonos*, usually indicated a person with a distinctive Christian ministry. In its meaning of "minister" it appears more frequently than many realize. In 1 Corinthians 3:5; 2 Corinthians 3:6; Ephesians 3:7; Colossians 1:23, 25; and 1 Timothy 4:6 it clearly means someone who ministers the gospel." [27] Bristow notes that Paul used the masculine form of the word here, just as it was used elsewhere in the New Testament to describe the office of a deacon.[28] The Word Bible Handbook says, "This is the same Greek word, deacon, used to identify Paul, Timothy, Tychicus [in Ephesians 6:21; Colossians 4:7], Epaphras [in Colossians 1:7], and the church leaders spoken of in 1 Timothy 3:8, 12! Most translations tend to blur this fact." [29]

2. **Prostatis.** The other word is *prostatis* which means "a woman set over others, a patroness, guardian or protectress." Most of the English translations just render it as "a help" or "a great assistance" or "a friend", which is extremely weak. None of these words carry the full impact of what *prostatis* really means! Indeed, the word belongs to

a word group with a strong connotation of authority and leadership. It was used in ancient Greek to describe divine beings.[30] Lenore Lindsey Mullican, who is an Assistant Professor of Modern Languages at Oral Roberts University, notes a source which defines the word as "exercising authority, to be a leader, to hold office, a leader, a chief, a protector."[31] Ryrie sheds more light on the meaning of *prostatis*. He says "All the New Testament references include to a greater or lesser extent the idea of having authority ... The meanings range from simple presiding to definite ruling." He goes on to add that the President of the council was often called the prostates and this Presidency was exercised by the chief Jew or chief religious person of the province. He further points out that the high priest who held the presidency of the Sanhedrin also held this title.[32]

Other women mentioned

In Romans 16, the apostle Paul also mentioned Tryphena, Tryphosa and Persis – all women who labored or worked hard in the Lord (verse 12). He also mentioned the mother of Rufus whom he said had been like a mother to him (verse 13), then Julia, and the sister of Nereus (verse 15).

Apparently Philemon had a house church, along with the woman Apphia and another man called Archippus (Philemon 1:1–2). Paul greeted the three of them, along with *"the church that meets in your home."* Swidler points out that the "your" is singular and concludes that Apphia was singled out by Paul apparently as a leader in that house church."[33]

Finally, we must make mention of the *"elect lady"* to whom 2 John is written. While some sources advocate that the term is probably just a euphemism for a church, other scholars believe it was written to a real person who probably pastored a church in her home. They base their conclusions on the grammar and the specific words used in the Greek.[34] The Spirit-Filled Life Bible explains that John writes "with instructions concerning whom she allows to minister in her 'house' (a designation for early church fellowships ...)."[35] Another study Bible notes that John may have used this title instead of her personal name in order to protect her from persecution.[36]

Official ministry by women in the early Church

Archeological evidence in the form of papyri and inscriptions from the first centuries suggest that women held ecclesiastical offices, according to Tucker and Liefeld. They conclude that "these texts provide a continuity of evidence for women as office-holders in the Church." [37] Karen Torjesen, in examining various "church orders" from the 3rd century which sought to define the practices of the Church, comments, "the controversies over women's ministries in the church orders teach us much about women's leadership. Women were evangelizing, baptizing, teaching, interpreting Scripture, doing visitation, functioning as leaders of groups within the church, and speaking out in the assembly. The *Statutes of the Apostles* show that women also shared in the eucharistic ministry." [38] There have even been some scattered references in various documents connecting women to the priesthood, and the walls Roman catacombs carry pictures of women "in authoritative stances, with their hands raised in the posture of a bishop." [39] Martha Looper has pointed out that after the 4th century, Eastern and Western Churches began to take separate paths. The Eastern Church, she maintains, stayed closer to its pure Hebrew roots for a longer period of time, with the result that women participated in the sacraments and in the priesthood well into the Middle Ages. [40] Torjesen, in her book *When Women Were Priests*, concludes,

> "Giorgio Otranto, an Italian professor of Church history, has shown through papal letters and inscriptions that women participated in the Catholic priesthood for the first thousand years of the Church's history. The last thirty years of American scholarship have produced an amazing range of evidence for women's roles as deacons, priests, presbyters, and even bishops in the Christian churches from the first through the thirteenth centuries." [41]

Corroboration through the writings of the Church Fathers

The writings of the Church Fathers in the early centuries of the Church also tend to corroborate that women were ministers and leaders in the early Church. This is in spite of the fact that most of these men were either Platonists or influenced greatly by the writings of the Greek philosophers, and subsequently holding the same disparaging view of women. Tertullian (born in A.D. 160) spoke of women having obtained "honor of ecclesiastical orders."[42] Clement of Alexandria is quoted as arguing that 1 Corinthians 9:5 was "not a reference to the wives of the apostles but to ministering women who accompanied the apostles in their ministry. He [Paul] refers to these ministering women (*diakonon gunaikon*), whom as fellow ministers (*sundiakonai*) the apostles took with them, 'not as wives, but as sisters'."[43] John Chrysostom recognized Priscilla as a teacher of Apollos, an evangelist who later became the pastor of the church in Corinth. Further, Chrysostom, Origen and Jerome all identified Junia as a woman, and Chrysostom specifically called her a woman apostle. Ryrie also quotes Origen, born in A.D. 185, in describing Phoebe as set in a ministry office in the church. His assessment of Origen's comments? "Evidently he believed that Phoebe occupied an official position."[44] Evidence for the official ministry of women in the early Church was also provided through correspondence between Pliny, governor of Bithnia, and someone called Trajan, in the year A.D. 111. Pliny wrote about two women slaves who had been arrested because they were Christians. He goes on to say that he submitted to torture to get information from these women "called by them 'deaconnesses'."[45] Ryrie shares this same evidence and concludes, "it is quite likely that these two female slaves were known in their own Greek-speaking community as *diakonoi*, i.e. deacons."[46]

Women presbyters, elders or priests

Ignatius, Bishop of Lyons, described (around A.D. 110) leadership of churches as a team ministry between bishops, priests and deacons. What he called "priests" was a later derivative of the Greek *presbyteroi* (or presbyter).[47] There is evidence from Paul's writings to Timothy (1 Timothy 5:1–2) that there were women presbyters as well as men presbyters. The word literally means "elder", but was also used to refer to members of the Sanhedrin as well as those who led churches. The word *presbeteros*, used for women in verse 1 is the same one used a few verses later (verse 17) which says, *"The elders who direct the*

affairs of the church well are worthy of double honor, especially those
whose work is preaching and teaching" (NIV). Kroeger cites the
usage of the terms *presbytera, presbutis,* and *presbytis* to refer
specifically to a female elder or "eldress." [48] Torjesen notes the
word, whether used to mean priest or elder, referred to a fully
ordained clergyperson.[49] She offers several examples of the
inscriptional evidence which prove women held this office.[50]
Torjesen also reveals the existence of a mosaic in a Roman
basilica which pictures four women. An inscription underneath
one of the women identifies as her as Theodora Episcopa. The
name means Bishop Theodora, using the feminine form of the
Latin word for bishop.[51]

Women deacons

There is evidence that there was an official order of deaconnesses in the Church. Swidler asserts, "Already in the lifetime of
Paul (death A.D. 63), the office of deacon was established ...
Women as well as men served in this 'ordained' office." [52] It was
not until about A.D. 100, that the term "deaconness" came into
use.[53] Swidler points out that the Council of Nicea (A.D. 325)
referred to women deaconnesses as part of the clergy. The
Council of Chalcedon (A.D. 451) gave guidelines on ordaining
of deaconnesses and made reference to them continuing in
their "liturgy". He also notes that the third century Didascalia
(a compilation of instructions on church practice) lauds the
importance of the ministry of deaconnesses, and mentions
that religious teaching (to other women) was part of it. The
Didiscalia likened the ministry of the deaconness to that of the
Holy Spirit.[54] Tucker and Liefeld note that in the Eastern
church, the ministry of the deaconnness lasted more than a
millennium. The cathedral at Constantinople had at one time
in the 6th century, forty deaconnesses under its supervision.[55]

The downward spiral into the Dark Ages

As the philosophy of the Greeks began to rear its head again to
oppress women through the teachings of the early Church
Fathers, the freedom and release gained by women through
the ministry of Jesus and during the first century of the Church
was gradually lost. As early as the second century, it was obvious

that the Church was moving closer and closer to the Dark Ages.
Hyatt points to the persuasion of Ignatius as being a deciding
factor in the rise of the institutional Church, with its emphasis
on authority, hierarchy, and position. She says that early in the
second century, "he designed a church structure like that of
the civil government" in a bid to establish and centralize
control over the various house churches. He was also apparently
very intense in his desire to promote the authority and prestige
of the bishop. She sadly concludes that history demonstrates
the success of his efforts.[56]

One of the earlier Church manuals, the Didache, written
sometime between the first and third century, shows no restrictions placed on the ministry of women and no controversy
surrounding the ministry of women.[57] The Didiscalia, a later
Church manual, mentioned deaconnesses and commended
them. However, by the time of its writing in the third century,
the deaconnesses were limited to ministering only to other
women. Things had already changed since the writing of the
Didache. The Didiscalia also maintained that "women are not
appointed by Jesus to teach and proclaim Christ".[58] Since the
historical record of the gospels show otherwise (a number of
women proclaimed Christ at His direction), and the historical
record of the early Church shows otherwise (Priscilla as an
example taught with the apostle Paul's hearty approval), we can
only assume that the writers of the Didiscalia were influenced
from another direction.

History records that by the 5th century, the order of the
deaconness was coming under more restriction by the Church.
Tucker and Liefeld share that the office of deaconess was
"wholly abolished" in the West in A.D. 533 when the synod
of Orleans decreed that "no woman shall henceforth receive the
benedictio diaconalis, on account of the weakness of this sex."[59]
By the twelfth century (the middle of the Dark Ages), this order
had all but disappeared in the Eastern Church.[60] Interestingly
enough, it was also in the twelfth century that the abbesses of
Kildare, a Celtic Christian community in Ireland, had the
dignity and honor of "Bishop" removed from their titles.[61] As
the Church moved through the Dark Ages, influenced more and
more by pagan thinking and tradition, it became increasingly
institutionalized and women were allowed less and less of a

place in ministry. As the Holy Spirit was quenched and a spirit of deception gained a greater foothold in the Church, the restrictions on women from ministry were given theological justification.

Summary

Historical evidence verifies that the ministry of women was prevelant during the first six hundred years of Christianity. The profusion of women involved in Church life and leadership began with the conception of the Church as men and women gathered together to pray and wait on God for the promised Holy Spirit. The Church was given life as the Holy Spirit was poured out on men and women alike on the day of Pentecost and was characterized by three major paradigm shifts in thinking.

1.   The resident empowerment and giftings of the Holy Spirit were now for *everyone,* not just a select few leaders.

2.   A new priesthood was established, composed of *all* believers, as Jesus fulfilled all the requirements for the priesthood in Himself.

3.   The wall of division which separated groups from one another, including men and women, was understood to be broken down by the atoning work of Christ on the Cross. Just as the veil of the temple was rent in two at the resurrection symbolizing the removal of the barrier between men and God, so the dividing wall was broken down which separated people from one another. The limitations, restrictions and prejudices that come with labeling and relegating people into certain categories were washed away by the stream of Divine blood which flowed from Calvary.

Luke was careful in the book of Acts to record how women played a part in the emerging Church – whether positively or negatively. A study of the entire New Testament brings to the forefront a number of women who figured prominently in the early Church. Some of these were Lydia, Dorcas, Damaris, Chloe, Nympa, Priscilla, Eunice, Lois, Euodia, Syntyche, Mary,

Junia, Phoebe and the "Elect Lady", all of whom are discussed in detail. Not only were they free to exercise and offer to the Church any giftings given by the Holy Spirit, but they also were free to function as pastors, teachers, apostles, prophetesses and evangelists.

There is archaeological evidence, as well as the writings of the early Church Fathers, to corroborate that women were involved in official ministry and leadership in the early Church. Paul's letters to Timothy record the existence of women presbyters or elders and bishops. There are also indications as well as inscriptional evidence, that women functioned as priests as well.

The most extensive role for women after the first century seems to have been that of the "deaconness". This order of ministry for women remained until the twelfth century in the east, but only until the sixth century in the west. It was abolished as an increasing amount of church organization and operation came under episcopal authority and the church became more and more institutionalized. As the Church moved into the Dark Ages, influenced increasingly by pagan thinking and tradition, women were given an ever declining place in ministry and leadership.

Chapter 8 notes

[1] John Temple Bristow, *What Paul Really Said About Women* (HarperCollins, San Francisco, 1988), p. 58.

[2] Ruth A. Tucker and Walter Liefeld, *Daughters of the Church* (Zondervan Publishing House, Grand Rapids, 1987), p. 96.

[3] Fuchsia Pickett, "Man and Woman Created to Co-Labor with God", *Spirit Led Woman* (June/July 1999).

[4] Susan Hyatt, *In the Spirit We're Equal* (Hyatt Press, Dallas, 1998), p. 80.

[5] Ruth A. Tucker and Walter Liefeld, *Daughters of the Church* (Zondervan Publishing House, Grand Rapids, 1987), p. 65.

[6] John Temple Bristow, *What Paul Really Said About Women* (HarperCollins, San Francisco, 1988), p. 54.

[7] Ibid., p. 56.

[8] F.F. Bruce, *Paul – Apostle of the Heart Set Free* (William B. Eerdmans Publishing Co., originally published by Paternoster Press Ltd., Exeter, 1977), p. 221.

⁹ Ibid., p. 258.

¹⁰ Ruth A. Tucker and Walter Liefeld, *Daughters of the Church* (Zondervan Publishing House, Grand Rapids, 1987), p. 69.

¹¹ John Temple Bristow, *What Paul Really Said About Women* (HarperCollins, San Francisco, 1988), p. 56.

¹² F.F. Bruce, *Paul – Apostle of the Heart Set Free* (William B. Eerdmans Publishing Co., originally published by Paternoster Press Ltd., Exeter, 1977), p. 251.

¹³ Leonard Swidler, *Biblical Affirmations of Women* (The Westminster Press, Philadelphia, 1979), p. 295.

¹⁴ Herb Hirt, "Godly Women Who Made a Difference", *Israel My Glory* (August/September 1996), p. 24.

¹⁵ John Temple Bristow, *What Paul Really Said About Women* (HarperCollins, San Francisco, 1988), p. 56.

¹⁶ Leonard Swidler, *Biblical Affirmations of Women* (The Westminster Press, Philadelphia, 1979), p. 296.

¹⁷ Ruth A. Tucker and Walter Liefeld, *Daughters of the Church* (Zondervan Publishing House, Grand Rapids, 1987), p. 72.

¹⁸ Leonard Swidler, *Biblical Affirmations of Women* (The Westminster Press, Philadelphia, 1979), p. 295.

¹⁹ International Standard Bible Encyclopedia, Volume III (Eerdmans Publishing Company, Grand Rapids, 1939, 1956), p. 2006.

²⁰ *The Spirit-Filled Life Bible*, Jack Hayford, General Ed. (Thomas Nelson, Nashville, 1991), p. 1714.

²¹ International Standard Bible Encyclopedia, Volume III (Eerdmans Publishing Company, Grand Rapids, 1939, 1956), p. 1781.

²² John Temple Bristow, *What Paul Really Said About Women* (HarperCollins, San Francisco, 1988), p. 57.

²³ Leonard Swidler, *Biblical Affirmations of Women* (The Westminster Press, Philadelphia, 1979), p. 299.

²⁴ Lenore Lindsey Mullican, "Women in Leadership, A Study in Paul's Views", *Restore!* (Winter 1999), p. 12.

²⁵ Kathryn Riss, "Women's Ministries in the Early Church", from *God's Word to Women* webpage, 1998.

²⁶ Leonard Swidler, *Biblical Affirmations of Women* (The Westminster Press, Philadelphia, 1979), p. 295.

²⁷ Ruth A. Tucker and Walter Liefeld, *Daughters of the Church* (Zondervan Publishing House, Grand Rapids, 1987), p. 72.

[28] John Temple Bristow, *What Paul Really Said About Women* (HarperCollins, San Francisco, 1988), pp. 56–57.

[29] Lawrence O. Richards, *The Word Bible Handbook* (Word Books, Waco, 1992), pp. 625–626.

[30] Ruth A. Tucker and Walter Liefeld, *Daughters of the Church* (Zondervan Publishing House, Grand Rapids, 1987), p. 73.

[31] Lenore Lindsey Mullican, "Women in Leadership, A Study in Paul's View", *Restore!* (Winter 1999), p. 13.

[32] Charles C. Ryrie, *The Place of Women in the Church* (The Macmillan Company, New York, 1958), pp. 87–88.

[33] Leonard Swidler, *Biblical Affirmations of Women* (The Westminster Press, Philadelphia, 1979), p. 297.

[34] Ruth A. Tucker and Walter Liefeld, *Daughters of the Church* (Zondervan Publishing House, Grand Rapids, 1987), pp. 74–75.

[35] *The Spirit-Filled Life Bible*, Jack Hayford, General Ed. (Thomas Nelson, Nashville, 1991), p. 1668.

[36] *The Word in Life Study Bible* (Thomas Nelson Publishers, Nashville, 1993), p. 863.

[37] Ruth A. Tucker and Walter Liefeld, *Daughters of the Church* (Zondervan Publishing House, Grand Rapids, 1987), pp. 91–92.

[38] Karen Torjesen, "Early Controversies Over Female Leadership", *Christian History* (Volume VII, No. 1, Issue 17), p. 24.

[39] Catherine Kroeger, "The Neglected History of Women in the Early Church", *Christian History* (Volume VII, No. 1, Issue 17), p. 11.

[40] Martha Looper, "Her Own Works Shall Praise Her", *Restore!* (Winter 1999), p. 42.

[41] Karen Jo Torjesen, *When Women Were Priests* (Harper, San Francisco, 1993), p. 2.

[42] Leonard Swidler, *Biblical Affirmations of Women* (The Westminster Press, Philadelphia, 1979), p. 313.

[43] Charles C. Ryrie, *The Place of Women in the Church* (The Macmillan Company, New York, 1958), p. 109.

[44] Ibid., p. 111.

[45] Ruth A. Tucker and Walter Liefeld, *Daughters of the Church* (Zondervan Publishing House, Grand Rapids, 1987), p. 94.

[46] Charles C.Ryrie, *The Place of Women in the Church* (The Macmillan Company, New York, 1958), pp. 102–103.

[47] Elaine Pagels, *Adam,Eve and the Serpent*   (George, Wiedenfeld and Nicolson, Ltd., 1988), pp. 57–58.

[48] Catherine Kroeger, "The Neglected History of Women in the Early Church", *Christian History* (Volume VII, No. 1, Issue 17), p. 11.

[49] Karen Jo Torjesen, *When Women Were Priests* (Harper, San Francisco, 1993), p. 5.

[50] Ibid., pp. 10, 19–20.

[51] Ibid., p. 10.

[52] Leonard Swidler, *Biblical Affirmations of Women* (The Westminster Press, Philadelphia, 1979), p. 309.

[53] Catherine Kroeger, "The Neglected History of Women in the Early Church", *Christian History* (Volume VII, No. 1, Issue 17), p. 11.

[54] Leonard Swidler, *Biblical Affirmations of Women* (The Westminster Press, Philadelphia, 1979), pp. 312–314.

[55] Ruth A. Tucker and Walter Liefeld, *Daughters of the Church* (Zondervan Publishing House, Grand Rapids, 1987), p. 133.

[56] Susan C. Hyatt, *In the Spirit We're Equal* (Hyatt Press, Dallas, 1998), p. 41.

[57] Karen Torjesen, "The Early Controversies over Female Leadership", *Christian History* (Volume VII, No. 1, Issue 17), p. 21.

[58] Ruth A. Tucker and Walter Liefeld, *Daughters of the Church* (Zondervan Publishing House, Grand Rapids, 1987), p. 109.

[59] Ibid., p. 133.

[60] Leonard Swidler, *Biblical Affirmations of Women* (The Westminster Press, Philadelphia, 1979), pp. 314–315.

[61] Peter Berresford Ellis, *Celtic Women* (Constable & Co. Ltd., London, 1995), p. 147.

Chapter 9

The Celtic Church:
A Model of 1st Century Christianity

"So continuing daily with one accord in the temple,
and breaking bread from house to house,
they ate their food with gladness and simplicity of heart,
praising God and having favor with all the people. And the Lord
added to the Church daily those who were being saved."
(Acts 2:46–47)

Over the past few years, I've been studying the Celtic Christianity that pervaded the British Isles before the Dark Ages. I previously thought that only Druids populated England in the centuries after the time of Christ – until we moved from the United States to the northeast of England. Then I began to discover that Christianity had been a pervasive force in the northeast at that time, with Christians operating in the gifts of the Spirit, especially prophecy, divine healing and miracles. It was a Christianity based more on community and relationship than on a central structure or hierarchy. There was an outward focus with a clear missionary emphasis and practice. It had life! Further, women were an integral part of the life of the Church, preaching, teaching, and leading communities of both men and women. As I have studied this Celtic Christianity alongside that of the early Church, the parallels have become more and more obvious. The Celtic Christianity of the 5th, 6th and 7th centuries was much more akin to the Christianity of the first century Church than the Roman Christianity that was introduced to England in A.D. 596. As Tucker and Liefeld point out, the Celtic Church remained (at least for a season) insulated from the restrictions that were beginning to be put upon women by Rome at this time, because of their independence from papal authority.[1] That all began to slowly change in A.D. 664 with the Synod of Whitby. However, until that time, the Christianity in Britain was thriving, alive, growing and supernatural.

Possible first century evangelization of Britain

David Gardner, in his book *The Trumpet Sounds for Britain*, asserts that Christianity was already in England and thriving when the Pope sent his emissary Augustine to evangelize the English in A.D. 596. He makes a good case for this, citing several facts. The first fact is that Roman legions first landed in Kent in A.D. 43. At that point, Britain became one of the forty-five provinces of the Roman Empire with an occupation of troops until A.D. 407. (Constantine issued an edict in A.D. 313 which paved the way for Christianity to become the state religion of the Roman Empire 70 years later). Gardner notes how God used the road systems of the Roman Empire to foster the spread of Christianity throughout the Roman Empire. This is a fact recognized by most Church historians. Gardner then cites historical sources which record that a British Christian Church sent Bishops to early Church councils during this time, and comments that Christianity would have needed to be quite well established by that time for such a thing to happen.[2] The historian Eusebius (A.D. 260–340) recorded that "the apostles passed beyond the ocean to the isles called the Britannic Isles", strengthening the case that Christianity came to Britain in the first century.[3]

Gardner also presents a case for Christianity to have arrived even earlier than the Roman conquest of A.D. 43. He shares that Julius Caesar made two peaceful exploratory trips to Britain in 55 and 54 B.C. which opened the way for visits from Roman colonists and traders to begin to penetrate Britain. One historian he quotes asserts that these colonists and traders established settlements in Britain. Gardner then notes that the Feast of Pentecost was attended by people *"from every nation under heaven"* (Acts 2:5) and suggests that some of those converted at that time (3,000 in one day) could have very well been merchants and traders who may have returned to Britain, carrying their newfound faith with them! [4] This sounds entirely plausible when one understands there was evidence of trade between the Celtic people and the Greeks as early as 550 B.C. [5] There is also evidence that the matriarchal society of the Celtic Britons was changed to a patriarchal one long before the birth of Christ, due to influence from Greek and Roman cultures. [6]

Gardner's point, he says, is to establish the *type* of Christianity that was first brought to Britain. If it truly came during apostolic times in the first century, then it would have been something very close to that of the early Church described in the New Testament, unpolluted by later prejudices, heresies, and institutionalization. [7] I was drawn to Gardner's thesis because this same conclusion had dawned upon me as I studied both the Celtic Church of Britain and the emerging Church of the New Testament. For a period of seventy years or so, there were two streams of Christianity operating in Britain concurrently – one was the Celtic version which operated independently of Rome (much to the papal frustration) and the other was the Roman version established by the Pope's emissary Augustine in A.D. 596. The Celtic version was entrenched in the west and the north of Britain and the Roman version in the south. A struggle for Roman supremacy ensued with the fate of the Celtic Church sealed at the Synod of Whitby in A.D. 664. King Oswy of Northumbria, made the decision that they would join with the Roman Church. A move of the Holy Spirit that had spanned several centuries was thereby quenched by the sterility of hierarchical rule, institutionalism and human control. From the Synod of Whitby onward, the light of the gospel was gradually extinguished. England moved steadily into the throes of the Dark Ages.

Women leaders in the Celtic Church

During the years that the Celtic Church thrived in the British Isles, its women leaders were particularly noteworthy. The women played as great a part in Church life and leadership as the men did. There is evidence that they performed "mass" and gave the sacraments. Brigid of Kildare and Beoferlic (Beverly of York) of the Celtic Church in Northumbria were both ordained as Bishops. [8] Celtic women leaders also led large monastic communities of both men, women and children. These were called "double monasteries" by some.

Brigid of Kildare (A.D. 455–525)

Brigid was raised in druidism before converting to Christianity and was named after the druid goddess of fertility. Brigid was known to be brazen and bold. One story describes her boldness and unconventionality. Upon being pestered by an unwanted suitor, she "thrust a finger into her eye, pulling it from the socket until it dangled on her cheek. Appalled, the suitor beat a hasty retreat." [9] After her conversion to Christianity, Brigid was ordained by Mel, the Bishop of Ardagh, who conferred upon her not only the office of priest but that of Bishop as well. Brigid first established a community of believers at Drumcree, then later at Kildare. She ruled a mixed community of both men and women. [10] It has been noted that Kildare was one of the most famous Christian communities in Ireland. The area was apparently a druid stronghold, famous for its magical oak trees. But in the center of this occult stronghold, God used Brigid to establish a stronghold of His kingdom where Christ was exalted. [11] Brigid traveled widely, preaching to both rich and poor, and speaking at Church synods. Miracles were also attributed to her ministry. [12] She became very well known, even beyond her native land, and was given the title "Mary of the Gaels." [13] Michael Mitton, in *Restoring the Woven Cord*, pays tribute to Brigid, noting, "The people of Ireland have traditionally respected Patrick and Brigid as their two greatest evangelists." [14]

Darerca of Killeavy

Darerca was baptized a Christian by Patrick [sometime after A.D. 432], who then asked her to take charge of teaching women converts. Later she stayed with Brigid at Kildare for a time, then went on to become Abbess of a site called Ard Conais' under the direction of Bishop Ibhair. Finally, she founded a new abbey at Killeavy, County Armagh. It too was a mixed community. She was well known for her miracles and exceptional organizational ability. Killeavy was considered one of the most influential centers for the gospel during this time in Ireland. Darerca is recognized to be one of the most influential women leaders during the time of Patrick. The center at Killeavy was taken over by a succession of women abbesses after her death.[15]

Aebbe

Aebbe was the sister of Kings Oswald and Oswy of Northumbria. All three had been raised by the Irish Celtic missionaries in Iona after their father was killed. Here they became Christians. When Aebbe returned to Northumbria in A.D. 634, she founded a mixed religious community at Coldingham, which stood for 50 years. After her death, a mysterious fire destroyed the monastery.[16]

Ide or Ita (died A.D. 570)

Ide, an Irish woman, was called "the bright sun of the women of Munster." She established a community at Limmerick and opened an ecclesiastical school there. One of her more famous pupils was Brendan the voyager (A.D. 486–578). The fact that Brendan studied there suggests that it was also a mixed community.[17]

Hilda of Whitby (A.D. 614–680)

Hilda's given name was originally Hild, meaning "battle" in Anglo-Saxon. She was born into the royal house of Northumbria in northeast England. Hilda was raised a pagan. After her father's murder, she was sent to live in the court of her relative, King Edwin. He had just married a second wife, Ethelburga from Kent, who had become a Christian and been baptized by Paulinus, the Pope's representative in Kent. After a few years, Edwin also became a Christian and was baptized along with his family and followers (including Hilda). Hilda apparently worked in a secular vocation until age 33. At this point she was inspired by the teaching of Aidan, the Celtic missionary from Iona who had established a religious community on the island of Lindisfarne off the Northumbrian coast. Hilda decided to become a nun and went to the south of England to stay with relatives in preparation for going to a convent in France. However, before she could leave, she was contacted by Aidan who begged her to return to Northumbria and establish a monastery of her own.

She was given some land for the monastery on the north bank of the River Wear as it entered the North Sea, called Monkwearmouth. Today the city of Sunderland sits on the spot. A few years later, in A.D. 649, Aidan appointed her the Abbess of Hartlepool farther down the northeast coast. Bede, the great chronicler of Christian history during this time, wrote that Bishop Aidan and other church leaders who knew Hilda's wisdom and love for God used to visit and advise her often while she was at Hartlepool. In A.D. 655, Hilda was given 1200 acres of land by King Oswy to establish a monastery at Whitby, called Streonshalh in Anglo-Saxon. In just seven short years, she built up the community at Whitby from nothing to a well-established community which became a center of learning and training for the priesthood. She trained clergy, sent out preachers and trained scribes to copy manuscripts, as well as directing and administrating a huge, bustling community of religious people, families, scribes, musicians, builders, fishermen, etc. A famous library was built at Whitby. Both abbeys at Whitby and Hartlepool were mixed communities of men and women under Hilda's leadership. Bede reveals that no fewer than five future Bishops were trained at Whitby under Hilda. The famous English poet, Caedmon, also studied under Hilda at Whitby.

The abbey at Whitby has great significance as the setting for the Synod of Whitby. Hilda hosted this historic church conference. Although she did not support the ruling to go with the Roman Church, she accepted it. She continued to establish the abbey in Whitby in strength, influence and reputation until she died in A.D. 680.

Bede comments that Hilda was a much loved woman, affectionately called "Mother" because of her grace and devotion. It is speculated that this is where the term "Mother Superior" originated. In addition to the abbeys at Monkwearmouth and Whitby, Hilda was involved in other "church planting" efforts. Prior to her death, she founded a new abbey, a "cell", at Hackness about 14 miles from Whitby. Hilda was succeeded as leader of the abbey at Whitby by Aelfleda, a woman that she had raised from infancy, trained and mentored. Aelfleda was Abbess over Whitby for thirty-six years.[18] Although Hilda was never ordained a Bishop, she was decidedly a Christian leader who stands out in history – a woman of power and influence, balanced by grace, dignity and the love of God.

I have heard of two legends that surround Hilda. One is that wild geese used to stop and rest in Whitby on their migratory flights to and from the Arctic. Their majestic descent has been described as paying tribute to Hilda. Interestingly enough, the wild goose (instead of the dove) is the Celtic symbol for the Holy Spirit. That the wild geese would choose to stop at Whitby seems somewhat poetic and perhaps spiritually significant when we consider that God has redemptive purposes for specific places. The second legend surrounding Hilda is that of snakes. It is said that she cleansed the area of all its snakes, throwing them over the cliffs to the beach below, where they were killed. The snakes then turned to stone and became the fossil ammonites that so prevail along the beaches below Whitby. I found this very interesting since snakes are a symbol for the demonic. That she may have aggressively cleansed the area of demonic spirits during her many years at Whitby somehow does not surprise me!

Summary

Celtic Christianity was a pervasive force in the British Isles during the centuries after the death of Christ. There is substantial evidence that Christianity was brought to Britain in the first century, perhaps even soon after the Pentecostal outpouring recorded in Acts 2. This Celtic Christianity, which pre-existed in Britain before the Roman Church arrived in A.D. 596, was a purer form of Christianity, exhibiting vivid spiritual life and growth. Celtic Christians operated in the gifts of the Spirit, especially prophecy, divine healing and miracles. The foundation of the Celtic Church was built on community and relationships rather than on a central structure or hierarchy. There was a clear missionary emphasis and practice. Further, women were an integral part of the life of the Church: preaching, teaching, and leading mixed communities of men and women.

There were a number of Celtic women leaders in the Church of the 5th, 6th and 7th centuries which are of note. They include Brigid, Darerca, Beoferlic, Aebbe, Ide (or Ita) and Hilda. Brigid and Hilda stand out as the two with the greatest degree of historical prominence. Brigid was renown for her boldness while Hilda, on the other hand, was renown for her grace and wisdom.

The thriving Celtic Church was dealt a death blow at the Synod of Whitby when the King of Northumbria elected to come under the authority of the Roman Church. The ripples from this historic decision spread outward to affect all of Britain and even the Church in Britain today. For women, it meant the gradual loss of liberty and involvement in Church leadership. The chains of bondage were once again placed upon God's women.

Chapter 9 notes

[1] Ruth A. Tucker and Walter Liefeld, *Daughters of the Church* (Zondervan Publishing House, Grand Rapids, 1987), p. 133.

[2] David E. Gardner, *The Trumpet Sounds for Britain* (Christian Foundation Publications, Cheshire, 1980), pp. 16–17.

[3] Ibid., p. 29.

[4] Ibid., pp. 18–27.

[5] Peter Berresford Ellis, *Celtic Women* (Constable & Co. Ltd., London, 1995), p. 76.

[6] Ibid., p. 30.

[7] David E. Gardner, *The Trumpet Sounds for Britain* (Christian Foundation Publications, Cheshire, 1980), pp. 29–30.

[8] Peter Berresford Ellis, *Celtic Women* (Constable & Co. Ltd., London, 1995), p. 142.

[9] Ibid., p. 147.

[10] Ibid., pp. 147–148.

[11] Michael Mitton, *Restoring the Woven Cord* (Darton, Longman and Todd, Ltd., London, 1995), p. 113.

[12] *Celtic Saints*, Ann Lockhart, Ed. (Pitkin Pictorials, Great Britain, 1995).

[13] Peter Berresford Ellis, *Celtic Women* (Constable & Co. Ltd., London, 1995), p. 146.

[14] Michael Mitton, *Restoring the Woven Cord* (Darton, Longman and Todd, Ltd., London, 1995), p. 113.

[15] Peter Berresford Ellis, *Celtic Women* (Constable & Co. Ltd., London, 1995), pp. 145–146.

[16] Ibid., p. 150.

[17] Ibid., pp. 151–152.

[18] Sylvia Mundahl-Harris, *St. Hilda and Her Times* (Caedmon of Whitby, England, 1997).

Chapter 10

A New Look at 1 Corinthians 11

"Give no offense, either to the Jews or to the Greeks
or to the church of God, just as I also please all men in all things,
not seeking my own profit, but the profit of many,
that they may be saved."
(1 Corinthians 10:32–33)

With these words in 1 Corinthians 10:32–33, the apostle Paul
leads into one of the most difficult passages for scholars and
those seeking to understand the function of women in the
Church. This difficult passage is found in 1 Corinthians 11:1–16
as follows:

> *"Follow my example, as I follow the example of Christ. I praise*
> *you for remembering me in everything and for holding to the*
> *teachings, just as I passed them on to you. Now I want you to*
> *realize that the head of every man is Christ, and the head of the*
> *woman is man, and the head of Christ is God. Every man who*
> *prays or prophesies with his head covered dishonors his*
> *head. And every woman who prays or prophesies with her head*
> *uncovered dishonors her head – it is just as though her*
> *head were shaved. If a woman does not cover her head, she*
> *should have her hair cut off; and if it is a disgrace for a woman*
> *to have her hair cut or shaved off, she should cover her head. A*
> *man ought not to cover his head, since he is the image and glory*
> *of God; but the woman is the glory of man. For man did not*
> *come from woman, but woman from man; neither was man*
> *created for woman, but woman for man. For this reason, and*

because of the angels, the woman ought to have a sign of authority on her head. In the Lord, however, woman is not independent of man, nor is man independent of woman. For as woman came from man, so also man is born of woman. But everything comes from God. Judge for yourselves: Is it proper for a woman to pray to God with her head uncovered? Does not the very nature of things teach you that if a man has long hair, it is a disgrace to him, but that if a woman has long hair, it is her glory? For long hair is given to her as a covering. If anyone wants to be contentious about this, we have no other practice – nor do the churches of God.'' (NIV)

Putting it in context

The general context for this passage is a letter written by Paul to the church at Corinth, which he established around A.D. 50–51 on his second missionary journey. Corinth was a large Greek city, a trade center infamous for its sensuality and sacred prostitution. Its name became a notorious proverb: "to Corinthianize" meant to practice prostitution. It was dedicated to the goddess Aphrodite, the goddess of love and the temple dedicated to her worship utilized the services of a thousand professional prostitutes. The spiritual climate in the city began to affect the church, which helps to explain the kind of problems the church there was facing.[1] Paul had begun to receive disturbing reports about what was going on in the Corinthian church, concerning morality, divisive factions, idolatry, etc. Paul sent Timothy to Corinth to try to correct some of the problems there. In addition, he also sent a letter, the epistle we know as 1 Corinthians.

The more specific context of the letter includes the chapters on either side. It is important to realize that the chapter divisions were not part of the original Greek manuscript. They were added by the translators and were meant to be helpful. Frequently, however, one chapter begins in the middle of a thought that was begun in the previous chapter. That is certainly the case here. In Chapter 10, he discusses idolatry, then moves on to the propriety of eating meat sacrificed to idols and the need to be sensitive to what will cause offense to the people around us. He says this in a number of different ways just before he gets to our difficult passage:

> *"All things are lawful for me, but not all things are helpful; all things are lawful for me, but not all things edify."*
> (1 Corinthians 10:23)

> *"Let no one seek his own, but each one the other's well-being."*
> (1 Corinthians 10:24)

> *" . . . whatever you do, do all to the glory of God."*
> (1 Corinthians 10:31)

> *"Give no offense, either to the Jews or the Greeks or to the church of God, just as I also please all men in all things, not seeking my own profit, but the profit of many, that they may be saved."*
> (1 Corinthians 10:32–33)

Paul then flows right into the first verse of chapter 11, saying "follow my example" or "have this same attitude yourselves" and goes on to talk about the propriety of how men and women wear their hair and cover their heads for public worship. His concern is still about giving offense to Jews and conservative Greeks! This is clear because at the end of our difficult passage he is still talking about what is proper (11:13), what is honorable or virtuous (11:14), and what is customary (11:15). Whatever Paul is saying in the difficult verses in between, we know it has something to do with propriety, cultural conventions and not giving offense, so that people might be saved. It is just a specific application of Paul's same theme from a few chapters back: *"to the weak I became as weak, that I might win the weak. I have become all things to all men, that I might by all means save some"* (1 Corinthians 9:22).

The problem

The primary problem with this passage is that some have tried to spiritualize it into something it was never meant to be – a treatise on the authority that men should have over women. The two texts most often used by those who believe the Bible teaches a hierarchy of authority, with men over women, are Ephesians 5:23 and 1 Corinthians 11:3. In referring to the Ten

Curses of Eve in the Babylonian Talumd, Bushnell points out the meaning of this passage has been partially perverted by the teaching of the rabbis. Curse number seven, that she is to be "wrapped like a mourner" and curse number eight, that "she dares not appear in public with her head uncovered" cast a shadow forward into the New Testament to influence interpretation of 1 Corinthians 11, according to Bushnell.[2]

Another problem with this passage is that it references a cultural decorum that is unfamiliar to us. Some legalists have read it as a prescription or rule for modern church life by requiring women to wear a covering on their heads or by forbidding women to cut their hair. When my husband Dave and I ministered in Mexico in an area that had been evangelized quite heavily by a leading denomination, all the women wore little handkerchief-like pieces of cloth pinned to the top of their heads. Our hearts went out to these precious women who we observed had many burdens of legalism placed upon them. Even in the area in which we now live in northern England, many churches still required women to wear hats inside the building up until only ten or fifteen years ago. These are just a few an examples which illustrate how emphatically we need the revelation of the Holy Spirit as we read and study the Scriptures.

A final difficulty with this passage is that there are a few verses which are terribly unclear, and they have left not a few scholars scratching their heads in puzzlement. We like to have everything spelled out for us nice and neatly, but it does not always work out that way, especially in translation work.

Analysis of the passage

First, it is widely accepted that Paul is dealing with the practical problem of hairstyle and head covering for public worship in this passage. Eerdman's Handbook to the Bible tells us that Greek women and men prayed bareheaded. But Roman and Jewish men and women prayed with their heads covered. Since Corinth was such a cultural mixture, it is not surprising that the church needed some guidance on this matter of propriety in public worship.[3] Liefeld says that when one looks at Paul's words about order, glory and honor, shame and dishonor, a clear picture emerges. "Paul is urging a sensitivity to contemporary moral

conventions..." Paul is concerned with avoiding any appearance of evil, that the gospel might not be hindered.[4] Bristow
agrees, advocating there is a transcultural "principle" behind
Paul's argument, which is "being sensitive to what message our
dress code and styles convey to others."[5]

Principle is important here. In this case, the principle
revealed in this passage is that our liberty in Christ is tempered
by the need to avoid offending others and bring glory to God,
that we might be honorable witnesses to the culture around us.
Some have great difficulty with the thought that Paul might
have been dealing with something culturally specific to that
time and place, and feel that it somehow cheapens the Word of
God or makes it less relevant to us today. We must realize,
however, that the principle remains intact, even though the
specifics may change. Recognizing this fact will actually
strengthen our confidence that the Word of God is relevant to
every age and every society.

A closer look at the difficult verses

*"Now I want you to realize that the head of every man is Christ,
and the head of the woman is man, and the head of Christ is
God."* (1 Corinthians 11:3)

At first glance, it appears that Paul is promoting a hierarchical
order here: God – then Christ – then man – then woman. But, as
Berkeley and Alvera Mickelson point out, Paul's word order
confirms that he was *not* teaching a chain of command. He
refers to Christ, the head of man, then man the head of woman;
then lastly God, the head of Christ.[6] This conclusion is echoed
by Payne[7] and Liefeld.[8]

Upon casual reading it might appear that Paul is speaking of
authority in this verse. When we say someone is the "head"
of someone else, we mean they have authority over them and
can tell them what to do. Payne notes that if we try to interpret
"head" here as "authority", we run into a problem. The present
tense of the Greek *estin* in this verse "requires that Christ
now in the present time after His resurrection and ascension
is under the authority of God." This is something called
"subordinationist Christology", which the Arians tried to use

to prove that Jesus was inferior to the Father.[9] A look at the Greek word that Paul used, however, reveals that he was speaking of something rather different. The word is *kephale*. Some scholars have assumed this word to mean something like "chief". But many have come to understand that it means "source", as in the headwaters of a river or a fountainhead.[10] In other words, *kephale* represents origin and source of life. With this understanding, we see that Paul was saying that Christ is the head or source of life for man. As Christ gave life to Adam, so He gives life to every man (1 Corinthians 8:6b). He is the head of His body the Church – our source of life. Then Paul says man is the head, or source of life for woman. She was brought out of *'adam*'s side and he is to lay his life down for her even as Christ laid His down for the Church (Ephesians 5). John Garr, writing from a Hebraic foundation, comments that, "Man was to be her head only in the sense that he was her source, that from which she was extracted."[11] Finally, Paul says, God is the head or source of Christ (which was Jesus' title on the earth and means "Anointed One"). Since the eternal second person of the Trinity came forth from the Godhead in the Incarnation, it is theologically sound to speak of His source as being God (John 8:42).[12] The understanding of *kephale* as meaning "source" here is underscored by Paul's reference in verses 8 and 12 to woman being "from" or "of" the man. The Greek word used is a primary preposition denoting origin.

Verses 4–6

> *"Every man praying or prophesying, having his head covered, dishonors his head. But every woman who prays or prophesies with her head uncovered dishonors her head, for that is one and the same as if her head were shaved. For if a woman is not covered, let her also be shorn. But if it is shameful for a woman to be shorn or shaved, then let her be covered."*
>
> (1 Corinthians 11:4–6)

Paul admonished the men to keep their heads uncovered because it would dishonor their head (Christ) to have it covered. Bushnell contends that the real purpose of this passage was to stop the practice of men veiling in worship. What she refers to as veiling is the wearing of the *tallith*. She describes it as a head covering worn by male Jews at morning prayer on week days, Sabbaths, holy days, and on other special occasions.[13] Bristow says it is also called a prayer shawl and was the head covering worn by the men in Paul's day.[14] The International Standard Bible Encyclopedia says the instruction for men to appear bareheaded was "diametrically opposed to the Jewish custom, according to which men wore the head covered by the *tallith* or prayer shawl..."[15]

This head covering was worn as a sign of subjection by a man, to "show that he is ashamed before God, and unworthy with open face to behold Him" according to Adam Clarke's Commentary.[16] It signified a man's unworthiness to look upon the face of the king.[17] It was also worn as a sign of man's guilt and condemnation before God and His law, according to Bushnell. She argues quite strongly that Paul is calling the men of Jewish background to dispense with this head covering since it is a symbol which "dishonors Christ" by nullifying His atoning work on the cross.[18] We are reminded that according to Romans 8:1, *"There is therefore now no condemnation to those who are in Christ Jesus."* Her argument is given credibility by several Old Testament accounts. When Haman was condemned by the king, his faced was then covered (Esther 7:8). Male head covering was also a sign of mourning.[19] David covered his head as a sign of mourning (2 Samuel 15:30), as did Haman when he found out he was in trouble (Esther 6:12). The plowmen who mourned over the severe drought also covered their heads (Jeremiah 14:4). As a sign of mourning, the male head covering would be dishonoring to Christ in terms of denying the inheritance of resurrection life and joy which He died to purchase for us. Payne considers a different aspect and argues that the man's head covering was also a dishonor because it "symbolizes a denial of the direct access to God that Christ has provided".[20] In 2 Corinthians 3:12–18, Paul wrote to the same group of believers in Corinth, saying,

"...the veil is taken away in Christ ... when one turns to the Lord, the veil is taken away. Now the Lord is the Spirit; and where the Spirit of the Lord is, there is liberty. But we all, with unveiled face, beholding as in a mirror the glory of the Lord, are being transformed into the same image from glory to glory, just as by the Spirit of the Lord."

Even Moses would take his veil *off* when he went before the Lord (Exodus 34:34–35). This was under the old covenant. Perhaps Moses had a clearer understanding of God's mind and heart than the rabbis, since the Scriptures tell us he understood God's ways in a way that others did not (Psalm 103:7).

Regarding the women, however, the situation was more complicated because of the implications to the women and their husbands. Bushnell comments that *not* wearing a covering could be dishonoring to a woman's head, her husband, because she would open herself to the charge of being an adulteress. Bushnell cites a passage from the oral law which identifies a woman as a "sinner" if she goes about with head uncovered. She also cites the Kethuboth and Sotah portions of the Talmud which state that a woman can be divorced, with loss of everything she brought with her into the marriage, if she is seen with her head uncovered. The Sotah goes even further to insist that it is a man's duty to get rid of a wife on the grounds of adultery if she were seen with her hair uncovered. Bushnell goes on to say, "A Jew, even if favorably disposed towards his wife's profession of Christianity, and towards the practice of unveiling in worship, might be compelled by his relatives or the synagogue authorities, much to his regret, to divorce his wife if she unveiled." She further notes that it was the custom in the case of a woman accused of adultery to have her hair shorn or shaven.[21]

Longnecker says that some women in the Corinthian church, in expressing their newly found Christian freedom, were dispensing with cultural conventions and subsequently causing the gospel to be confused with paganism. He comments, "perhaps their enthusiastic praying and prophesying with hair hanging loose was reminiscent of the pagan prophetesses giving voice to their oracles in disheveled frenzy. Or perhaps their appearance in the congregation with hair cut short and heads uncovered suggested the styles of the city's prostitutes."[22] He feels that Paul's primary concern is that a Christian woman would be mistaken for a heathen or confused with a prostitute.[23] The Jewish prostitutes wore their hair flowing loose and the Greek prostitutes wore theirs cut short or "shorn".[24]

Finally, Paul's comments about cutting or shaving the hair *if* she is not covered and *if* that is a shame or disgrace, to cover it, are extremely difficult to interpret in a way that make sense. No respectable woman in either culture, Greek or Jewish, would cut or shave her hair. And it was always a shame or disgrace at that time, in both cultures, because it denoted a woman who was sexually loose in one way or another. Various scholars have made an attempt at making sense out of this verse, usually coming up with something rather different, but I have not found any interpretation of verse 6 that is satisfactory. Certainly, further study is needed regarding this particular statement.

Verses 7–12

"A man ought not to cover his head, since he is the image and glory of God; but the woman is the glory of man. For man did not come from woman, but woman from man; neither was man created for woman, but woman for man. For this reason, and because of the angels, the woman ought to have a sign of authority on her head. In the Lord, however, woman is not independent of man, nor is man independent of woman. For as woman came from man, so also man is born of woman. But everything comes from God."   (1 Corinthians 11:7–12)

When Paul says man is the glory of God and woman (or the wife) is the glory of the man (or her husband), he is using the Greek word *doxa*. It means praise, splendor, brightness, or outshining. The context in which he is speaking is that of *kephale*. As man was made in the image and likeness of God and Christ is his source of life, so man is the glory of God. As woman was taken out of Adam and her husband is also her head or source of life in that he is to lay his life down for her, she is the glory of her husband. She is not the distraction of men as the Stoics claimed, nor the downfall of men, nor an object or possession to be owned and used. Rather, she is his glory! It reminds me of Proverbs 12:4 which says, *"An excellent wife is the crown of her husband."* The word translated as "excellent" here is a Hebrew word more specifically meaning one who is strong, efficient and forceful like an army. Man did not come from or originate in the woman, but she was taken out of and originated in the man. Therefore, she is his glory, the bejeweled crown upon his head. She was created for him as *'ezer kenegdo* (see Chapter 3), a help equal in terms of adequacy and fit together, one corresponding to him as a mirror image, and who would be strong and powerful on his behalf.

For this reason, *"and because of the angels,"* Paul says, *"the woman ought to have a sign of authority upon her head,"* or so it has been translated in English (1 Corinthians 11:10, NIV). But what Paul says in the Greek is that the woman has *exousia* on her head. It means "power, authority, right to choose, liberty". Liefeld points out that recent scholarship on this passage has resulted in this verse being understood to mean that the woman *possesses* authority rather than being forced to have a symbol of her *husband's* authority on her head. He says that in 1907 W.M. Ramsay called this passive sense "a preposterous idea which a Greek scholar would laugh at anywhere except in the New Testament, where (as they seem to think) Greek words may mean anything that commentators choose."[25] Bushnell traces the concept that it was a veil worn on her head to Valentinus, a second century gnostic. She says Clement of Alexandria and Origen passed on the teaching.[26] Bristow echoes the nonsense of this by commenting that *exousia* is not a piece of clothing! He notes that the use of the word *epi* with *exousia* means "authority over someone or something" such as "authority on earth" and "authority over demons". He understands Paul to be saying that since woman is the glory or splendor of man, she has been given spiritual authority, right and liberty over herself. She is no longer the property of her father or husband. And that this spiritual authority was witnessed and affirmed by the angels as they announced the resurrection of Jesus to the women first and commissioned them to be witnesses of this to the other disciples.[27] Bushnell thinks Paul mentions angels here because Jesus talked about the angels beholding the face of the Father in heaven (Matthew 18:10). She said if they can stand before the Father with no intervening veil and behold His face, then Paul is arguing that women should be able to as well.[28]

Paul then proceeds to counter balance his earlier statement about the woman coming from the man with a statement that the man also comes out of the woman [through birth] and that men and women are really interdependent and all have their origin in God. Richards says of this verse, "Neither sex is adequate or whole without the other, and so neither can be more important than the other."[29] Payne notes that these statements of man/woman interdependence "tell strongly against the 'authority' interpretation" of this passage.[30] It also removes the whole "secondary creation" argument which people try to use from this passage to justify the domination of women – that since Eve was created second, she is inferior to Adam and he has authority over her. Paul makes a point of saying that not only did woman come out of man, but man also comes out of woman. If Eve were inferior to Adam because she was brought forth from him, then every man is inferior to his mother for the same reason![31] Finally, he says, all have their origin in God. He is the Creator, the Designer, the Source for both man and woman.

Verses 13–16

> *"Judge among yourselves. Is it proper for a woman to pray to God with her head uncovered? Does not even nature itself teach you that if a man has long hair, it is a dishonor to him? But if a woman has long hair, it is a glory to her; for her hair is given to her for a covering. But if anyone seems to be contentious, we have no such custom, nor do the churches of God."*
>
> (1 Corinthians 11:13–16)

Bushnell asserts that the apostle is making a statement here, not asking a rhetorical question. She says this should read: "It is proper [or fitting or OK] for a woman to pray to God with her head uncovered." She notes that Greek does not alter the word order between a statement and a question like the English does. What makes the difference in this case is the punctuation. The original Greek text had no punctuation, as we know. It was supplied and placed by the translators.[32]

The normal English rendering of the next sentence as a question is "an absurdity," according to Bushnell. She asserts that it should read, "There is nothing in the nature of hair itself to teach that if man has long hair it is a dishonor to him." She notes that no artist would paint a picture of Jesus with short hair and asks if Jesus' hair is dishonorable or shameful to Him?[33] Also, the Nazirite vows dictated that a man not cut his hair (Numbers 6:5–6; Judges 13:5). Since this was a consecration to God of one's life in a special way, it is doubtful that long hair on a Jewish man was considered dishonorable or disgraceful. Further, with respect to the Greeks, we find that the people of Achaia, where Corinth was located, were noted for their long hair.[34] Bearing in mind that Paul was writing to a mixed congregation of Jews and Greeks, the evidence would support Bushnell's translation here.

Paul goes on to say that a woman's long hair is a glory or *doxa* to her – her praise, glory, splendor, outshining and that it *is* her covering (or veil). It seems that he is striking a blow to the whole concept of a special covering or veil, saying that a woman's hair provides that for her naturally. There is evidence that the Greek matrons wore no special covering or veil, but wore their long hair bound up in braids or with pins on top of their heads.[35] Payne says Hurley argued convincingly that the head covering Paul was recommending was hair modestly done up over the head.[36] Finally, the apostle concludes that if anyone wants to be contentious about it, there is no official custom or rule regarding veiling or head coverings among the Christian churches. The New American Standard Bible reads, *"no other custom"*, but there is a footnote advising the reader that it could also read, "no such custom", which is how the NKJV and NAB translate it. The Greek word *toioutos* translated "other" by the NASB, but as "such" in the other versions never means "other" anywhere else in the New Testament. It always means "such." Therefore, *"we have no such custom"* appears to be a more accurate translation of the apostle Paul's words concerning head coverings.

Final considerations – impact on Christian life and practice

By using the same phrase and words ("praying or prophesying") for both men and women, Paul defined the ministry of both men and women in a balanced and equal way. He dismantles the argument which people use to justify the restriction of women from preaching or teaching. Some have used this passage in 1 Corinthians 11 to argue that Paul allowed women to pray or prophesy, but not to preach or teach. Yet, Jamison, Fausset and Brown describe "prophesying" here as "preaching in the Spirit."[37] Adam Clarke allows that prophesying involves edification, exhortation and comfort according to 1 Corinthians 14:3. He goes on to say that this involves all aspects of exhortation, even preaching.[38] Finally, even the Puritans recognized "prophesying" as inclusive of preaching. According to William Perkins in his 16th century work, *The Art of Prophesying*, "There are two parts to prophecy: preaching the Word and public prayer. For the prophet has only two duties. One is preaching the Word and the other is praying to God in the name of people ... preaching the Word is prophesying..."[39]

Another interesting thing about this passage is that it illustrates the practical outworking of the paradigm shifts in thinking towards women that were initiated by Jesus. Whereas Jewish women from the Intertestamentary period onward were allowed little or no part in the services, we see here that Christian women were taking an active part! It gives us greater insight into the daily life of the first century Church, and the liberty accorded women in public ministry.

Finally, Paul unknowingly exposed the faulty reasoning of the "traditional" interpretation of 1 Corinthians 14:34, which is another passage often used to support the traditional view of women's participation in the life of the Church. Because 1 Corinthians 11:1–16 conveys the usual practice for women to be actively involved in public worship, prayer and prophecy, the injunction in 1 Corinthians 14:34 *cannot* be interpreted to mean that women are supposed to keep silent in church and are not permitted to speak!

Summary

The meaning of the 1 Corinthians 11:1–16 passage is not nearly as obvious as it might appear or as simple as what has often been taught. Contextually, it appears in a letter sent by Paul to bring some guidelines to the church in Corinth, which was multicultural and filled with people coming out of paganism. The discussion that Paul began in chapter 10, deals with how the Church was to operate in sensitivity to cultural conventions, so as to not give offense to the people around them. It is a passage specifically dealing with propriety in public worship, on the part of both men and women, and shows clearly that women were involved in public prayer and prophecy in first century services or gatherings.

In looking more closely at the difficult verses, we concluded that the husband is the head of the wife, in the sense that he is her origin (Eve was taken from Adam's side) and the one who is to lay down his life for her. Men were encouraged to refrain from head coverings because of the significance of these coverings in Judaism. Wearing them denied the atoning work of Jesus on the Cross. Women, however, were encouraged to wear a head covering, even if it was long hair neatly wound up on top of their heads, so as to appear chaste and not be mistaken for prostitutes or cultists. Women were told they were the glory or splendor of man – the crown over and around him in an interdependent relationship where woman comes from man, man comes from woman, but both "come from God." Thus, God is the ultimate source of both. The concept that woman is inferior to man or subject to him because of her secondary creation is dispelled in these verses. Similarly, the authority on the woman's head is not her husband's authority over her, but is understood to mean that she *possesses* authority.

In the final verses of the passage, it has been proposed that Paul was not asking a question, but making the statement that it is acceptable for a woman to pray with her head uncovered. The sentence structure in the Greek would not have changed, the only difference being the punctuation supplied by the translators. Either way, the verses in question deal with first century propriety. It's a moot point! God's truth is timeless and unchanging, and applicable to any culture.

The important principle in this passage is our liberty in Christ should be tempered in such a way that we bring glory to God, avoid offense, and be honorable witnesses to the culture around us. This principle is found over and over again in the writings of the New Testament. In no way does this passage promote a hierarchical order, the authority of the husband over the wife, or the inferiority of the woman or subjugation to man because she was created second, as has been so often taught.

Chapter 10 notes

1 *The Spirit-Filled Life Bible*, Jack Hayford, General Ed. (Thomas Nelson, Nashville, 1991), pp. 1717–1718.

2 Katherine C. Bushnell, *God's Word to Women* (1923, reprinted by Ray Munson, N. Collins NY), par. 106.

3 *Eerdman's Handbook to the Bible* (Eerdmans Publishing Company, Grand Rapids; Lion Publishing, Hertfordshire, 1973), p. 593.

4 Walter Liefeld, "Women, Submission and Ministry in 1 Corinthians" in *Women, Authority and the Bible*, Alvera Mickelsen, Ed. (InterVarsity Christian Fellowship, 1986), pp. 141–142.

5 John Temple Bristow, *What Paul Really Said About Women* (HarperCollins, San Franciso, 1988), p. 86.

6 Berkeley and Alvera Mickelsen, "What Does Kefale Mean in the New Testament?" in *Women, Authority and the Bible*, Alvera Mickelsen, Ed. (InterVarsity Christian Fellowship, 1986), p. 107.

7 Philip Barton Payne, "Response" in *Women, Authority and the Bible*, Alvera Mickelsen, Ed. (InterVarsity Christian Fellowship, 1986), p. 128.

8 Walter Liefeld, "Women, Submission and Ministry in 1 Corinthians" in *Women, Authority and the Bible*, Alvera Mickelsen, Ed. (InterVarsity Christian Fellowship, 1986), p. 137.

9 Philip Barton Payne, "Response" in *Women, Authority and the Bible*, Alvera Mickelsen, Ed. (InterVarsity Christian Fellowship, 1986), p. 127.

10 Marianne MeyeThompson, "Response" in *Women, Authority and the Bible*, Alvera Mickelsen, Ed. (InterVarsity Christian Fellowship, 1986), p. 91.

11 John D. Garr, "The Biblical Woman", *Restore!* (Winter 1999), p. 7.

12 Philip Barton Payne, "Response" in *Women, Authority and the Bible*, Alvera Mickelsen, Ed. (InterVarsity Christian Fellowship, 1986), p. 126.

13 Katherine C. Bushnell, *God's Word to Women* (1923, reprinted by Ray Munson, N. Collins NY), par. 240.

14 John Temple Bristow, *What Paul Really Said About Women* (HarperCollins, San Franciso, 1988), p. 85.

15 International Standard Bible Encyclopedia, Vol. II (Eerdmans Publishing Company, Grand Rapids, 1939, 1956), p. 1348.

16 Adam Clarke, *Commentary on the Holy Bible* (Baker Book House, Grand Rapids, 1967), p. 1109.

17 James M. Freeman, *Manners and Customs of the Bible* (Whitaker House, Springdale, PA, 1996), p. 206.

[18] Katherine C. Bushnell, *God's Word to Women* (1923, reprinted by Ray Munson, N. Collins NY), par. 240–241.

[19] James M. Freeman, *Manners and Customs of the Bible* (Whitaker House, Springdale, PA, 1996), p. 145.

[20] Philip Barton Payne, "Response", in *Women, Authority and the Bible*, Alvera Mickelsen, Ed. (InterVarsity Christian Fellowship, 1986), p. 127.

[21] Katherine C. Bushnell, *God's Word to Women* (1923, reprinted by Ray Munson, N. Collins NY), par. 242–243.

[22] Richard N. Longenecker, "Authority, Hierarchy and Leadership Patterns in the Bible" in *Women, Authority and the Bible*, Alvera Mickelsen, Ed. (InterVarsity Christian Fellowship, 1986), p. 72.

[23] Ibid., p. 78.

[24] John Temple Bristow, *What Paul Really Said About Women* (HarperCollins, San Franciso, 1988), p. 86.

[25] Walter Liefeld, "Women, Submission and Ministry in 1 Corinthians" in *Women, Authority and the Bible*, Alvera Mickelsen, Ed. (InterVarsity Christian Fellowship, 1986), p. 145.

[26] Katherine C. Bushnell, *God's Word to Women* (1923, reprinted by Ray Munson, N. Collins NY), par. 251–259.

[27] John Temple Bristow, *What Paul Really Said About Women* (HarperCollins, San Franciso, 1988), pp. 87–88, 111.

[28] Katherine C. Bushnell, *God's Word to Women* (1923, reprinted by Ray Munson, N. Collins NY), par. 248.

[29] Lawrence O. Richards, *The Word Bible Handbook* (Word books, Waco, 1982), pp. 644–645.

[30] Philip Barton Payne, "Response", in *Women, Authority and the Bible*, Alvera Mickelsen, Ed. (InterVarsity Christian Fellowship, 1986), p. 128.

[31] John Temple Bristow, *What Paul Really Said About Women* (HarperCollins, San Franciso, 1988), pp. 59–60.

[32] Katherine C. Bushnell, *God's Word to Women* (1923, reprinted by Ray Munson, N. Collins NY), par. 249.

[33] Ibid.

[34] Adam Clarke, *Commentary on the Holy Bible* (Baker Book House, Grand Rapids, 1967), p. 1110.

[35] John Temple Bristow, *What Paul Really Said About Women* (HarperCollins, San Franciso, 1988), p. 81.

[36] Philip Barton Payne, "Response", in *Women, Authority and the Bible*, Alvera Mickelsen, Ed. (InterVarsity Christian Fellowship, 1986), p. 128.

[37] Jamison, Fausset and Brown, Vol. III (Eerdmans Publishing Co., Grand Rapids, Reprinted 1993), pp. 313–314.

[38] Adam Clarke, *Commentary on the Holy Bible* (Baker Book House, Grand Rapids, 1967), p. 1109.

[39] William Perkins, *The Art of Prophesying* (first published in Latin 1592; in English 1606; Banner of Truth Trust, Edinburgh, 1996).

Chapter 11

What Was Paul Really Saying in 1 Timothy 2:11–15?

"I desire therefore that the men pray everywhere, lifting up holy hands, without wrath and doubting; in like manner also, that the women adorn themselves in modest apparel, with propriety and moderation, not with braided hair or gold or pearls or costly clothing, but, which is proper for women professing godliness, with good works. Let a woman learn in silence with all submission. And I do not permit a woman to teach or to have authority over a man, but to be in silence. For Adam was formed first, then Eve. And Adam was not deceived, but the woman being deceived, fell into transgression. Nevertheless she will be saved in childbearing if they continue in faith, love, and holiness, with self-control."
(1 Timothy 2:8–15)

This passage is important to address in our study of women in ministry because evangelicals who restrict women in preaching, teaching or filling positions of authority in the Church consider 1 Timothy 2:11–12 the strongest biblical text in support of their position.[1] Indeed, Catherine Kroeger says no passage has been used more consistently than this one to prohibit women leadership in the Church.[2] Also, the mention of Eve's "secondary creation" in this passage is important because of the rabbinic argument that it requires woman's submission to man. While the argument may be rabbinic in origin, it is very much alive and well today in the Christian Church. Spencer quotes a resolution from the 1984 U.S. Southern Baptist Convention that excluded all women from pastoral functions and ordination based on the submission God supposedly requires because man was first in creation and woman was first in the fall.[3] This same issue has, in the past few years, raised its head again in the Southern Baptist Convention, causing much furor and debate.

The background and context of Paul's letters to Timothy

Because the letters to Timothy were personal, addressing problems known to him and to Paul, the apostle did not always spell things out or fully describe the nature of the situation. It is probable that Paul wrote this first letter around A.D. 64, sending it to his young associate in Ephesus, where Timothy was pastoring. We do know these "pastoral epistles" as they are called, were written in part to help Timothy (and Titus) deal with those who propounded false teaching. He mentions this false teaching at the beginning of the letter (1 Timothy 1:3–7), throughout the body of the letter, at the end of the letter (1 Timothy 6:20–21), and in his second letter to Timothy as well. The Kroegers note the letters really addressed "churches under siege" and that more than 20% of the material in these epistles deals with the false teachers and their heretical doctrine.[4]

Ephesus was the fourth largest city in the Roman Empire. It lay on the western coast of what is now Turkey. This western coastal area of Asia Minor was called Iona and was predominently Greek. Because of its Greek heritage, philosophy and debate were characteristics of Ephesian society. There was a vigorous Jewish community in Ephesus as well. Ephesus, like Corinth, was a center for cult worship, with a huge temple erected to the goddess Artemis, known as Diana to the Romans. This temple was one of the "seven wonders of the world". The history of goddess worship there was well entrenched prior to the Greeks" arrival in 1000 B.C. The extent to which this cult of Artemis/Diana permeated Hellenistic society is seen in the fact that by the second century A.D., "there was a shrine to Artemis Ephesia in every Greek city throughout the Mediterranean region and that in private devotion she was the most worshipped of the gods." It is likely that the spiritual climate which existed in Ephesus and the surrounding area accounted for the heresy addressed in these epistles and specifically in the prohibition against women teaching.[5]

John Bristow notes, "it is almost certain that the false teachings that concerned Paul in his letters to Timothy were those of Gnosticism."[6] He elaborates that these false teachings were "characterized by useless speculations and the desire for controversy (1 Timothy 1:4; 6:4; 2 Timothy 2:23), a denigration of marriage and a demand for dietary abstinence (1 Timothy 4:3), immoral practices (1 Timothy 4:2), a great attention given to genealogies and myths (1 Timothy 1:4; 4:7; compare Titus 1:14; 3:9), and a denial of the resurrection of the body (2 Timothy 2:18). This list fits one heresy: Gnosticism."[7] Catherine and Richard Kroeger agree that the false teaching was probably the product of incipient Gnosticism.[8] F.F. Bruce offers support for this thesis in noting that incipient Gnosticism existed in the first century and that it also affected the Corinthian and Colossian churches.[9]

Though Gnostic cosmologies often varied, a Gnostic version of the story of Adam and Eve was common. Eve was "always a potent force". She had the ability to procreate without male assistance, rendering men unnecessary and unimportant. She pre-existed Adam and gained knowledge that she later imparted to him. Man was formed from Eve's side; she created Adam and gave him life. She was involved in creation and became mother of everything, giving birth to both gods and men. Further, Adam was deluded and then liberated with knowledge from the enlightened Eve.[10] We can see how the centuries of goddess worship in Iona laid a foundation for receptivity to Gnosticism. The goddess was considered all-sufficient, creator, source of life, and men were likewise considered unnecessary and un-important.[11] Both Gnosticism and goddess worship taught the superiority of the female and advocated dominion over the male. In that sense, they were anti-marriage, anti-motherhood and anti-feminine.

An analysis of the passage

> *"I desire therefore that the men pray everywhere, lifting up holy hands, without wrath and doubting; in like manner also, that the women adorn themselves in modest apparel, with propriety*

and moderation, not with braided hair or gold or pearls or costly clothing, but, which is proper for women professing godliness, with good works."   (1 Timothy 2:8–10)

As with 1 Corinthians 11:1–16, which we reviewed in the previous chapter, the context of 1 Timothy 2:8–15 has to do with balancing liberty with convention, so as not to give offense or hinder the spread of the gospel. A few verses earlier, Paul had stated God's desire for all men to be saved and come to a knowledge of the truth (2:4) and that Jesus gave Himself a ransom for all (2:5). As he begins verses 8–10, he says, *"I desire **therefore**..."* referring to the previous verses. Richard Longenecker comments, this passage was necessary for "decorum to avoid confusion, arguments and violation of the sensitivities of others."[12] David Scholer likewise says Paul is addressing behavior here out of a concern for propriety and notes numerous other verses within the pastoral epistles which express concern for the reputation of the Church within the larger Greco-Roman society.[13] We know that Paul was very much concerned about giving offense. He advised Timothy to be circumcised, not because it made him more holy or righteous, but simply to avoid offending the Jews since Timothy's mother was Jewish![14]

Verses 11–12

"Let a woman learn in silence with all submission. And I do not permit a woman to teach or to have authority over a man, but to be in silence."   (1 Timothy 2:11–12)

At first glance, this verse looks overwhelming! It's really not surprising that so many have interpreted it in the traditional way, because it seems so clear in the English. Not so in the Greek. The Kroegers maintain that a major doctrinal position regarding women in leadership rests on this one verse (verse 12). And the understanding of this verse is dependent on the translation of one verb, which is only used once in the New Testament.[15]

First, let's look at verse 11. *"Let a woman learn"* was a whole new concept to the Jews and the Greeks, one of those paradigm shifts in thinking which took place as the emerging Church affected its rite of passage from the old covenant to the new covenant. Embedded here is an assumption that women are to be taught the Word of God. If we are not aware, the shocking significance of this assumption could pass right by us. Now, how was she to learn? In what manner? The English says *"in silence with all submission."* What does the original text say? It uses the Greek word *hesuchia*, which means quietness, tranquility, peace, harmony and agreement. It suggests a restful quietness as in meditation or study. Bristow defines it as "being quiet in order to listen with studious attention."[16] It does not mean to refrain from talking or to not speak. It does, however, paint a picture which is in sharp contrast to the cries, shrieks and frenzy which were part of the pagan worship out of which many of these women were saved.[17] *Hesuchia* is used four times in the New Testament: Acts 22:2; 2 Thessalonians 3:12; 1 Timothy 2:11, 12.

She is also to learn *"with all submission."* What does the original text say? The Greek is the noun form of *hupotassomai* which is a voluntary willingness to be responsive to the needs of others, to be considerate, willing to serve and honor one another. It is the opposite of self-centered or selfish or grasping.

Bristow comments that Paul's desire for women to be educated in the faith was both "radical in thought and difficult in execution." He reminds us that "women were not used to listening to lectures or theological concepts, or studying at all." So there was a need to instruct them in proper protocol.[18] In verse 11, he instructs them to learn in a quiet, studious manner, receptive to and respectful of not only the Word of God, but others.

Now let's take a look at verse 12. Scholer argues that Paul's statements in verses 11–12 are ad hoc instructions intended for a particular situation, directed at a particular group of women. Some object to this and argue that Paul could have been more specific, if that were the case. Scholer, however, reminds us that Paul would not have spelled out a situation that he and Timothy both understood intimately. He points out that Paul did not do this with his discussion of meat offered to idols either.[19]

Scholer goes on to advocate that Paul's *practice* in regards to women's ministry in the Church is the key factor in understanding these two verses. Analysis shows that women were just

as active in ministry, including teaching, as the men.[20] This was
with Paul's approval and encouragement, I might add.
1 Corinthians chapters 11–14 have some bearing on our understanding of this verse. In Scholer's professional view, these
chapters make prophecy the "functional equivalent" of authoritative teaching. He cites recent studies which "clearly indicate"
that "prophetic utterance and prophecy did function as authoritative teaching within Paul's churches."[21] Since 1 Corinthians
11 shows clearly that women were actively involved in public
ministry, praying and prophesying, any prohibition against
teaching for women in general which we might read into this
passage is suspect indeed!

Paul also says here he does not permit a woman *"to have
authority over a man"*, as the English reads. Here is where we get
to the tricky Greek verb, *authentein*, which occurs only once in
the whole New Testament. Scholer argues strongly that if Paul
were referring to the normal exercise of authority he would
have used *exousia/exousiazo* as he normally did. The choice of
such an unusual verb indicates Paul intended a different nuance
of meaning.[22] Kroeger similarly notes that "the concept of
ruling or exercising authority over another occurs frequently
in the New Testament, but always in other words."[23] Since
authentein means to domineer or usurp authority in a very
negative sense, Scholer sees the injunction in this verse as
directed against women involved in false teaching who have
abused proper exercise of authority in the Church by usurpation
and domination of the male leaders and teachers in the church
at Ephesus.[24] Howard Morgan says *authentien* had coarse sexual
overtones as well, and quotes John Chrysostom, a Church
Father from the fourth century, in a commentary on this verb.
Chrysostom used the expression "sexual license" in describing
its implied meaning.[25] Paul's injunction begins to make sense in
light of this understanding! Jezebel's control and seduction of
believers as she flouted her Gnostic heresies (Revelation 2:20–
22) was an example of the kind of situation Paul was addressing.
Jezebel was not the wife of King Ahab as some assume. She was a
first century prophetess from Thyatira, a multicultural trade
center steeped in pagan worship, much like Ephesus. It should
be noted that the risen Jesus did not say that it was wrong for
Jezebel to be teaching or prophesying. What He called her to

repent of was leading people into sexual immorality and eating meat sacrificed to idols *through* her teaching and prophesying.

Catherine Kroeger spells out the different shades of meaning of *authenteo*:

1. to begin something, to be primarily responsible for a condition or action (especially murder);

2. to rule, dominate;

3. to usurp power or rights from another [Note: "usurp" means to seize power without right. It is from a Latin root meaning to seize.];

4. to claim ownership, sovereignty or authorship.[26]

She then expands on this last shade of meaning and quotes the French etymologist Pierre Chantraine. He suggests that the noun form of the word basically means instigator or originator.[27] She goes on to say that the word could imply a claim of authorship – to represent oneself as the author, originator or source of something.[28] This sounds very much like the teaching of the Gnostics. In Gnostic theology, Eve was represented as the originator and source of life for Adam and all mankind. Kroeger goes on to apply the meaning of *authentein* to 1 Timothy 2:12, and suggests it could read this way, "I do not allow a woman to teach nor to represent herself as the originator or source of man."[29] The pieces continue to fall into place and this verse begins to make more sense!

Finally, Paul ends verse 12 with an exhortation *"to be in silence."* Again, it is the Greek word *hesuchia*, meaning restful quietness or to be quietly attentive. As Kroeger sums it up, "women are asked to learn with an attitude of receptivity and, at the end of verse 12, to be in harmony rather than on a collision course with the truth of the Word."[30]

Verses 13–14

> *"For Adam was formed first, then Eve. And Adam was not deceived, but the woman being deceived, fell into transgression."*
> (1 Timothy 2:13–14)

Kroeger explains that verses 13 and 14 supply the *reason* for the constraint found in verse 12. It is because these women were teaching Gnostic (or pre-Gnostic) versions of the Adam and Eve story that contradicted the biblical account. The Gnostic versions promoted Eve as the source of Adam. They also pictured Eve as Adam's instructor, an enlightened one who was a mediator of divine revelation and knowledge or "gnosis" brought by the serpent, rather than one who was deceived and fell into sin as a result.[31] Bristow agrees, noting that Gnostics would lay no blame on Eve at all, seeing the fall as humankind's great leap forward into grasping knowledge and finding enlightenment.[32]

Here, Paul simply counters the false teaching with the truth – that Eve was utterly deceived in listening to the serpent and fell into transgression against the will of God as a result. Paul is not promoting the inferiority of women as a result of Eve's "secondary creation", nor disqualifying women from ministry as a result of Eve's deception. These conclusions have been read *into* this verse by those looking for evidence to support their bias. We could add that if the label on Eve is "gullible", then the label on Adam would be "rebellious", because he disobeyed knowingly. If Eve is then disqualified by her naivety, would not Adam also be disqualified by his rebellion? [33]

Verse 15

> "Nevertheless she will be saved in childbearing if they continue in faith, love, and holiness, with self-control." (1 Timothy 2:15)

This is a difficult verse to translate, one that has left many scholars scratching their heads in bewilderment. We know, in studying the full breadth of the Scriptures, that Paul is not saying women are saved through procreation. We know that salvation by grace through faith is not limited to men only. Also, the switch from "she" to "they" is confusing. The verb *sothesetai* ("will be saved") is singular, whereas the second verb *meinosin* ("to abide or remain") is plural. Some have suggested that the singular "she" refers to Eve, and "salvation through childbearing" makes reference to the salvation that would come through the seed of the woman, the Messiah.[34]

Kroeger may shed some light on this verse. She notes that, "Childbearing and marriage were forbidden by certain Gnostic groups because they pulled the soul-atoms back into material bodies instead of liberating them to ascend to their ultimate source." Some of the Gnostics also "engaged in ritual promiscuity and forcibly aborted any accidental pregnancies, eating the fetus in a sacramental meal." She further notes that other Gnostics taught that Jesus came to do away with childbearing and still others taught that femininity was a bondage; women must become men in order to be saved.[35]

Once again, an understanding of the Gnostic heresy with which Paul was dealing may help us to make sense out of what at first appeared to be an incomprehensible verse. Paul may have intended it to be a counter to the Gnostic false teaching which assaulted marriage, childbearing, and feminine virtues. In fact, there is the implication that they will find wholeness (one aspect of salvation) through embracing their God-given femininity and the godly virtues of faith, love, holiness and self-control.

Some personal thoughts regarding verse 15

As I looked at this confusing and bewildering verse 15, I had a little conversation with the Lord. As we talked, I began to see it in a new way. I'm not a Greek scholar, so I can't verify from a language standpoint how valid this interpretation might be. I will say that something in my spirit leaped! It all happened as I began to look at the individual Greek words used. First, I looked at "nevertheless" and saw that it was a conjunction that meant the equivalent of "but". It was directed back to the sentence before in which Paul had just finished saying Eve fell into transgression. Now, he is saying, she fell into sin *but* ... which presupposes something good is coming! It was bad news, but now there is good news! I then went on to examine the word translated "saved". This is a form of the Greek verb *sozo*, which means to be healed, delivered, rescued, made whole. Then I looked at the word for "childbearing". It literally means to bring forth or bear children. But the children it designates are *teknon*. I know from my studies on sonship that *teknon* are not infants or even toddlers. The word is used to refer to those who are old enough to be trained in the Father's business as apprentices – or, as we would call them, "disciples". We often speak of birthing and raising up spiritual children in the Kingdom. We call the women who seem to be good at this

"Mothers in Israel." Why is it so hard for us to see that Paul may never have been talking about natural birth here at all? Next I looked at the Greek word translated "if" and that is exactly what it means, without any other rival possibilities. I went on to the word for "continue" and found that the Greek paints a picture of a conditional abiding or remaining in. However, what was interesting was that it was in the aorist tense, which encompasses past, present and future. He was qualifying his statement with the condition that we abide and keep on abiding in the virtues listed.

Next I looked at each one of these virtues we are to abide and keep on abiding in. "Faith" or the Greek word *pistis*, has an emphasis on complete trust and total confidence in God wrapped up in its meaning. It is so much more than deciding to believe or some kind of mental assent. It's being sold out completely to the Lord, willing to put every aspect of our life in His hands! "Love" is the Greek word *agape*, which is God's love in us. It is the love that has been shed abroad in our hearts by the Holy Spirit. It is the love which is selfless and seeks not its own. It is the love which causes a person to lay down their life for their friends. It is the love which motivated Jesus as he healed the sick, lifted up the crushed, set at liberty the oppressed and pulled the scales off the eyes of the blind! The Greek word translated "holiness" means consecrated to God, set apart for His use. It's the picture of offering ourselves as the living sacrifices mentioned in Romans 12:1–2. Finally, "self-control" is from a Greek word that means sound of mind, temperate, stable, steady – *not flaky!* I could really relate to this one because I have known lots of flaky women in my years in the ministry.

To put it all together, then, the thought behind verse 15 would read something like this: Even though Eve sinned and really blew it, nevertheless, woman (singular) will experience healing, freedom and wholeness through her obedience to the Lord in bringing forth and making disciples *if* God's women (plural) abide and keep on abiding in complete trust and confidence in God, in His perfect love, in that place of willingness to die to self and be yielded to His purposes, and in the steadiness and stability which comes from the empowerment of His Spirit within us.

This understanding of verse 15 may be borne out by the very next sentence which Paul writes. Remember, the chapter divisions were added by the translators. He goes on to say that if anyone desires the office of a bishop, they aspire to a good work. Most translations say "any man", because the translators assumed it would be a man. But the Greek word used is genderless and means anyone. Paul has just finished speaking of how women could enter into and begin to walk in God's redemptive purposes for them, despite Eve's transgression. He then flows right into some of his thoughts on leadership and some of the qualifications for those who would like God to use them as leaders in the Body of Christ. What could be more natural?

Summary

The key to understanding the passage in 1 Timothy 2:8–15 is an awareness of the goddess worship and Gnostic heresies which permeated Ephesus and influenced the women who were coming into the Church from pagan backgrounds. The passage is presented within a context of exhorting the believers to be honorable witnesses for Christ, living epistles read of all men who would reveal Him to the world so that people might be saved.

In looking at the difficult verses, we discovered a number of things. One was that Paul's exhortation about how women were to learn, does *not* mean in silence under a forced subjection to a higher authority. What Paul does seem to be encouraging in women is the quiet, respectful, listening attitude of the attentive student who approaches learning about God's heart, mind, will and purposes with a humble and submissive heart.

Another thing we discovered is that the arguments which use verse 12 to prohibit women teaching or operating in positions where they might have authority over men, hang on one Greek verb which is used nowhere else in the New Testament. Paul did not use the normal word for "authority", but rather an obscure word which has some other shades of meaning. It has more the connotation of domineering and *usurping* or *seizing* authority. It can also imply a claim of authorship or origin. The Gnostic heresies, interestingly enough, promoted Eve as the source or origin of Adam and as the Enlightened One who brings light and life to all mankind. The word *authentein* can also have coarse, sexual overtones, implying seduction and the promotion of sexual license. John Chrysostom, a Church Father from the fourth century, understood it to have this meaning.

Finally, we looked at some different ways in which the last verse might be read which are non-traditional, but consistent with the Greek and with the cultural and historical context in which the passage was written. We considered that Paul may have been sharing good news with women believers, showing them how they could walk in God's redemptive purposes of healing, freedom and wholeness through the birthing and discipling of spiritual children. This understanding of the verse fits and is appropriate within the general context of this portion to Paul's letter to Timothy.

Chapter 11 notes

[1] David M. Scholer, "1 Timothy 2:9–15 and the Place of Women in the Church's Ministry" in *Women, Authority and the Bible*, Alvera Mickelsen, Ed. (InterVarsity Christian Fellowship, 1986), p. 193.

[2] Catherine C. Kroeger, "1 Timothy 2:12 – A Classicist's View" in *Women, Authority and the Bible*, Alvera Mickelsen, Ed. (InterVarsity Christian Fellowship, 1986), p. 225.

[3] Aida Besacon Spencer, *Beyond the Curse* (Hendrickson, Peabody, MA, 1985), p. 19.

[4] Richard C. Kroeger and Catherine C. Kroeger, *I Suffer Not a Woman – Rethinking 1 Timothy 2:11–15 in Light of Ancient Evidence* (Baker Book House, Grand Rapids, 1992), p. 42.

[5] Catherine C. Kroeger, "1 Timothy 2:12 – A Classicist's View" in *Women, Authority and the Bible*, Alvera Mickelsen, Ed. (InterVarsity Christian Fellowship, 1986), pp. 226–228.

[6] John Temple Bristow, *What Paul Really Said About Women* (HarperCollins, San Francisco, 1988), p. 74.

[7] Ibid., p. 73.

[8] Richard C. Kroeger and Catherine C. Kroeger, *I Suffer Not a Woman – Rethinking 1 Timothy 2:11–15 in Light of Ancient Evidence* (Baker Book House, Grand Rapids, 1992), p. 42.

[9] F.F. Bruce, *Paul – Apostle of the Heart Set Free* (William B. Eerdmans Publishing Co., originally published by Paternoster Press, Ltd., Exeter, 1977), pp. 179, 408–409, 413, 417.

[10] Catherine C. Kroeger, "1 Timothy 2:12 – A Classicist's View" in *Women, Authority and the Bible*, Alvera Mickelsen, Ed. (InterVarsity Christian Fellowship, 1986), pp. 232–235.

[11] Ibid., pp. 232–234.

[12] Richard N. Longenecker, "Authority, Hierarchy and Leadership Patterns in the Bible" in *Women, Authority and the Bible*, Alvera Mickelsen, Ed. (InterVarsity Christian Fellowship, 1986), p. 78.

[13] David M. Scholer, "1 Timothy 2:9–15 and the Place of Women in the Church's Ministry" in *Women, Authority and the Bible*, Alvera Mickelsen, Ed. (InterVarsity Christian Fellowship, 1986), pp. 197–198.

[14] *The Spirit-Filled Life Bible*, Jack Hayford, General Ed. (Thomas Nelson, Nashville, 1991), p. 1839.

[15] Richard C. Kroeger and Catherine C. Kroeger, *I Suffer Not a Woman – Rethinking 1 Timothy 2:11–15 in Light of Ancient Evidence* (Baker Book House, Grand Rapids, 1992), p. 12.

[16] John Temple Bristow, *What Paul Really Said About Women* (HarperCollins, San Francisco, 1988), p. 71.

[17] Jimmilea Berryhill, "First Century Woman", *Restore!* (Winter 1999), p. 23.

[18] John Temple Bristow, *What Paul Really Said About Women* (HarperCollins, San Francisco, 1988), pp. 70–71.

[19] David M. Scholer, "1 Timothy 2:9–15 and the Place of Women in the Church's Ministry" in *Women, Authority and the Bible*, Alvera Mickelsen, Ed. (InterVarsity Christian Fellowship, 1986), pp. 203–204.

[20] Ibid., p. 205.

[21] Ibid., p. 207.

[22] Ibid., p. 205.

[23] Catherine C. Kroeger, "1 Timothy 2:12 – A Classicist's View" in *Women, Authority and the Bible*, Alvera Mickelsen, Ed. (InterVarsity Christian Fellowship, 1986), p. 229.

[24] David M. Scholer, "1 Timothy 2:9–15 and the Place of Women in the Church's Ministry" in *Women, Authority and the Bible*, Alvera Mickelsen, Ed. (InterVarsity Christian Fellowship, 1986), p. 205.

[25] Howard Morgan, "Anointed for Service, Robbed of Opportunity", *Restore!* (Winter 1999), p. 20.

[26] Catherine C. Kroeger, "1 Timothy 2:12 – A Classicist's View" in *Women, Authority and the Bible*, Alvera Mickelsen, Ed. (InterVarsity Christian Fellowship, 1986), p. 225.

[27] Ibid., pp. 229–230.

[28] Ibid., p. 231.

[29] Ibid., p. 232.

[30] Catherine C. Kroeger, "1 Timothy 2:12 – A Classicist's View" in *Women, Authority and the Bible*, Alvera Mickelsen, Ed. (InterVarsity Christian Fellowship, 1986), p. 237.

[31] Ibid., pp. 237–238.

[32] John Temple Bristow, *What Paul Really Said About Women* (HarperCollins, San Francisco, 1988), p. 75.

[33] Gretchen Gaebelein Hull, "Response" in *Women, Authority and the Bible*, Alvera Mickelsen, Ed. (InterVarsity Christian Fellowship, 1986), p. 25.

[34] Roger Nicole, "Biblical Authority and Feminist Aspirations" in *Women, Authority and the Bible*, Alvera Mickelsen, Ed. (InterVarsity Christian Fellowship, 1986), p. 48.

[35] Catherine C. Kroeger, "1 Timothy 2:12 – A Classicist's View" in *Women, Authority and the Bible*, Alvera Mickelsen, Ed. (InterVarsity Christian Fellowship, 1986), p. 243.

Chapter 12

Headship in Ephesians 5:21–33

"Submit to one another out of reverence for Christ.
Wives, submit to your husbands as to the Lord. For the husband is
the head of the wife as Christ is the head of the church, his body,
of which he is the Savior. Now as the church submits to Christ, so
also wives should submit to their husbands in everything.
Husbands, love your wives, just as Christ loved the church and gave
himself up for her to make her holy, cleansing her by the washing
with water through the word ... In this same way, husbands ought
to love their wives as their own bodies. He who loves his wife loves
himself. After all, no one ever hated his own body, but he feeds and
cares for it, just as Christ does the church – for we are members of
his body. For this reason a man will leave his father and mother
and be united to his wife, and the two will become one flesh." This
is a profound mystery – but I am talking about Christ and the
church. However, each one of you also must love his wife as he
loves himself, and the wife must respect her husband."
(Ephesians 5:21–33 NIV)

Ephesians 5:23 and 1 Corinthians 11:3 are the two primary
verses which Christians use to advocate that the Bible teaches a
hierarchy of authority, with men (or husbands) over women (or
their wives) as the "head". This passage in Ephesians has further
been used to justify the domination of husbands over wives
because of Paul's discussion about submission. Men are fond of
quoting that wives are to submit to their husbands, conveni-
ently ignoring the next verse which tells them to love their
wives the same way Jesus loved the Church and gave up His very
life for her. Even so, this passage has much more to say to us, if

we will examine some of the Greek words used. There are three key words used here that paint a picture somewhat different from the traditional interpretation of this passage. They are the words translated into English as "head", "submit", and "love".

"Head" – ruler or source of life?

In Chapter 10, we looked briefly at the Greek word that was translated "head" in 1 Corinthians 11. It is the same word here – *kephale*. Let's take a more in depth look at the word in this chapter. Lawrence Richards, in his Word Bible Handbook, comments on Ephesians 5:

> "Like many other Bible terms, the concept of headship has been warped by importing secular notions. To call someone head of a corporation or project identifies him as a person with control over others. But the New Testament term is not used in this sense. Instead the biblical emphasis is on the head as 'source' or 'origin'. Thus Jesus, as 'head over everything for the church' (Ephesians 1:22) is seen as source and sustainer of life of his body ... Headship does not speak of power but of serving!" [1]

Earlier in Ephesians 4:15–16, Paul substantiated that this concept of Jesus as the source of life is what he meant when he wrote *"... from him* [as the head] *the whole body, joined and held together by every supporting ligament, grows and builds itself up in love."* The understanding of *kephale* as meaning "source of life, top or crown, originator and completer" [2] fits when we look at the larger context. Philip Payne concurs by noting that "the idea of authority was not normally associated with the word for 'head' in Greek thought." He also notes that the Greeks believed the heart, not the head, was the central governing place of the body, the seat of control and the seat of intelligence." [3] So the word *kephale* would not have been the word used if Paul were describing one who governs, controls or directs in the husband–wife relationship.

Payne's point is borne out by Berkeley and Alvera Mickelsen who claim to have studied "the most complete Greek–English lexicon (covering Homeric, classical and koine Greek) in current existence", a two-volume work of over 2,000 pages published first in 1843. In regards to the word *kephale*, they said the list of possible meanings included the literal meaning (the literal, physical head of a man or animal) and 25 figurative meanings. *None* of the figurative meanings included the concept of authority, leader or anything similar.[4] Payne actually argues that they have understated the case. He notes that another prominent lexicon lists 48 separate English equivalents of the figurative meaning of *kephale*. "None of them implies leader, authority, first or supreme".[5] He also cites a number of sources from the first and second century who used *kephale* to clearly mean "source of life."[6] The Mickelsens noted that the Septuagint (the Greek translation of the Old Testament) only used *kephale* as a rendering of the Hebrew *ro'sh*, meaning "leader or chief", 4% of the time (8 instances out of 180). "*Kephale* would have been the natural word to use in all 180 instances if the word had been commonly understood to mean 'leader or chief'. Its rare usage indicates that translators knew that *kephale* did not commonly carry this meaning."[7] It must be pointed out that Paul was a Greek-speaking Jew who grew up in a Greek-speaking city. He would have had an understanding of what the word conveyed to the people of his day. We can only conclude, then, that he was *not* conveying any idea of hierarchy, authority, prominence or control.

I think it is very possible that what we have done is confuse Jesus' role as Savior with that of Lord. As Savior, He is head of His body the Church. We are one with Him and He is our source of life. He makes us whole, completes us, transforms us. He is our Bridegroom, the lover of our souls with whom we have a deep, spiritual union. He is our friend, our brother, our lover. We give Him our time, our love, our hearts. As Lord, however, He is our master. He now owns us instead of the devil. We are his "bondservants". We give Him worship, reverence and obedience as the Lord. I think it very possible that we have read into this passage our understanding of Christ as Lord, when Paul was speaking of His role as our Head, as our source of life and the One who completes us.

Berkeley and Alvera Mickelson explain that the head–body metaphor used by Paul in Ephesians is speaking of interdependence not a chain of command. They note that the Scriptures

which present Christ as "head" of the Church do not emphasize His authority over the Church, but rather His oneness with
the Church. In Ephesians 5, they observe, this oneness is
applied to husband and wife. They summarize by saying that
Christ's headship of the Church could be illustrated this way:
"Christ loved the church and gave himself up for her ... that he
might present the church to himself in splendor ... Christ gave
himself up to enable believers (the church) to become all that
we are meant to be ... so the husband is to give himself up to
enable (bring to completion) all that his wife is meant to be.
The husband is to *nourish* and *cherish* his wife (verse 29) as he
does his own body, even as Christ nourishes and cherishes the
church."[8] Fuchsia Pickett says it all with her gracious description of the biblical "head". She says, "A godly leader will have
abandoned the macho, domineering image that is a reflection
of his carnal nature and adopted the attitudes and behavior of
Christ-modeling sacrifice, giving and caring."[9]

"Submit" – what it really means

We have a context for Paul's discussion about submission in
Jesus' talk about relationships among believers in Mark 10:42–
45. His emphasis was that relationships were to be characterized
by servanthood, not the exercise of authority. Jesus said in this
passage,

> *"You know that those who are supposed to rule over the
> Gentiles lord it over them, and their great men exercise author-
> ity over them. But it shall not be so among you; but whoever
> would be great among you must be your servant, and whoever
> would be first among you must be slave of all. For the Son of
> man also came not to be served but to serve, and to give his life
> as a ransom for many."* (Mark 10:42–45 RSV)

In Ephesians 5:21, Paul similarly speaks of mutual submission, which is the theme and the thread throughout the
remainder of this passage which discusses headship, wifely
submission and love. The Mickelsens note that the word for
"submit" does not appear in verse 22 "in the better Greek
manuscripts". This means, as they point out, that the meaning

is brought down from verse 21, making the context of the verse the mutual submission required of all Christians.[10] This mutual submission to one another is a *major theme* of the New Testament. This idea is mentioned also in 1 Peter 3:7; 5:5; Philippians 2:3–4; Romans 12:10; 13:1–7 and 15:2.

Payne brings out that in verses 28–32 of Ephesians 5, Paul is focusing on the unity of the head and the body. "As Christ and the church are one body, so husband and wife are one flesh ... Paul bases his appeal for submission on the loving nature of the head–body relationship in which the head is the source of life."[11] The Mickelsens agree that Paul's emphasis here is unity, stating that it is obvious from his quotation of Genesis 2:24 (where the husband is to leave parents, cleave to his wife and become one flesh with her).[12] This is clear in his statement that the man who loves his wife loves himself (verse 28), thereby equating the two as one.

In speaking of "submission", what does the Greek convey here? The word Paul used is *hupotassomai*. John Bristow comments that in using the middle voice, Paul was emphasizing the voluntary nature of being subject to. He was requesting that wives voluntarily, willingly and actively submit to their husbands.[13] It is noteworthy that the apostle used a form of the same word in 1 Timothy 2:11, when he was writing to Timothy in Ephesus. Both 1 Timothy and Ephesians address the peculiar attitudes of the women in Ephesus who had been influenced to some degree by the goddess worship and Gnostic heresies. The Gnostic teachings were perhaps the most deadly since they used Christian words and symbolism. These teachings constituted an assault on marriage, as man was rendered unnecessary and unimportant in Gnostic cosmologies.[14]

In what way were wives called to submit to their husbands in Ephesians 5? As we saw in the previous chapter of this book, the word *hupotassomai* suggests a voluntary willingness to be responsive to the needs of others, to be considerate, willing to serve and honor one another. It can also mean to give allegiance to, tend to the needs of, be supportive of, be responsive to, and to place oneself at the disposition of. Bristow notes that it is also a military term referring to taking position in a group of soldiers in the sense of returning to the line, joining his fellows, being supportive of them and fulfilling his part of the assignment. For this reason, "Paul could tell all the members of the Church to be subject to (*hupotassomai*) one another ... For *hupotassomai* is not a ranking of persons as ruler and being ruled. It is a concise appeal for the Church to have its members live out their call to be 'the body of Christ and individually members of it' ... to be willing to 'bear one another's burdens and so fulfill the law of Christ' (Galatians 6:2). What is true of the Church, Paul added, is true of marriage."[15] It is really describing the mutual submission required in teamwork, whether it is a team of many, or a team of two.

To dispel the popular concept that this word means "to obey", there is a Greek word which carries the idea of dutiful obedience. It is used a few verses later in Ephesians 6:1 to convey the thought of children obeying their parents. It is important that Paul did *not* use this word in speaking of husbands and wives. It is also important that he did *not* use the word *peitharcheo*, which describes obedience to someone in authority.[16]

Husbands "love" your wives

Paul exhorted husbands three times in this passage to love their wives. Guidelines for Scripture interpretation clearly note that any repetition of statements or commands in the Scripture are a cause for special attention. Repetition is a red flag waving at us which says, "Pay particular attention here!" Paul must have been adamant about getting his point across! He used the Greek word *agapao*. Bristow notes that this word fits with Paul's use of *hupotassamai* because "both involve giving up one's self interest to serve and care for another's. Both mean being responsive to the needs of the other ... Wives are to *hupotassomai* their husbands; husbands are to *agapeo* their wives."[17]

I think the apostle may not have been legislating behavior here so much as he was trying to bring a revelation of what husbands and wives both need from one another. In other words, he was telling us *how* we can "in honor prefer one another" in a way that is meaningful to each spouse. Men, because of the nature of their insecurities, need respect, honor and support. Women, because of the different nature of their insecurities, need to know they are loved, valued and cherished.

Paul defines the actions that show this kind of *agape* love by again referring to Christ and the Church. The actions involve loving his wife "as he loves his own body" and "as he loves himself." They also involve laying down his life to serve her even as Christ laid down His life for the Church. This is not dying in the physical sense of course, but dying to self.

The divine call to men is to be willing to lay down control, self-centeredness, personal ambitions and fleshly desires. It is also a call to nurture, lift up, support and release their wives. The divine call to women is to respect, support, honor and lift up their husbands, with a heart to bless and minister to their needs. The call to *both* is *"in honor preferring one another"* (Romans 12:10). My very wise mother-in-law commented once on the number of divorces today. She said her observation is that so often, it seems like the primary dissatisfaction in the relationship is that each spouse feels that they are giving more than the other. "Why don't people just go into the relationship willing to each give 75%? Then no one would feel used and abused and it would work out just fine!" I think she might be on to something biblical!

Summary

The real essence of Ephesians 5:21–33 is found in the three key words which the apostle Paul used: "head", "submit", and "love". In studying these words in the Greek, we find that they do not advocate a hierarchy of authority.

The word rendered "head" is *kephale*. A number of scholars have argued, quite extensively and thoroughly, that the traditional understanding of *kephale* as an authority or ruler is not supported by various lexicons which cover both Homeric, classical and koine Greek. The way in which the Septuigint translators handled this word strengthens their case that the word does not convey any idea of hierarchy, authority, prominence or control. Rather, *kephale* (head) is used in the sense of origin, source of life, and completer.

Hupotassomai is the Greek word translated "submit" in this passage. It describes the voluntary willingness to be responsive to the needs of others, to be considerate, willing to serve and honor one another. It is also refers to a person taking their position in a group of soldiers in the sense of returning to the line, joining one's fellows, being supportive, and fulfilling their part of the assignment. It does not imply ranking or hierarchy. For this reason, Paul could tell all the members of the Church to *hupotassomai* one another. It is really describing the mutual submission required in teamwork, whether it is a team of many, or a team of two such as husbands and wives.

The third key word the apostle Paul used was the verb *agapao* in describing the husband's part in the marriage relationship. He repeated it three times, which alerts us that he was calling attention to this admonition. Paul defined the actions which show this kind of love as a man loving his wife "as he loves his own body" and "as he loves himself." He also defined it as laying down his life to serve her as Jesus laid down His life for the Church.

Finally, we saw that in this passage the apostle was calling both husband and wife to a place of mutual submission, in honor preferring one another. Using different words, he called *each* to give up their self-interest to serve the other. He encourages us that the service of love and submission in the Holy Spirit will dissolve the barriers and walls of alienation erected by sin, allowing husbands and wives to join together in unity and truly be one flesh.

Chapter 12 notes

[1] Lawrence O. Richards, *The Word Bible Handbook* (Word Books, Waco, 1982), p. 685.

[2] Berkeley and Alvera Mickelsen, "What Does Kefale Mean in the New Testament?" in *Women, Authority and the Bible*, Alvera Mickelsen, Ed. (InterVarsity Christian Fellowship, 1986), p. 105.

[3] Philip Barton Payne, "Response" in *Women, Authority and the Bible*, Alvera Mickelsen, Ed. (InterVarsity Christian Fellowship, 1986), pp. 119–120.

[4] Berkeley and Alvera Mickelsen, "What Does Kefale Mean in the New Testament?" in *Women, Authority and the Bible*, Alvera Mickelsen, Ed. (InterVarsity Christian Fellowship, 1986), pp. 100–101.

[5] Philip Barton Payne, "Response" in *Women, Authority and the Bible*, Alvera Mickelsen, Ed. (InterVarsity Christian Fellowship, 1986), pp. 118, 122.

[6] Ibid., pp. 124–125.

[7] Berkeley and Alvera Mickelsen, "What Does Kefale Mean in the New Testament?" in *Women, Authority and the Bible*, Alvera Mickelsen, Ed. (InterVarsity Christian Fellowship, 1986), pp. 102–104.

[8] Ibid., p. 109.

[9] Fuchsia Pickett, "Male and Female Created to Co-Labor with God", *Spirit Led Woman* (June/July 1999).

[10] Berkeley and Alvera Mickelsen, "What Does Kefale Mean in the New Testament?" in *Women, Authority and the Bible*, Alvera Mickelsen, Ed. (InterVarsity Christian Fellowship, 1986), p. 108.

[11] Philip Barton Payne, "Response" in *Women, Authority and the Bible*, Alvera Mickelsen, Ed. (InterVarsity Christian Fellowship, 1986), p. 130.

[12] Berkeley and Alvera Mickelsen, "What Does Kefale Mean in the New Testament?" in *Women, Authority and the Bible*, Alvera Mickelsen, Ed. (InterVarsity Christian Fellowship, 1986), p. 109.

[13] John Temple Bristow, *What Paul Really Said About Women* (HarperCollins, San Francisco, 1988), p. 40.

[14] Catherine C. Kroeger, "1 Timothy 2:12 – A Classicist's View" in *Women, Authority and the Bible*, Alvera Mickelsen, Ed. (InterVarsity Christian Fellowship, 1986), pp. 232–235.

[15] John Temple Bristow, *What Paul Really Said About Women* (HarperCollins, San Francisco, 1988), pp. 40–41.

[16] Ibid., p. 39.

[17] Ibid., p. 42.

Chapter 13

A Fresh Look at
1 Corinthians 14:33–35

"For God is not the author of confusion but of peace, as in all the churches of the saints. Let your women keep silent in the churches, for they are not permitted to speak; but they are to be submissive, as the law also says. And if they want to learn something, let them ask their own husbands at home; for it is shameful for women to speak in church."
(1 Corinthians 14:33–35)

The difficulties with the traditional interpretation

1 Corinthians 14:33–35 is another Pauline text which at first glance appears to say one thing quite clearly, yet upon closer examination says something completely different! The first indicator we should have that all is *not as it appears* is that the English translation suggests an attitude and conviction on the part of the apostle Paul that is in complete opposition to New Testament practice. It is even in opposition to Paul's own practice! We saw that women were consistently involved in ministry and leadership in the early Church. Further, 1 Corinthians 11 makes it clear that women were actively involved in public worship, prayer and prophecy. In defining what constitutes prophecy, we previously noted in Chapter 10 that prophesying has been accepted among the most traditional of scholars, and even among the Puritans of the 16th century, to include Spirit-led preaching. Additionally, in verses 30–31 of

1 Corinthians 14, Paul says *all* (includes both genders) may prophesy *"that all may learn and all may be encouraged."* The NIV translation puts it this way, *"that everyone may be instructed and encouraged."* Two Greek words used here are *manthano* which means "to learn or increase in knowledge", and *parakaleo*, which means "to admonish, beseech, exhort, encourage or instruct". Paul's description of the purpose of prophecy actually involves teaching and what we would call "ministry". It makes no sense that Paul would give instructions regarding this public ministry of women in 1 Corinthians 11, and then a few pages later in the same letter forbid women to talk at all in public gatherings. Further, we know from various New Testament passages that Paul was supportive of Priscilla's ministry of preaching and teaching, as well as the many women he commended in his epistles for their roles in sharing the gospel of Jesus Christ.

Additionally, the Greek word translated "church" here is *ekklesia*, which refers to a group of Christians not a meeting place. The "churches" of the New Testament period were not edifices dedicated to a solemn and ritualistic religion, but were groups of Christians who met in homes. We know from the historical record of the New Testament that a number of these house churches met in the homes of women (for example, Lydia, Mary, Priscilla, Nympha, etc.) and were probably led, at least in part, by these women as well. It makes no sense that Paul would be saying these leaders or hostesses were not allowed to talk in their own homes or to talk in any gathering together of Christians, which is what *ekklesia* really means. Let's take a closer look at this passage and see if, by examining the context of it and the original language, we can come to a better understanding of what Paul was trying to communicate.

Historical and grammatical context

Corinth was a huge Greek city, a trade center infamous for its sensuality and sacred prostitution, and dedicated to the Greek goddess Aphrodite (Venus to the Romans). Aphrodite was associated closely with the Phoenician goddess Astarte (Ashtoreth). The apostle Paul wrote this letter to the church in Corinth because the spiritual climate in the city was beginning to affect the church [1] and as an answer to a letter written to him from the Corinthian church (1 Corinthians 7:1). Eerdman's Handbook to the Bible calls 1 Corinthians "essentially a practical letter which throws light on the many problems facing a newly established community in a pagan environment notorious for its immorality." [2] Many of the Christians in this city had formerly been involved in cult worship. This worship was characterized by religious frenzy and exchange of sex roles.[3] A popular encyclopedia notes that Corinthians were notorious for "their love of pleasure and lax morals." [4] This describes what we would today define as "hedonism". It is characterized by lack of rules, discipline or propriety. Anything goes. If it feels good, do it ... or say it! Such was the historical context for this epistle to the Christians at Corinth.

The context of these verses within Paul's letter is a chapter in which Paul discusses the use (or abuse) of spiritual gifts and the corresponding order (or disorder) within public gatherings where the gifts are in operation. Just before these verses, Paul makes the statement, *"For you can **all** prophesy one by one, that **all** may learn and **all** may be encouraged"* (1 Corinthians 14:31, emphasis added). After this section which we are examining, he goes on to conclude, *"Therefore, brethren, desire earnestly to prophesy, and do not forbid to speak with tongues. Let all things be done decently and in order"* (verses 39–40). Clearly, then, the verses in question have to do with the operation of spiritual gifts and the orderliness of their operation.

In discussing the context of the passage, John Bristow points out that the central theme of Paul's remarks is really confusion. He notes that the Greek word used is *akatastasia*, which Paul used to describe in 2 Corinthians 6:4–5 the tumultuous situations he had experienced. Jesus used the same word to describe coming destruction in Luke 21:9. Bristow maintains that Paul was sharing with the church in Corinth that "he did not want *akatastasia* in their public worship and then gave instructions for orderliness..." [5] Richard Longenecker concurs that the avoidance of confusion is the purpose of this passage.[6] It helps if we remember that ecstatic cries, shrieks and religious frenzy were part of the pagan worship out of which were coming the new converts in Corinth.[7]

Key words in the original language

Perhaps the key to these verses lies in the original Greek. What words were used? Bristow maintains that clarity comes in taking a closer look at Paul's choice of words translated "silence" and "speak". He notes that Paul did not use the word *phimoo*, meaning "forced silence", or *hesuchia* that refers to "quietness, stillness or harmony". Rather, he used the verb *signao* which describes either a "voluntary silence", such as the silence of the apostles and elders when they listened to a report from Paul and Barnabas (Acts 15:12) or a "requested silence", such as when the beggar was told to quit yelling (Luke 18:39). It was also used when a crowd was told to be quiet (Acts 12:17). He notes that "*signao* is the kind of silence asked for in the midst of disorder and clamor." [8]

Bristow relates an experience shared by Kari Jorjesen Malcom, whose parents were missionaries in northern China. The women in their missions church were coming out of paganism, and tended to use the gathering time together as a time to catch up on the latest gossip and news. She says, "Their only concept of an assembly was a family feast where everyone talked at once." It was chaos and her mother used to exclaim that it couldn't be more like Corinth! Bristow maintains that Paul was merely telling these untaught, noisy women to "hush up".[9] Interestingly enough, the root of *sigao* is a word meaning "to hiss or to hush", and several references translate it as "holding one's peace." [10]

Bristow's conclusion is corroborated by the fact that Paul spoke this *same* injunction for silence, using this *same* verb, to prophets and tongue-speakers in 1 Corinthians 14:28–30. For this reason, Liefeld concludes that the silence Paul was imposing upon the women in verse 34 was not a universal silence but one "dictated by circumstances, in this case the time for judging prophecies." [11] This is very important! He used the exact same words, telling them not to speak and to keep silent. Yet we do not try to establish a doctrine from his words in these verses and teach that all those with prophetic words or tongues should always and at all times remain silent. Why do we do so regarding his admonitions to the women?

The second word that Paul used which offers some clarity here is the word translated "speak". It is the Greek verb *laleo*.

Bristow notes that there are some 30 words in the Greek which signify speaking, all with various shades of meaning. He notes that, "like the other verbs, *laleo* can denote the act of saying something quite important. But of all the verbs that can be translated 'speak', only *laleo* can also mean, simply 'talk'. If someone wished to write in Greek the sentence 'Please do not talk during the prayers,' the verb would have to be *laleo* ... Paul was telling them that it is shameful for women to keep talking during the worship services."[12]

Why would Paul's comments be directed only towards the women? Roger Nicole states the obvious: because they were the principle source of this particular disruption![13] This first letter to the Corinthians is full of the apostle's corrections and adjustments, aimed at a long list of problems and abuses that had come to his attention. In these verses, he is merely addressing another one of these problems, *not* establishing a general directive and policy for women in the Church. The fact that he ends the verses with a comment about women (or wives) asking their questions at home (instead of in the meeting) strengthens our understanding that Paul was addressing the specific situation of confusion and disorder during the flow of spiritual gifts within the worship services.

Paul goes on to bolster his request by referring to a law which calls upon women to submit or *hupotassomai*. This is a word we have looked at previously in Chapters 11 and 12, in regards to 1 Timothy 2:11–12 and Ephesians 5:21–33, respectively. *Hupostassomai* means literally "to stand under". It speaks of yielding to one another and a voluntary willingness to put oneself under others by being responsive to their needs, to be considerate of them, to be willing to serve and honor one another, to be supportive of, and to be willing to work together as a team. It is the opposite of being "me-oriented", self-centered, self-assertive or grasping. Trombley says regarding this verb, "*Huppotasso* is a Spirit-filled, Spirit-controlled believer taking the second seat rather than the first, submitting to others rather than lording it over others. It's having the mind of Christ."[14] Philippians 2:5–8 defines the mind of Christ as the willingness to come as a servant, and the willingness and humility to lay down one's own life for others.

In Ephesians 5, it is within the larger context of Christians submitting one to another (verse 21) that he goes on to encourage wives to submit to their husbands with a self-sacrificing honor and respect, and husbands to love their wives with a self-sacrificing love which lifts them up and puts them first. In 1 Timothy 2, we discovered that Paul was speaking specifically to the behavior of women within the learning environment. He urged them to learn with a quiet, attentive attitude that was respectful and submissive, not only to those around them but also to the Word of God.

Here in 1 Corinthians 14:33–35, the apostle is illuminating another specific situation where believers, women in particular, need to submit to one another. Within this context of the operation of spiritual gifts in the public worship gathering, he encourages the noisy women to hush up, consider other people and ask their questions at a better time and place.

So says what law?

A number of scholars have questioned this "law" to which Paul refers in verse 34. Traditionalists such as Matthew Henry [15] and Dake [16] assume this law refers to Genesis 3:16, and the subordination of woman to man that they infer God was making in this verse as a judgment upon her for "making" Adam sin. However, to give Dake credit for moving beyond the traditional viewpoint, he notes in his remarks on this passage that Paul is really dealing with "lawlessness" and "confusion". He goes on to say,

> "Among people who have inspirational experiences of prophecy, tongues and interpretation of tongues, it is very easy for one to claim that the Holy Spirit is moving upon him and that he should not quench the Spirit ... This attitude of being determined to obey the Spirit leads to abuses of such gifts many times, causing much confusion in the church. Let no man claim to be moved by the Spirit who acts disorderly and causes confusion ... This does not contradict the fact that women were free to pray and prophesy in the church (1 Corinthians 11:15, 13; Acts 2:16–21; 21:9; Joel 2:28–32)."

Dake also notes that Paul's directive to the women to be quiet, asking their questions at home, referred only to their desire to learn, "not their desire to preach, pray, testify or prophesy anything."[17]

Other scholars, those who embrace what we would call non-traditional viewpoints, decry the fact that there is no such "law" anywhere in the biblical record. Liefeld points out, "No single Old Testament text stands clearly behind this prohibition."[18] Bristow comments,

> "This last phrase, 'as also the law says,' has confused scholars. Some translators print *Law* with a capital L, as if *the law* here refers to the law of Moses. But nowhere in the Old Testament is there any command for women to remain silent during worship. Nor is there any such law known to have existed in Corinth or any other pagan city. Some Bibles have a cross-reference to 1 Timothy 2:11. But that passage could not be the *law* to which Paul makes reference, since when he wrote to the Corinthians, he had yet to write to Timothy!"[19]

Trombley agrees that these verses in 1 Corinthians 14 totally conflict with the attitude and practice of the apostles as recorded in the New Testament, and that there is no such Old Testament law as that referred to in such a perplexing way by the apostle Paul. He suggests that the "law" to which Paul refers is the oral law of the rabbis, which *did* insist that women remain silent in public.[20]

While I recognize that Trombley has identified a viable possibility, I think it also possible that the "law" to which Paul refers is a spiritual law embodied within this new covenant sealed by the blood of Jesus. As we look carefully at the meanings of the words in Greek which Paul used, they actually convey only what we would consider appropriate, sensitive, Spirit-led behavior. There was obviously a need to lift up a new standard of relating to one another in gathering together for worship due to the large number of converts from paganism. The new standard was governed by the "law" of love, which puts others before oneself.[21]

Think about it for a minute! The law of the world is to look out for yourself and step on others to climb to the top. The ethos of the world is "might makes right". But under grace, the law of love establishes a different ethos: "right makes might" – that spiritual power is inherent in the righteousness and morality of our God who is love. James 2:8 says this "royal *law*" is to *"love your neighbor as yourself"*, in other words treat others the way you would like them to treat you. This spiritual law calls every Christian to submit to one another (Ephesians 5:21), in honor preferring one another (Romans 12:10). *"Let each of us please his neighbor for his good, leading to edification"* (Romans 15:2). Galatians 6:2 describes lifting up one another and focusing on their needs as fulfilling the *"law* of Christ".

My grandfather frequently joked about something he called "the boardinghouse reach". He had been a locomotive engineer in the 1920s and 30s, and his travels frequently required him to stay in what were then called boardinghouses. He said that there was only a limited supply of food to put out on the table, and if one didn't jump in and grab their share, they would be left with an empty stomach. He would joke about his bad table manners, reaching across others at the table to grab a dish. He attributed his manners to spending so much time in these boardinghouses. The "boardinghouse reach" is a surprisingly accurate picture of the attitude of the world that often permeates our lives before Christ. I think it is an accurate picture of what was happening in the Corinthian church. Paul was lifting up a different standard in 1 Corinthians 14:33–35 to countermand the boardinghouse reach kind of attitude and behavior. He called not only women, but all those who would prophesy or speak in tongues, to be respectful and considerate of others during the worship services. He called them to prefer others before themselves and to help maintain peace and orderliness as the gifts of the Spirit flowed within the congregation.

Summary

The context of verses 33–35 within chapter 14 in this first letter to the Corinthians is the *key* to understanding and rightly applying these verses to our Christian walk. We find that these verses occur in the middle of a discourse about the release of spiritual gifts within the services. The apostle Paul was addressing the specific problem of disorder and confusion in the services. He proceeds to bring balance and guidelines to ensure the gifts were released, but "decently and in order."

The Greek words the apostle used are ones that describe Spirit-led behavior within any gathering of Christians. They are words that illustrate how we are to prefer, respect, honor, and submit to one another in love. Just a few verses earlier, in 1 Corinthians 14:28, 30 Paul used the same words to provide guidelines for those with prophetic words and tongues. Again, he was dealing with this same problem of disorder and chaos in the services. He used the exact same words, telling them not to speak and to keep silent. Yet we do not try to establish a doctrine from his words in these verses and teach that all those with prophetic words or tongues should always and at all times remain silent.

There is some question as to what "law" Paul refers to in this text. There is no Old Testament law that dealt with these issues of women being silent and submissive in worship services. It's possible that he was making reference to the oral law in which the rabbis did restrict women's involvement. But it is also possible, given the various shades of meaning of the words which he used, that he was speaking of the law of love, which was the new standard of relating to one another under grace. It has been suggested that the apostle was calling all who had something to say to be respectful and considerate of others during the services and to help maintain peace and orderliness as the gifts of the Spirit were released in their midst.

Chapter 13 notes

[1] *The Spirit-Filled Life Bible*, Jack Hayford, General Ed. (Thomas Nelson, Nashville, 1991), pp. 1717–1718.

[2] *Eerdman's Handbook to the Bible* (Eerdmans Publishing Company, Grand Rapids; Lion Publishing, Hertfordshire, 1973), p. 575.

[3] Walter L. Liefeld, "Women, Submission and Ministry in 1 Corinthians" in *Women, Authority and the Bible*, Alvera Mickelsen, Ed. (InterVarsity Christian Fellowship, 1986), p. 151.

[4] Microsoft (R) Encarta "Corinthians", Copyright (c) 1994 Microsoft Corporation. Copyright (c) 1994 Funk & Wagnalls Corporation.

[5] John Temple Bristow, *What Paul Really Said About Women* (HarperCollins, San Franciso, 1988), p. 61.

6 Richard N. Longenecker, "Authority, Hierarchy and Leadership Patterns in the Bible" in *Women, Authority and the Bible*, Alvera Mickelsen, Ed. (InterVarsity Christian Fellowship, 1986), p. 78.

7 Jimmilea Berryhill, "First Century Woman", *Restore!* (Winter 1999), p. 23.

8 John Temple Bristow, *What Paul Really Said About Women* (HarperCollins, San Franciso, 1988), pp. 62–63.

9 Ibid., p. 64.

10 W.E. Vine, *An Expository Dictionary of New Testament Words* (Fleming H. Revell Company, Old Tappan, NJ, 1940), pp. 31, 170.

10 W.E. Vine, *An Expository Dictionary of New Testament Words* (Fleming H. Revell Company, Old Tappan, NJ, 1940), pp. 31, 170.

11 Walter L. Liefeld, "Women, Submission and Ministry in 1 Corinthians" in *Women, Authority and the Bible*, Alvera Mickelsen, Ed. (InterVarsity Christian Fellowship, 1986), p. 150.

12 John Temple Bristow, *What Paul Really Said About Women* (HarperCollins, San Franciso, 1988), p. 63.

13 Roger Nicole, "Biblical Authority and Feminist Aspirations" in *Women, Authority and the Bible*, Alvera Mickelsen, Ed. (InterVarsity Christian Fellowship, 1986), pp. 45–46.

14 Charles Trombley, *Who Said Women Can't Teach* (Bridge Publishing, South Plainfield, NJ, 1985), p. 150.

15 Matthew Henry, *A Commentary on the Whole Bible Volume Six* (Fleming H. Revell Company, New York), p. 583.

16 *Dake's Annotated Reference Bible* (Dake Bible Sales, Lawrenceville, GA, 1961, 1963), p. 187 of the New Testament.

17 Ibid.

18 Walter L. Liefeld, "Women, Submission and Ministry in 1 Corinthians" in *Women, Authority and the Bible*, Alvera Mickelsen, Ed. (InterVarsity Christian Fellowship, 1986), p. 149.

19 John Temple Bristow, *What Paul Really Said About Women* (HarperCollins, San Franciso, 1988), p. 65.

20 Charles Trombley, *Who Said Women Can't Teach* (Bridge Publishing, South Plainfield, NJ, 1985), pp. 43–50.

21 John Temple Bristow, *What Paul Really Said About Women* (HarperCollins, San Franciso, 1988), p. 65.

Chapter 14

Out of the Darkness and into the Light of Christ

"Arise, shine; for your light has come!
And the glory of the Lord *is risen upon you.*
For behold, the darkness shall cover the earth,
and deep darkness the people;
but the Lord *will arise over you,*
and His glory will be seen upon you."
(Isaiah 60:1–2)

The Dark Ages began to come to a grimy close the day in 1517 when a young man named Martin Luther posted 95 theses to the door of a church in Wittenberg, Germany. His actions, challenging the heresies of the medieval Church, hailed the beginning of what is known as the Reformation. With reformation, came restoration of an understanding of justification by faith alone, the authority of the Scriptures, and the priesthood of the believer. While practice didn't change quickly, a work of the Spirit was beginning in the heart of the Church. As that work of the Spirit has continued, an understanding of the spiritual and functional equality of women within the Body of Christ has slowly unfolded, with the Father prodding and stirring His women onward, thrusting them forward to fulfill their destinies in Him.

In this chapter, we will look at the gradual unveiling after the Reformation of God's heart and mind towards women and their place in the Body of Christ. We will examine briefly how the Reformation changed the status of women in the Church and how it did not. Finally, we will look at some of the post-Reformation sects and movements which opened the prison doors for women, releasing them into ministry in a way that had not happened since the first century.

The Middle Ages

During the millennium known as the Dark Ages of the Church, which spanned a period of time historians refer to as the Middle Ages, the involvement of women in official ministry within the Church came to an almost complete standstill. A major reason for this was the increasing institutionalization of the Church under a male religious hierarchy. Furthermore, this hierarchy was steeped in a theology that had its roots in a Greek (pagan) philosophy which saw women as weak and worthless, yet also very dangerous to men. The resultant mindset was given strength by the ongoing tension in the relationship between men and women which had existed since the fall of man. Because women were seen as a threat to male dominance, they were increasingly shut out of a role within the institutionalized Church.

An interesting story which gives some background concerning women in medieval times is that of "Pope Joan" or "Papess Johanna". There is increasing evidence that an Englishwoman, the daughter of two missionaries from a Dorset village, deceived the entire Roman Catholic hierarchy to become Pope John VIII in A.D. 855. She took on the appearance of a young man and was educated at a Benedictine monastery in the north of Germany. She became known as "John the English" well-known lecturer and expert in the liberal arts, who taught at a medieval university called the Trivium. Her deception was only exposed when, after two-and-a-half years of rule, she began to give birth during a papal procession in Rome. A Catholic mob vented their anger at this deceit by killing her, and a new Pope John VIII was subsequently installed. The Vatican tried to keep the story hidden, but news of it leaked out and the story was passed on through the generations. A modern researcher has found 500 separate accounts of her papal term, and brought to light a bizarre test of gender that was introduced by the papacy to avoid any repetition of this deception. Future popes were required to sit in a chair with a hole in the seat. Through this hole, a cardinal would reach up and verify the sex of the papal candidate.[1] Tucker and Liefeld, although skeptical themselves, note that the story of Papess Johanna was widely accepted during the late medieval period. In fact, a bust of her was placed alongside the busts of other popes during the early fifteenth century and her existence cited as fact at the Council of Constance.[2]

Despite the story of Joan's unique rise to the Papacy, women were kept on a very short leash during the Dark Ages. As one text sums up,

> "The Roman Catholic Church was deeply committed to a position of male domination in spiritual matters. Women had a place in the Church, but that place was clearly defined as one that carried with it no official authority. By their own leadership ability and charismatic influence, women on occasion overcame this disability, but whatever role they attained almost always remained within the confines of monasticism."[3]

Changing attitude towards women in the Reformation

Church historians note that the sixteenth century was a time of upheaval in Christendom, as Renaissance thinking challenged the dogma and tradition of the times. The role of women in the Church was included in this challenge. Renaissance humanists and Christian reformers began to depart from the misogynist thinking that had characterized attitudes towards women during the Dark Ages, and endowed women with a somewhat greater worth and dignity.

The reformers still had their prejudices, however. These prejudices were partly the result of the culture of the time and partly the result of theology based on the teaching of the early Church Fathers, whose disparaging views on women were influenced by Plato and the Greek stoic philosophers. Tucker and Liefeld note, "Although Martin Luther had proclaimed the priesthood of all believers, it apparently did not occur to him or to his fellow Reformers what the ramifications would actually mean for the

Church." They continue on to say that regarding the role of women, "whether women themselves could hold the clerical office was not even seriously considered ... the Reformers were clearly not anxious to be innovators in this area."[4]

The attitude towards women was changing, however, as the Holy Spirit stirred the hearts of men during the Reformation. Tucker and Liefeld note that *Martin Luther*, while a man of his time in many respects, attacked those who disdained women as inferior or as a necessary evil. He had an understanding unique to his time of women's value and dignity as equal bearers of the image of God. He supported female education, encouraged greater freedom for women in the marriage relationship, and even opened up the idea of the role for women in public ministry. He suggested that if no men were available, it might be necessary for women to preach.

Nevertheless, Luther still wrestled with the biases of the men of his day, and it was obvious from his writings that he generally considered women to be inferior to men because Eve was deceived by the serpent and therefore the "weaker vessel". He saw woman as initially created equal in all things to Adam, but dropping to an inferior state after the fall. Luther saw the subjection of women to men as a necessary result of the punishment imposed on Eve for her sin. He also read the controversial passages in the Pauline epistles as injunctions against women teaching.[5]

John Calvin's view of women in the Church remains a source of debate. Most of his relationships with women were political, with French noblewomen whom he exhorted to stand strong against opposition in their support of the Huguenots. Some of his writings seem to indicate that he viewed the controversial Pauline texts as simply promoting decorum and edification, rather than divine law. But in other writings, he took a very derogatory and sometimes scathing view of women as "defective", "weak" and "contemptible".[6] His teaching on sovereignty, predestination, and government supported an authoritative and hierarchical model, which left women forbidden to baptize, speak or teach in the Church.[7]

Scottish *John Knox*, by contrast, very outspokenly denounced women in leadership. His hostility towards women had apparently been invoked by two Catholic queens, Mary Tudor of

England and Mary Guise of Scotland, who had brought persecution to Protestants under their rule. He offended many with his diatribes, and made statements like, "woman in her greatest perfection was made to serve and obey man." Nevertheless, Knox admitted his dependence upon women in spiritual matters. He had a very close woman friend and confidante in London whom he praised "for nourishing and confirming him in the faith." He confided on one occasion that he was "in desperate need of her spiritual counsel".[8]

The Reformation served to begin a process of unlocking the chains of bondage from God's women, though it never removed them. As Lutz points out, "The Reformers improved attitudes towards sex and gave dignity and spirituality to marriage. But at no time in history had ministry for women been so limited as in the Reformation. Women were now devoid of service even in monasteries and religious orders, and found little avenue for ministry outside their homes and children."[9] Others note that the position of women changed very little in society and in the established churches (Catholic, Anglican, Lutheran, Reformed, Congregationalist, Puritan, etc.) in the centuries which immediately followed the Reformation.[10] There were bright spots, but things did not really begin to open up again for women within the Body of Christ until some years after the Reformation when radical sects began to spring up. These sects were willing to take things a step further than the Reformers by putting their theology into practice.

Susan Hyatt sees a correlation in the openness of the Reformers to the moving of the Holy Spirit, and their openness to women's involvement. She notes that the rejection of the *charismata* in the Reformation appeared to coincide with the rejection of women. "Where the Holy Spirit is silenced, it appears that the women are also silenced. When the Holy Spirit is secondary, it seems that women are also secondary."[11] If we look at various movements within the Church historically, I believe study will verify the veracity of her observations.

Post-Reformation sects – lifting off the chains

It was not until the rise of non-conformist Protestant sects outside the established churches in the late 16th, 17th and 18th centuries that women began to experience some release within the churches.[12] Interestingly enough, many of these sects were considered "non-conformist" because they did not quench the Spirit! We will now look at a few of these sects and their influence on changing attitudes towards women:

English Baptists, founded by John Smyth in the early 17th century, recognized the place of women in public ministry. Smyth wrote in 1609 that women deacons should be elected, approved and ordained by the Church. Women preachers were also fairly common among the early Baptist congregations.[13]

Another group of non-conformists, called the *Fifth Monarchists*, was known for permitting women an active role in ministry. They were a small yet highly visible sect which arose in England in the mid-16th century. Their founder and leader, John Rogers, strongly supported the equality of women within the Church and their right to preach publicly. He used biblical arguments to defend his position, as well as his own observation regarding the godly nature and wisdom exhibited among Christian women.[14]

A sect known as the *Cevenols*, *Camisards* or the *French Prophets* was another sect well-known for allowing women to minister alongside men. This sect's style of worship was charismatic/pentecostal in the sense that it was exuberant and included singing, dancing, shaking, shouting, speaking in tongues and prophesying.[15] They arose in France in the 17th and 18th centuries, but were forced to flee to England to avoid persecution. There they became known to many of the English leaders including John Wesley.[16] They also had an indirect influence on Ann Lee, who founded the Shaker movement in the United States.[17]

One of the most well known sects that developed in 17th century England was the *Quakers* or *Society of Friends*. George Fox, the founder, strongly defended the involvement of women in ministry. He challenged those who would limit women in ministry, using scriptural arguments to back up his claim. Quaker women boldly and courageously faced much opposition to their beliefs and their freedom to minister, often suffering persecution, imprisonment and even hanging in the case of Mary Dyer, a New England Quaker.[18] According to Hyatt, "This biblically-based, Spirit-oriented Christianity threatened the rigid hierarchical social pattern promulgated by the state Church and Puritans who held to a medieval, hierarchical worldview. It threatened the authority by which these religious systems controlled people."[19] Interestingly enough, the Friends movement was very open to the Holy Spirit. Quaker writings reveal the operation of the gifts of the Spirit in their midst.[20]

The rise of *Methodism* in 18th century England helped to solidify the position of women in public ministry in the sects outside the established churches. While John Wesley initially "took a very conservative stand" on the place of women in ministry, his convictions changed over time and by the 1770s he was supporting his women leaders in their preaching. Tucker and Liefeld note that "Wesley eventually became so convinced of the rightness of women's ministry that he openly encouraged women to preach..."[21] Some of the early Methodist women, under Wesley's leadership, became itinerant preachers. One of the best known was Sarah Crosby, who was an itinerant minister for over 20 years in the north of England.

After Wesley's death, prejudice against women began to arise again within Methodism and opportunities for women to publicly minister declined somewhat with the lack of Wesley's support and backing.[22] Perhaps this was because Wesley had retained the hierarchical structure of the Church of England in his Methodist societies.[23] Perhaps the inherent corruption of institutionalism eventually began to burden down women once again under weight of suppression. Thankfully, God's plan was not to be stopped! Coming moves and revivals would release God's women again.

Reform and revivalism – open doors for women

The post-Reformation revival movements helped to re-open doors for women into ministry. Church historian Richard Riss has stated, "Women and lay people have found a greater place for leadership during times of revival than at other periods in the history of the church."[24] Maybe this is because during revivals and awakening movements, the focus is on God and not on tradition! Perhaps it is also true because the Holy Spirit lifts up women, and where there is an openness and yielding to the Holy Spirit, women are released.

Riss has surveyed literally hundreds of revivals that took place in the British Isles and in North America from the time of the Puritans until the present day. The biggest and most influential revivals, in terms of releasing women into ministry, were the North American Great Awakening and its counterpart in Britain – the Evangelical Awakening of the early 18th century, and the North American Second Great Awakening and its counterpart in Britain – the Second Evangelical Awakening of the late 18th to early 19th centuries. Methodism sprang out of the Evangelical Awakening in the early 18th century. The Holiness movement, which began about mid-19th century in America and emphasized the need for revival, provided the rise in revival activity for years to come. There was also a parallel Healing Movement at the same time, which further served to open doors wider for women's ministry.[25]

Tucker and Liefeld reveal that the revivals and sectarian movements began to bring change to the rigidity of Puritanism, which "loosened up" American religion, providing greater opportunities for women within the religious community.[26] They declare that "without female involvement, the Great Awakenings might never have transpired." It was women's prayer meetings that fostered these revivals and it was mostly women who attended the meetings.[27] Tucker and Liefeld note that it was during the Second Great Awakening (late 18th century and early 19th century) "that female lay ministries began to flourish." They observe that the women were not seeking professional religious careers, only to serve God and impact society in a meaningful way. As a result, "during the early 19th century, there was a tremendous increase in women's involvement in lay ministries."[28]

Similar things were going on across the Atlantic in Britain as a result of both the Evangelical Awakenings, with lay ministries also springing up there. These lay ministries involved not only every aspect of social work but spiritual ministry as well. Home mission societies sprang up which were founded and directed by women who had a vision to reform their cities. Tucker and Liefeld note that "it was out of the reform movement that Sunday schools emerged."[29]

The Sunday School movement

The Sunday School movement, which began in England in the 1780s, would never have flourished without women. Its most active agents and most of its teachers were women. In the early years of the movement, it was often opposed by clergy for this very reason.[30] The growth rate of this movement was astounding, despite the opposition. One woman in England, Hannah More, organized Sunday schools that accommodated approximately 20,000 children. In Sweden, under the leadership of Lady Ehrenborg, the movement grew from the 1850s to include 25,000 teachers and more than 300,000 pupils in 50 years.[31]

Foreign missions movements

The missions movement of the 19th century offered women fantastic opportunities for meaningful ministry – and many leaped at this opportunity. On the mission field, they could freely minister in ways that they could not minister so freely at home. They could evangelize, preach, plant churches, pastor, establish apostolic networks, train ministers of the gospel and the list goes on. It has been noted that by 1915, there were more than *3 million* women on the membership roles of some 40 women's missions societies.[32] Tucker and Liefeld observed in 1987, however, that "in spite of the fact that there were vast numbers of women involved in foreign missions, both at home and abroad, and that women had a powerful effect on the modern missionary movement, little mention is made of their contributions in the history-of-missions texts."[33] Thankfully, this situation has changed over the past fifteen years! There is now a selection of books for the Christian reader to choose from which share the historic accomplishments and the many sacrifices of God's women on the mission field.

Summary

During the period of the Dark Ages, the involvement of women in ministry almost came to a standstill. The main reason was the institutionalization of the Church and a theology rooted in the pagan teachings of the Greek philosophers. The Dark Ages came to a close with the advent of the Reformation in the early 16th century. Yet the Reformation brought only a glimmer of light. Church practice did not change to any great degree. The Reformation was, however, the beginning of a work of the Spirit within the Church which continued in the centuries to come.

A possible correlation between an openness to the moving of the Holy Spirit and the freedom for women to minister was identified. In the Reformation, the gifts of the Spirit were quenched, as were the giftings of women. In contrast, it was noted that when the Holy Spirit was allowed to move in the various revival movements, women found a greater place of leadership than at any other time.

The rise of the non-conformist sects after the Reformation in the late 16th, 17th and 18th centuries opened a door for the release of women to minister. Not bound by the traditional thinking and limitations of the established denominations, these sects recognized the place of women in public ministry and actively encouraged it. Some of these sects included the English Baptists, the Fifth Monarchists, the Camisards or French Prophets, the Quakers or Society of Friends and Methodism. Many of these experienced *charismata* and manifestations of the Holy Spirit in their midst.

The revival and awakening movements helped to bring more liberty to women within the Church. They were also influential in thrusting women forward into ministry. The most significant ones in terms of impact upon women were probably the 18th century Great Awakening in North America and its counterpart, the Evangelical Awakening in Britain, and the Second Great Awakening and Second Evangelical Awakening in the late 18th and early 19th centuries. It was noted that the Great Awakenings might never have happened without the female involvement and undergirding in prayer. One movement almost solely sustained by women was the Sunday School movement. Another was the missions movement of the 19th century. By 1915, more than 3 million women were on the membership roles of the various missions societies.

Chapter 14 notes

[1] Christopher Morgan, "Riddle of Joan the 'She Pope' May Be Solved", *The Sunday Times* (London, March 22, 1998), p. 15.

[2] Ruth A. Tucker and Walter Liefeld, *Daughters of the Church* (Zondervan, Grand Rapids, 1987), pp. 139–140.

[3] Ibid., p. 140.

[4] Ibid., pp. 172–173.

[5] Ibid., pp. 173–175.

[6] Ibid., pp. 175–176.

[7] Susan C. Hyatt, *In the Spirit We're Equal* (Hyatt Press, Dallas, 1998), p. 68.

[8] Ruth A. Tucker and Walter Liefeld, *Daughters of the Church* (Zondervan, Grand Rapids, 1987), pp. 177–178.

[9] Lorry Lutz, *Women As Risk-Takers for God* (World Evangelical Fellowship in assoc. with Paternoster Publishing, Carlisle, Cumbria, 1997), p. 13.

[10] Ruth A. Tucker and Walter Liefeld, *Daughters of the Church* (Zondervan, Grand Rapids, 1987), pp. 207–216.

[11] Susan C. Hyatt, *In the Spirit We're Equal* (Hyatt Press, Dallas, 1998), p. 70.

[12] Ruth A. Tucker and Walter Liefeld, *Daughters of the Church* (Zondervan, Grand Rapids, 1987), pp. 207, 218.

[13] Ibid., p. 224.

[14] Ibid., p. 225.

[15] Edith Deen, *Great Women of the Christian Faith* (Harper and Row Publisher, 1959, reprinted by Barbour and Company, Uhrichsville, OH), p. 161.

[16] Ruth A. Tucker and Walter Liefeld, *Daughters of the Church* (Zondervan, Grand Rapids, 1987), p. 226.

[17] Edith Deen, *Great Women of the Christian Faith* (Harper and Row Publisher, 1959, reprinted by Barbour and Company, Uhrichsville, OH), p. 161.

[18] Ruth A. Tucker and Walter Liefeld, *Daughters of the Church* (Zondervan, Grand Rapids, 1987), pp. 227–228.

[19] Susan C. Hyatt, *In the Spirit We're Equal* (Hyatt Press, Dallas, 1998), p. 94.

[20] Ibid., p. 96.

[21] Ruth A. Tucker and Walter Liefeld, *Daughters of the Church* (Zondervan, Grand Rapids, 1987), p. 242.

[22] Ibid.

[23] Susan C. Hyatt, *In the Spirit We're Equal* (Hyatt Press, Dallas, 1998), pp. 131–132.

[24] Richard M. Riss, *A Survey of 20th Century Revival Movements in North America* (Hendrickson Publishers, Peabody, MA, 1988), p. 6.

[25] Ibid., pp. 17–24.

[26] Ruth A. Tucker and Walter Liefeld, *Daughters of the Church* (Zondervan, Grand Rapids, 1987), p. 245.

[27] Ibid., pp. 245–246.

[28] Ibid., p. 247.

[29] Ibid., p. 249.

[30] Ibid.

[31] Ibid., p. 291.

[32] Ibid.

[33] Ibid.

Chapter 15

Women Preachers, Teachers and Leaders

"And I urge you also, true companion,
help these women who labored with me in the gospel . . .
whose names are in the Book of Life."
(Philippians 4:3)

I used to think that God didn't start using women much in ministry until the 20th century. In my arrogant and ignorant modern mind, I thought that anything before 1900 was still the Dark Ages! I was in for a shock when I began to research and found out how many women over the past 500 years have stood firmly against all odds to answer the call of God on their lives.

The Lord has used many women in the centuries since the Reformation to build and expand the kingdom of God. While there have been perhaps hundreds of thousands of women involved in post-Reformation ministry, we will examine the lives of just a few of these women who stand out as beacons of light in the retreating darkness. For each one of these, there are *many, many more* who labored unceasingly to spread the gospel. It is my prayer that the testimonies left by these women will be an encouragement to God's women today, to stir us to greater boldness in our faith and greater determination to fulfill the purposes of God in our generation!

Sixteenth, seventeenth and eighteenth centuries

After the Reformation, one of the first women to step out and test the waters of religious freedom was *Anne Hutchinson*

(1591–1643). She is cited as the first and most well known woman preacher in colonial New England. Anne's father was an independent thinker and non-conformist minister in Northampton, England, who was imprisoned for his unorthodox preaching. Anne remained in the established Church through marriage and the birth and rearing of 14 children. She then broke with the established Church and later moved with her family to America in search of greater religious freedom. She is described as a deeply sincere woman, upright and blameless, but determined to follow the leading of the Holy Spirit rather than a list of legal rules.[1]

In Boston, she opened her home to women, holding meetings in her living room where she shared from the Scriptures and prayed for the sick. These meetings have been described as "so popular ... that soon the large numbers of women who attended could no longer fit in Anne's living room, and she had to hold extra meetings to accommodate them all. Her critics charged that she frequently had as many as sixty women in attendance."[2] Her growing leadership among women began to cause animosity with the local clergy. She made matters worse by speaking very frankly in challenging the rigid Calvinist theology of the Puritans. She also claimed to know God's voice and hear Him speaking to her.

She was put on trial in 1637, at age 46 and pregnant with a 16th child, for "holding unorthodox opinions." Many of her "opinions" are freely taught today and extolled as "good Bible teaching". She defended with dignity her scriptural interpretation, but was sentenced to four months in prison and banishment from Massachusetts Bay Colony. She and her husband subsequently moved to Rhode Island, but the Boston group sent a delegation to Rhode Island to warn the church there against Anne. Due to a campaign of harassment and threats against the whole family, they planned to move deeper into the wilderness to escape the persecution. Before they could move, however, Anne's beloved husband of 30 years died. He had supported Anne through all of the persecution, saying "I am more nearly tied to my wife than to the church ... She is a dear saint and servant of God."[3]

The family moved soon after his death to a frontier area within the Dutch colony of New Amsterdam (New York) where there would be protection by the Dutch from the Massachusetts Bay persecutors. Here, one year later, the family was attacked and massacred by Indians. One of the Puritan ministers, upon hearing of the deaths, claimed, "Thus the Lord heard our groanes to heaven, and freed us from the great and sore affliction."[4] I find it incredibly sad that these ministers were actually praying for the demise of this poor woman. Doesn't it illustrate how low sin has brought the human race? In contrast are the words on a plaque erected to Anne's memory in Boston in 1904. She is described as one of "bold spirit" and "a persuasive advocate of the right of Independent Judgement."[5]

Margaret Fell (1614–1702) is considered to be almost as important in the early years of the Quaker movement as its founder, George Fox. After the death of Margaret's husband, Judge Thomas Fell, she later married George Fox, and continued in a team ministry together with him for 22 years until his death. Margaret, like her first husband Judge Fell, was a member of the English nobility and resided at Swarthmoor Hall near Morecambe Bay in Lancashire. With her husband's approval, Swarthmoor Hall was opened up to the Quakers as a place of refuge and renewal.

After Thomas' death, she continued to hold illegal religious meetings on the estate. Quaker men described her as "a precious jewel in the hands of the Lord" and one "filled with a spirit of wisdom, meekness, sincerity and supplication."[6] Edith Deen describes her as possessing a pioneering spirit, boundless energy, kindness, courage, strength and an ability to inspire love in those who met her. She says that Margaret preached, taught, wrote, organized and dispensed hospitality, bringing enthusiasm and stability to the growing movement.[7] Margaret also organized women's meetings to help equip women to serve God more ably. These meetings were very controversial and drew much criticism.[8]

For her beliefs and involvement with the Quakers, Margaret was imprisoned three times, once for as long as four years. Because of these imprisonments and those of her second husband, George Fox, they were seldom together during the years of their marriage. Tucker and Liefeld write that their marriage was one "of common interest but little togetherness. They lived missionary lives, preaching and travelling, and were frequently, though never together, in prison."[9] Though they loved each other deeply, they were willing to sacrifice their time together for the good of God's kingdom.

Margaret wrote 16 books and many pamphlets. One of these is an early apologetic for the right of women to share in public ministry entitled *Women's Speaking Justified by the Scriptures*, first published in 1666.[10] This pamphlet was "packed full of Scriptures from Genesis to Revelation relating to women in ministry." It was the "Magna Carta for Quaker women", according to some historians.[11] After George Fox's death, Margaret still influenced the Quaker movement, working hard to keep the teaching pure and free from encroaching legalism.[12]

Madame Jeanne Guyon (1648–1717) was a wealthy wife, member of high French society, and mother of five children who was imprisoned in the Bastille for her religious beliefs. She was also an itinerant evangelist, the author of 40 books including a 20-volume commentary on the Bible, and one of the leading exponents of Quietism, a movement which encouraged Christians to spend time in the presence of God rather than focus on a religion of works. John Wesley said of her, "We may search many centuries before we find another woman who was such a pattern of true holiness."[13] According to Edith Deen, she "taught a religion not of ceremony but of the heart, of affections rather than form, not of creeds but of God."[14]

At age 34, after the death of her husband, she took her youngest child and began an itinerant ministry through the towns of France and Switzerland, evangelizing and sharing with others the faith she had found. Her chief mission, according to Deen, was to teach that holiness is based on faith.[15] Tucker and Liefeld note that her ministry was largely one of personal evangelism.[16] She ministered to the downtrodden, the more educated and even to the nobility. She was the first woman to ever enter the monastery of the Grande Chartreuse. There she shared on justification by faith, and on faith as the foundation of the whole inward Christian life.[17]

Many miracles were associated with her preaching and healing ministry.[18] Church leaders began to become jealous of her popularity with the people in both France and Switzerland, and denounced her as a heretic because some of her teaching did not conform to official Church doctrine. They also said "it was the business of priests to pray, and not of women."[19] She was persecuted heavily, her books publicly burned and was finally arrested and imprisoned for 7 years for her commitment to the message she felt the Lord had given her to proclaim. The last two years of her imprisonment were spent in solitary confinement in the Bastille.[20] Her trust in the Lord was so unwavering and her relationship with Him so strong during this time in prison, that she was able to compose beautiful hymns extolling her contentment, freedom from care, and happiness in God's presence.[21]

19th century evangelists and preachers

Tucker and Liefeld explain that the 19th century women preachers were usually involved in movements that would be considered "sectarian". In England this included the Quakers, Primitive Methodists, and Bible Christians. In America, it included the Quakers, Freewill Baptists, Free Methodists, as well as various groups connected with the holiness or deeper life movements. They also note that each of these movements "emphasized direct communion with God, the leading of the Spirit, and the call to ministry over and above clerical counsel, church bylaws, and ordination."[22] Some of these 19th century preachers included: Mary Savage, Sally Parsons, Clarissa Danforth, Jerena Lee, Salome Lincoln, Mary Cole, Phoebe Palmer, Hannah Whithall Smith and Catherine Booth, to name but a few.

Phoebe Palmer (1807–1874), known to some as "the Mother of the Holiness Movement", is referred to by Tucker and Liefeld as "the most influential woman in nineteenth-century Methodism." As they share in their book *Daughters of the Church*, "hundreds of Methodist preachers, including at least two bishops and three who were later to hold that office, were sanctified under Mrs. Palmer's influence."[23] Richard Riss mentions her in his history of revival movements, noting that she ministered during the 1830s to 1850s, promoting holiness in her Tuesday meetings and as a speaker at camp meetings. She was known for her doctrinal stand on entire sanctification.[24] She apparently had great influence outside of Methodist circles, especially among Congregationalists, Episcopalians, Baptists and Quakers. Besides preaching and teaching, she played an instrumental role in establishing a church and a mission project in New York which provided schooling and religious training as well as housing poor families. Further, she edited a magazine called *The Guide to Holiness*, which had a circulation of about 30,000.[25] Like Priscilla (Acts 18:26), Phoebe Palmer was also involved in team ministry with her husband. Tucker and Liefeld record that Phoebe and her husband Walter teamed up in full-time evangelistic ministry. At the time of her death, she was credited with having led 25,000 people into a salvation experience with Jesus Christ. Despite the way in which God used her however, Phoebe's view of women in ministry was a very traditional one. She viewed her own ministry as unique and did not encourage other women into leadership.[26]

It was actually criticism of Phoebe Palmer's preaching in England that propelled *Catherine Booth* (1829–1890) to speak out in defense of women in ministry. In her booklet, *Female Ministry; Or, Women's Right to Preach the Gospel*, Catherine emphasized the biblical precedents for women in ministry as well as the personal leading of the Holy Spirit.[27] As a child, Catherine's interests focused on Church history and theology. By the age of 18, she was already grappling with theological issues. By age 23, she was teaching a Sunday School class and mentoring 15 teenage girls. She was also an analytical thinker with very decided ideas about things. She sided with the reformers in the Methodist movement at this time because she felt they more clearly emphasized the need for salvation and holiness.[28]

Catherine's ministry began in Gateshead, in the north of England, where her husband was the local New Connexion Methodist minister. She found that people were very open to her as she visited their homes and shared the gospel with them. This discovery led to her initiation of a systematic course of house-to-house visitation two evenings a week and ministry to alcoholics, mostly men.[29] The real turning point came, however, when her husband William entered a period of protracted illness and therapy. His absence forced Catherine to assume the leadership role not only for their church in Gateshead, but also for the circuit of churches in the area. She was so successful in this ministry that at the quarterly meeting of the circuit, a resolution was made that, when William returned to his duties, they would like William to preach one Christmas message and Catherine the other. He and Catherine shared the responsibility of preaching that Christmas day in 1860 and began what would be 30 more years of team ministry. As Green notes in his biography of Catherine Booth, she "was well on her way toward fulfilling her principle vocation – preaching the gospel."[30] Catherine was usually well received. She wrote, "I have every reason to think that the people receive me gladly everywhere, and that prejudice against female ministry melts away before me like snow in the sun."[31]

After beginning a Christian mission in London, the seed which was later to blossom into the Salvation Army, it was Catherine who was the travelling speaker and promoted the ministry as well as supported the family with her earnings. As a result "at this time the name of Catherine Booth was far better known in London circles than was that of William Booth."[32] She also undertook the editing of the mission's magazine, writing many of the articles, and authored a number of books on practical Christianity which are still read and treasured today. Under the direction of William and Catherine, the mission took a theological stand for women in ministry, incurring criticism in the process. They did not waver in their commitment to this principle, however.[33] Green notes that in speeches and writings from the time, it is clear that both William and Catherine were seen as the founders of the Salvation Army.[34] Edith Deen paints Catherine as "quite literally the mother of this Army, nurturing it in its infancy and seeing it through almost 3 pioneering decades."[35] Catherine was in her own words, "one of the most timid and bashful disciples the Lord Jesus ever saved," yet she boldly pressed on to become a powerful model for women in ministry.[36]

Hannah Whitall Smith (1832–1911) was raised an American Quaker, but became well-known through the "deeper life" movement. In 1865, she and her husband, Robert Pearsall-Smith, moved to New Jersey where they experienced and embraced the revivalism that was happening there. They both became very involved in evangelistic activities, preaching, writing tracts, and leading people to the Lord.[37] Charles Cullis, who was a leader in the Healing Movement, persuaded the couple to conduct his 1876 faith convention. According to Riss, the Smiths had been active leaders in the higher life movement in Britain, a movement which emphasized holiness and deeper spiritual life. Their involvement led to the founding of the Keswick Convention.[38] As of this writing, the Keswick Convention is still meeting annually in the Lake District of England. Hannah is best remembered for her popular book, *The Christian's Secret of a Happy Life*, published in 1875. This book has been translated into many languages and is still in print today.

Richard Riss, in his survey of revival movements, also puts a spotlight on the ministry of some other women who lived and ministered through the nineteenth and into the early twentieth century. He mentions *Elizabeth Mix*, a black woman healed under the ministry of Ethan O. Allen sometime after 1846. Ethan Allen was one of the leaders in the nineteenth century Healing Movement and later worked with A.B. Simpson. Elizabeth became one of his first assistants. She and her husband traveled with him until they launched out in their own healing ministry.[39] Riss also mentions *Carrie Judd Montgomery* who entered into a healing ministry after experiencing a divine healing herself. She was a promoter of the Pentecostal experience and was given a platform for ministry within the Holiness Movement by A.B. Simpson, the founder of the Christian and Missionary Alliance denomination.[40] *Maria Woodworth-Etter* is another well-known woman minister from this period who is mentioned by Riss. He calls her "one of the most outstanding evangelists of this era." She was involved in ministry for 6 years before she began to preach divine healing. It is said that the accounts of the revivals which took place in the next 5 years could easily fill a book. People fell under the power of the Holy Spirit in her meetings, and almost always came to Christ as a result. After 35 years of itinerant ministry, she founded and pastored an independent pentecostal church in Indianapolis, Indiana.[41] The first student to receive the gift of tongues at Charles Parham's Bible school in 1901 inTopeka, Kansas was a woman. *Agnes N. Ozman*, notes Riss, helped to ignite the Pentecostal Movement of the early twentieth century.[42]

Tucker and Liefeld also mention a few other women ministers of this era. One is the black scrub woman, *Amanda Smith* (1837–1915), who became a preacher and revivalist in Methodist circles. She was born a slave, but after the civil war, became an evangelist who traversed the country preaching to all races. She spent time evangelizing in England, India and Africa. Says Amanda, "The thought of ordination had never once entered my mind, for I had received my ordination from Him ... "[43]

Ellen G. White (1827–1915), the founder of Seventh-Day Adventism, is another mentioned by Tucker and Liefeld. She was considered a prophetess, receiving many revelations and testimonies which became the foundational doctrines of her writing and teaching. They note that by 1910, she had over 130,000 followers.[44] Her book, "Steps to Christ", is well known today even outside of Adventist circles. While some may question the orthodoxy of some of the Adventist doctrine, it is clear that Ellen G. White has had a profound influence as a teacher and leader in the Body of Christ.

The ministry of *Frances Willard* (1839–1898) was also examined by Tucker and Liefeld. She became well known as one of the temperance leaders of the nineteenth century. She founded and directed WTCU, the largest nineteenth century women's organization. She ministered occasionally with Dwight L. Moody during his Boston campaign, conducting afternoon Bible "lectures" and speaking at women's meetings. He even invited her to preach upon one occasion. By the 1880s, Willard had become a vocal advocate for an equal role for women in the Church. Her book, *Woman in the Pulpit*, presented a strong defense of women in ministry. Tucker and Liefeld note that "she also confessed to her own calling in life and encouraged other women not to be intimidated as she had been ... " She wrote that her dearest wish was to break down the barriers of prejudice that keep God's women from preaching the unsearchable riches of Christ.[45]

Finally, *Antoinette Brown* is another whose ministry should be mentioned. She had the distinction of being the first woman preacher officially ordained in America. This was during the period of 1853–1854. She was ordained by the denomination when she took the pastorate of a Congregationalist church in New York. She had six daughters and wrote ten books during her lifetime.[46] In the later years of her life, she planted another church in New Jersey, where she ministered for 20 years until her death.[47]

Tucker and Liefeld note that "as late as 1888, when Willard published her classic, *Women in the Pulpit*, there were only an estimated twenty women in the United States serving as pastors." They point out, however, that there were an estimated 500 women evangelists, around 350 Quaker women "preachers" and many women Salvation Army officers. Most of these women ministers tried to stay out of the limelight and avoid arguments over their controversial role. One Methodist pastor wrote, "I have gone forth, never allowing myself to be drawn into an argument on the subject, and never saying a word in personal defense, but I knew all the time the Lord would send somebody to take care of the defense."[48]

Denominationally, interesting things were happening in the 19th century with regards to women's rights and roles. The Quakers had always promoted women in preaching ministries. During this time, meeting houses began to spring up all over the western United States, largely as the fruit of women itinerant evangelists.[49] One Wesleyan Methodist leader, Luther Lee, was a strong public advocate of women in ministry. He argued that the early church prophetesses were, by the nature of prophecy, preachers and public teachers of religion, thereby laying a biblical foundation for women in public ministry.[50] In 1891, the Wesleyan Methodists voted to leave it up to local conferences as to whether to allow women's ordination to the ministry or not.[51] The Free Methodists, although not ordaining women, did allow women to preach and conduct evangelistic services. The founder of the denomination, B.T. Roberts, was a staunch supporter of women in ministry. He published a book entitled *Ordaining Women* in 1891, in which he justified his position from a biblical standpoint.[52]

The Brethren church in America was one of the "most progressive evangelical sects regarding women" in the 19th century. After their split from the German Baptist Brethren in the early 1880s, they moved quickly to officially open the way for women into church leadership. By 1894, resolutions had been passed which favored equality of men and women in the church and inclusion of women as pastors and missionaries. In 1890, Mary M. Sterling was ordained and received credentials from the denomination. She entered into an itinerant evangelistic ministry, at one point preaching 207 sermons in 187 days.

She was so well received that she was even asked to preach the Sunday morning sermon one year at the General Conference.[53]

The Church of God (Anderson, Indiana) was another American denomination that led the way in 19th century women's ministries. From the beginning, women were prominent in ministry and in leadership. It is estimated that 25% of the movement's leaders were female. Tucker and Liefeld quote historian John Smith as writing, "Forty years before the time of women's suffrage on a national level, a great company of women were preaching, singing, writing and helping to determine the policies of this religious reform movement."[54]

A.B. Simpson, the founder of the Christian and Missionary Alliance denomination in 1887, was criticized for his "open policy" for women in ministry. His response to one of his critics was thus, "Dear brother, let the Lord manage the women. He can do it better than you, and you turn your batteries against the common enemy."[55] Yes, Mr. Simpson said it well over 100 years ago. Let's get on with fighting our common foe!

Following the Pentecostal movement

The early years of the 20th century saw little change for women within established mainline churches. However, it was a different story within the sectarian movements! They offered many opportunities for women. Some of the most influential voices in the Body of Christ during this time were those of women. The understanding that the Holy Spirit was meant to be poured out on "all flesh" opened the way for women in greater positions of ministry and leadership in churches affected by the holiness and pentecostal movements.[56] Riss records that of the 12 elders appointed to the Apostolic Faith Mission which developed out of the Azusa Street meetings, 6 were women.[57]

Marie Burgess and *Jessie Brown* were sent in 1907 by Charles Parham, one of the leaders in the Pentecostal revival, to establish a work in New York City. Revival spread from their church, Glad Tiding Hall, into other parts of New York state and New Jersey. Marie Burgess later married Robert Brown, and together they served as pastors in the city for many years.[58]

Florence Crawford preached in Portland, Oregon in 1906, where she was so successful that the pastor turned over the pastorate to her! A tremendous revival occurred at the church soon after she became the pastor, which grew to a membership of over 1,000 in 3 years. By 1966, her apostolic ministry had grown to include 42 churches serving 4,764 members.[59]

Dr. A. Maude Royden was an advocate for women's rights within the Church of England during this period. One of her contemporaries called her, the "world's greatest woman preacher." She was not allowed ordination through the Anglican church, but preached in both Anglican and free churches, became assistant pastor of a Congregational church in London, founded an independent mission work with another pastor, established a radio ministry and conducted preaching and lecture tours in the United States, Australia, New Zealand, India and China. She wrote a number of books, including *The Church and Women*. A staunch Anglican all her life, she remained optimistic about increasing freedom for women to minister within the Church.[60]

Aimee Semple McPherson, senior pastor of the famed Angelus Temple in Los Angeles, California and founder of the International Church of the Foursquare Gospel denomination, was one of the most influential church leaders of the early 20th century. *Time* magazine called her "the most spectacular woman U.S. evangelist since Billy Sunday."[61] She began her ministry on the mission field in Hong Kong with her husband Robert Semple. Upon his death, she returned to the United States, where she married Harold "Mack" McPherson. She gained a reputation as an evangelist in many parts of eastern Canada and along the eastern seaboard of the United States. She and her husband eventually divorced, but Aimee's reputation as an evangelist continued to grow. Her meetings in Montreal in 1920 were described as "the greatest revival in the history of Quebec."[62] She conducted her first healing service in 1921 which proved to be a turning point in her ministry. From there, she established the Angelus Temple in Los Angeles. By the mid-1980s, the number of Foursquare churches had risen to almost 800 and the number of foreign mission stations to 2,000.[63] Before her death, she had personally baptized over 100,000 people.[64]

Mid-century women church leaders

Probably the most well-known woman preacher of the mid-20th century was *Kathryn Kuhlman* who began a ministry in 1946 which continued until her death in 1976. Many present day church leaders claim to have been greatly influenced by the ministry of Kathryn Kuhlman, including Benny Hinn [65] and Roberts Liardon [66] In the 1920s, she began preaching at the age of 16, and carried on an evangelistic ministry for decades. She was also involved in the founding of the Denver Revival Tabernacle in 1935.

Kathryn began preaching divine healing and holding healing services in 1947. The healings that took place launched her into a 30 year healing ministry, although she was never officially involved with the leaders of the 1940s Healing Movement. [67] She was often criticized for her flamboyance and for her ministry as a woman. These efforts only increased interest in her meetings, however. After one particularly scathing attack upon her in Ohio, more than 20,000 people attended her meeting the following Sunday. [68] Kuhlman was an ordained minister who baptized, performed marriages and conducted funerals. She was known as a "strong leader who demanded high performance from those who worked with her." [69]

Henrietta Mears came into the limelight in the mid-1940s. She began as director of Christian Education at First Presbyterian Church of Hollywood, California. It has been said "she spoke with the authority of a person who had just stepped from the presence of God." [70] In two-and-a-half years, she increased the Sunday School enrollment from 450 to over 4,000. She was a well respected Bible teacher who, according to one source, "produced more than one generation of some of the most prominent Presbyterian ministers in America." Some of her more well-known proteges included Bill Bright, the founder of Campus Crusade for Christ and Dick Halverson, pastor of an influential Presbyterian Church in Washington D.C. [71] She was the developer of the Forest Home Conference Center which impacted university students from around the country, sending them home with a determination to win their fellow students to Christ. [72] When demands for her Sunday School curriculum began to come in from all over the country, she founded the well-known publishing house, Gospel Light Publications.[73]

Myrtle Beall pastored an Assembly of God church in Detroit, Michigan. She was an important leader in the Latter Rain Movement of the late 1940s and early 1950s. From her church, revival spread to many other congregations in the United States. Riss says that what happened at her church precipitated a *nationwide* revival.[74] This revival had a lasting impact upon Charismatics and Penecostals outside of denominations, and became an important influence in the Charismatic Renewal of the 1960s and 1970s.[75]

Latter years of the twentieth century

Since the 1960s, there have been so many women involved in teaching, preaching and leading churches in the Body of Christ, that it would be very difficult to select only a few to highlight. This list includes women from around the world. Where would we begin?

At the same time, however, it may be important to share an alarming trend brought to public attention by Ruth A. Tucker, a well respected Church historian who is on the faculty of several Bible schools and seminaries. She has voiced concern over a trend she sees in evangelical circles. "It is often assumed," she writes, "that opportunities for women in ministry have expanded over the past century ... Interestingly, an almost opposite trend has occurred over the past century in most 'sectarian' evangelical bodies." She goes on to give an example from a book by Janette Hassey. The example involved a letter in the 1927 Moody Bible Institute (MBI) *Alumni News* from 1913 graduate, Mabel C. Thomas. Ms. Thomas, who was called to pastor a church in Kansas, praised MBI saying that she "could not have met the many and varied opportunities for service" without her training there. Tucker then reveals that female students at MBI and other evangelical institutions are today barred from pastoral training courses because of their gender. She asks *why* such an enormous shift has occurred since the turn of century in these circles and answers with one word, "institutionalism". She goes on to explain, "In their formative years virtually all sectarian movements throughout Church history have depended upon the ministry of women and lay men. But once these groups become established and seek to legitimize their ministry, women ... are excluded from office and leadership roles."[76]

While Tucker identifies this trend in evangelical circles, we can point to a different trend in mainline denominations, as well as pentecostal/charismatic denominations and networks. Not everyone advocates the involvement of women in ministry for biblical reasons, however. I have noticed that frequently, the reasons given seem to have more to do with sociological conformity and a desire to be politically correct than they do with a commitment to what the Bible teaches. My personal conviction is that if we are going to support the involvement of women in ministry, let's do it for the right reason! Let's be upfront about our commitment to the inerrancy of the Scriptures and our understanding of God's purposes for women that we see revealed in the Scriptures. Otherwise, we just reinforce the misunderstanding and confusion that continues to permeate the issue of women in ministry. My hope is that this book will be one of many resources enabling Christian men and women to offer sound biblical justification for their support of women in teaching, preaching and leadership roles within the Church.

Summary

A surprising number of women were used by the Lord as leaders, preachers and teachers in the post-Reformation era. Even as early as the 16th century, women were thrust into positions of ministry, with the full support of their husbands. Many of these women were also prolific writers, writing pamphlets, tracts, books and even multi-volume commentaries on the Scriptures. Large numbers of these women were also imprisoned for their unswerving commitment to the Lord and determination to respond to the leading of His Holy Spirit.

These women preachers were frequently invited to preach and given a platform by the male founders and leaders of sectarian movements. These same sectarian groups, now established evangelical denominations, today frequently restrict women's involvement in ministry more than they did at the beginning of the century. The question arises, "Are we moving forward or backwards?" Ruth Tucker identifies the institutionalization of these groups as the primary reason for the decreasing liberty of women within their ranks to lead, preach or teach. This is just a repeat of the same pattern which has occurred throughout Church history, beginning in the second century with the institutionalization of the Church birthed at Pentecost!

On a more encouraging note, however, it was pointed out that there is a different trend within mainline and charismatic/ pentecostal circles. More and more women are being recognized by these churches as able ministers, and released into ministry with the blessing and support of the churches and church leaders.

A caution was brought that we base our support of women's ministry not on a desire to stay current with modern trends, but on what the Bible says. It is important that we offer sound biblical justification for our position in order to avoid further contribution to the misunderstanding and confusion surrounding the issue of women in ministry.

Chapter 15 notes

[1] Edith Deen, *Great Women of the Christian Faith* (Harper and Row Publisher, 1959, reprinted by Barbour and Company, Uhrichsville, OH), p. 107.

[2] Ruth A. Tucker and Walter Liefeld, *Daughters of the Church* (Zondervan, Grand Rapids, 1987), p. 221.

[3] Edith Deen, *Great Women of the Christian Faith* (Harper and Row Publisher, 1959, reprinted by Barbour and Company, Uhrichsville, OH), p. 114.

[4] Ruth A. Tucker and Walter Liefeld, *Daughters of the Church* (Zondervan, Grand Rapids, 1987), p. 223.

[5] Edith Deen, *Great Women of the Christian Faith* (Harper and Row Publisher, 1959, reprinted by Barbour and Company, Uhrichsville, OH), p. 116.

[6] Ibid.

[7] Ibid., p. 117.

[8] Lorry Lutz, *Women As Risk-Takers for God* (World Evangelical Fellowship in assoc. with Paternoster Publishing, Carlisle, Cumbria, 1997), p. 15.

9 Ruth A. Tucker and Walter Liefeld, *Daughters of the Church* (Zondervan, Grand Rapids, 1987), p. 230.

10 Lorry Lutz, *Women As Risk-Takers for God* (World Evangelical Fellowship in assoc. with Paternoster Publishing, Carlisle, Cumbria, 1997), p. 16.

11 Ruth A. Tucker and Walter Liefeld, *Daughters of the Church* (Zondervan, Grand Rapids, 1987), p. 230.

12 Ibid., p. 232.

13 Edith Deen, *Great Women of the Christian Faith* (Harper and Row Publisher, 1959, reprinted by Barbour and Company, Uhrichsville, OH), p. 130.

14 Ibid., p. 131.

15 Ibid., p. 136.

16 Ruth A. Tucker and Walter Liefeld, *Daughters of the Church* (Zondervan, Grand Rapids, 1987), p. 214.

17 Ibid., p. 215.

18 Ibid., p. 216.

19 Ibid., p. 215.

20 Ibid., p. 216.

21 Edith Deen, *Great Women of the Christian Faith* (Harper and Row Publisher, 1959, reprinted by Barbour and Company, Uhrichsville, OH), p. 139.

22 Ruth A. Tucker and Walter Liefeld, *Daughters of the Church* (Zondervan, Grand Rapids, 1987), p. 258.

23 Ibid., p. 261.

24 Richard M. Riss, *A Survey of 20th Century Revival Movements in North America* (Hendrickson Publishers, Peabody, MA, 1988), pp. 18–19.

25 Ruth A. Tucker and Walter Liefeld, *Daughters of the Church* (Zondervan, Grand Rapids, 1987), p. 262.

26 Ibid., p. 263.

27 Ibid., p. 264.

28 Roger J. Green, *Catherine Booth* (Baker Book House, Grand Rapids, 1996; reprinted by Monarch Publications, Great Britain), pp. 23, 29, 32, 36–37.

29 Ibid., pp. 92–93.

30 Ibid., p. 97.

31 Ibid., p. 143.

[32] Ibid., p. 159.

[33] Ibid., pp. 169–171.

[34] Ibid., pp. 174–175.

[35] Edith Deen, *Great Women of the Christian Faith* (Harper and Row Publisher, 1959, reprinted by Barbour and Company, Uhrichsville, OH), p. 218.

[36] Ruth A. Tucker and Walter Liefeld, *Daughters of the Church* (Zondervan, Grand Rapids, 1987), p. 265.

[37] Edith Deen, *Great Women of the Christian Faith* (Harper and Row Publisher, 1959, reprinted by Barbour and Company, Uhrichsville, OH), p. 379.

[38] Richard M. Riss, *A Survey of 20th Century Revival Movements in North America* (Hendrickson Publishers, Peabody, MA, 1988), pp. 21–22.

[39] Ibid., p. 18.

[40] Ibid., pp. 22–23, 78.

[41] Ibid., pp. 23–24, 74.

[42] Ibid., pp. 26–27.

[43] Ruth A. Tucker and Walter Liefeld, *Daughters of the Church* (Zondervan, Grand Rapids, 1987), pp. 270–271.

[44] Ibid., pp. 276–277.

[45] Ibid., pp. 272–274.

[46] Edith Deen, *Great Women of the Christian Faith* (Harper and Row Publisher, 1959, reprinted by Barbour and Company, Uhrichsville, OH), p. 378.

[47] Ruth A. Tucker and Walter Liefeld, *Daughters of the Church* (Zondervan, Grand Rapids, 1987), pp. 280–281.

[48] Ibid., p. 279.

[49] Ibid., p. 285.

[50] Ibid., pp. 281, 286.

[51] Ibid., p. 286.

[52] Ibid., pp. 286–287.

[53] Ibid., p. 287.

[54] Ibid., p. 288.

[55] Ibid., pp. 287–288.

[56] Ibid., p. 359.

[57] Richard M. Riss, *A Survey of 20th Century Revival Movements in North America* (Hendrickson Publishers, Peabody, MA, 1988), p. 59.

[58] Ibid., pp. 66, 80.

[59] Ibid., p. 70.

[60] Ruth A. Tucker and Walter Liefeld, *Daughters of the Church* (Zondervan, Grand Rapids, 1987), pp. 378–379.

[61] Ibid., p. 365.

[62] Richard M. Riss, *A Survey of 20th Century Revival Movements in North America* (Hendrickson Publishers, Peabody, MA, 1988), pp. 86–87.

[63] Ruth A. Tucker and Walter Liefeld, *Daughters of the Church* (Zondervan, Grand Rapids, 1987), p. 367.

[64] Michal Ann Goll, *Women on the Front Lines*, Destiny Image Publishers, Shippensburg, PA, 1999), p. 89.

[65] Benny Hinn, *Good Morning Holy Spirit* (Thomas Nelson Publishers, Nashville, TN, 1990), pp. 2–13.

[66] Roberts Lairdon, *God's Generals* (Albury Publishing, Tulsa, OK, 1996), p. 271.

[67] Richard M. Riss, *A Survey of 20th Century Revival Movements in North America* (Hendrickson Publishers, Peabody, MA, 1988), pp. 102, 110–111.

[68] Ruth A. Tucker and Walter Liefeld, *Daughters of the Church* (Zondervan, Grand Rapids, 1987), pp. 392–393.

[69] Ibid., p. 393.

[70] Richard M. Riss, *A Survey of 20th Century Revival Movements in North America* (Hendrickson Publishers, Peabody, MA, 1988), p. 127.

[71] Ruth A. Tucker and Walter Liefeld, *Daughters of the Church* (Zondervan, Grand Rapids, 1987), pp. 393–394.

[72] Richard M. Riss, *A Survey of 20th Century Revival Movements in North America* (Hendrickson Publishers, Peabody, MA, 1988), p. 128.

[73] Ruth A. Tucker and Walter Liefeld, *Daughters of the Church* (Zondervan, Grand Rapids, 1987), p. 394.

[74] Richard M. Riss, *A Survey of 20th Century Revival Movements in North America* (Hendrickson Publishers, Peabody, MA, 1988), pp. 117–118.

[75] Ibid., p. 124.

[76] Ruth A. Tucker, "How Faith Mission Pioneers Understood Women's Roles", *Priscilla Papers* (Christians For Biblical Equality, Volume 10, Number 2, Spring 1996), p. 1.

Chapter 16

Restoration and Blessing

"Behold, I will do a new thing,
now it shall spring forth;
Shall you not know it?
I will even make a road in the wilderness
and rivers in the desert."
(Isaiah 43:19)

God is always doing a new thing! Because He is always moving us towards completion, perfection, and purity, we are constantly undergoing a process of restoration and renewal. Like the Israelites following the cloud by day and the pillar of fire by night in the wilderness, following the Lord means leaving former things behind and embracing the new. It means being willing to move on to a new place as we endeavor to follow the leading of the Holy Spirit – a new place of understanding and revelation, a new place of vision, and a new place of practice. I believe that many of the problems we see in the Church today in terms of our ineffectiveness, our inability to manifest the heart and the power of God, and our irrelevance to the world around us, are the result of camping around various watering holes in the wilderness journey since the Reformation. Times of revival, renewal, and moves of God in the past have been like watering holes that released the many sectarian movements which have become today's denominations and church networks. We have stopped at various places in the journey towards oneness in Christ, saying in effect, "Well, we've come far enough. We've arrived." We have not been willing to move on to follow the presence of the Lord when He has tried to take us further.

Acts 3:20–21 tells us that heaven must retain, hold, or keep Jesus until the restoration of all things which God has spoken through His prophets since the world began. Jesus isn't coming back until God's restoration process is complete. The Lord still has a great deal of restoring to do! As the Body of Christ, we haven't advanced since the first century. That statement might come as a surprise to many. But the reality of the situation is that we are still recapturing much of the life and power that was lost by the Church in the Dark Ages.

The health of the body

The Church is not healthier than it was in the first century. In fact, institutionalism has made it corrupt and diseased. So many parts of the Body aren't working that it is largely incapacitated. The members which are working often aren't working together. Rather, they are frequently working against each other – pulling and pushing and competing with one another while the world looks on in confusion and disgust. We are a grotesque caricature of what the Body should be!

The Divine Physician desires to bring healing and wholeness to the Body of Christ, both individually and corporately. He longs to set us free from every chain of bondage, even those chains we have put upon ourselves. He is passionate in His love and desire for us, and wants to see each member of the Body be all that we were created to be. He waits with anticipation to see each member of the Body fulfill their divine purpose and destiny. As individual members step into and begin to walk in this purpose and destiny, the corporate vision that God has for the Body of Christ will be fulfilled. He has ordained a process of restoration for His Church, but it requires our cooperation.

When are we going to listen to the Lord and follow His prescriptions? The need to submit to God's plan and process of restoration is imperative in this hour. He's coming for a Bride without spot or wrinkle. Our own efforts have so bound and contorted us that we cannot function the way He ordained the Body to function, and our robes of righteousness look like twisted, wrinkled rags. We have stabbed and cut to pieces *our own members*. The Church is filled with people who are not functioning according to their giftings and callings because we have limited them to only those functions *that we have deemed appropriate* to their age, gender, or level of training. The Church is trying to operate according to operating manuals written *by the Church*. We need the mind of the Lord. We need His heart. We need so desperately to understand His ways and His purposes!

The Word and the Holy Spirit

We must come back to a place where we give equal emphasis to the Word of God and the Spirit of God. I see churches that preach the Word and make no room for the Spirit. They are dry, rigid and often miss the heart of God. The letter without the Spirit kills, doesn't it? These churches are raising up modern-day Pharisees who go through all the right motions and then miss Jesus when He shows up. They are not tuned into the Spirit of God who came to reveal Jesus. I also see segments of the Church who are bouncing off the ceilings "in the Spirit", but have no foundation in the Word to keep their feet on the ground. There is no ability to judge what is of God and what is not. There is no capacity to judge between the holy and the profane, because they don't know the Word. We desperately need to come back to a place of *balance*, where we give equal place to the Word and the Spirit!

In giving equal place to the Word, however, it is still import-ant that we rely on the Holy Spirit for our interpretation and understanding of the Word. If we do not, we are merely teaching the doctrines of men and calling it "Bible". Jesus spoke of this very situation when He lamented in Mark 7:7, *"in vain do they worship me, teaching for doctrines the command-ments of men"* (KJV). It is imperative that we depend upon the Holy Spirit and be led by Him in our study of Scripture. Susan Hyatt ends her book, *In the Spirit We're Equal* with a plea:

> "the need is obvious and the need is now ... it demands that we – both men and women – bring our theologies, our attitudes, and our actions into agreement with the Author of the Book – the Holy Spirit." [1]

Because we have *not* been listening to the Holy Spirit, He is quenched in our services. We *go* to church but we don't know how to *be* the Church. A large segment of the Body of Christ is forbidden to operate in their giftings and callings, and we are trying to operate according to a secular system of organization and government which has killed much of the life the Church had once had. Many of the sectarian groups which were spawned by past seasons of revival or renewal, and have become established denominations or networks, have lost to institutionalism the life of the Spirit they once possessed. C. Peter Wagner comments on the dysfunctional nature of the modern Church as he opens his book, *Churchquake!*, "Structures that were originally developed to facilitate the evangelism, Christian nurture, worship, social service and ministry in general are now considered by some as the *causes* of much inefficiency and ineffectiveness in the same areas. Dysfunctionalism has been setting in." [2] He goes on to list and discuss institutional factors that have caused and perpetuated denominational decline. [3]

Organism not organization

The Body of Christ was meant to function as an organism, not an organization. It was only in the second and third centuries that man's ways began to prevail, and the Church became structured more like the Roman civil government. Previously, it functioned as a living, growing organism. *How* did the Church function in the first century?

First, leaders operated out of a servanthood model, not an authority model. The servanthood model is based on Jesus' definition of leadership. He did not come to be served but to serve, by laying down his life for others (Matthew 20:28). He also told His disciples that if they desired to be first or to lead, then they must be willing to put their own interests last and be the servant of all (Mark 9:35). The servanthood model is not hierarchical with the leader at the top telling everyone else what to do. Instead the leader is underneath, lifting everyone else up and encouraging them forward to release them into God's plan and purpose for their lives.

Secondly, members of the Body in the first century functioned primarily according to giftings and callings rather than according to human assignments of title or position. Because the Holy Spirit was directing and coordinating everything, the members of the Body functioned smoothly and efficiently together towards the common goal of reaching the lost and hurting people around them with the good news.

Finally, the early Church was *united*. Luke's account, called the Acts of the Apostles, records eight different times that the people were "in one accord". They were joined together in fellowship through the blood of Jesus, and were of one mind and spirit.

The Church was *not* focused on perpetuating an institution like it is today. It's a sad fact that there is so much empire building happening in the Church these days. Many local fellowships and networks of churches focus almost solely on building their own empires, expending huge amounts of effort and using any justification to perpetuate the institution. People are used to build ministry, rather than ministry being used to build people. Local churches compete with one another for what they consider to be their piece of the pie. What has happened to the biblical concept of working together to build the kingdom of God? I'm reminded of Paul's words to the church at Philippi, urging them, *"fulfill my joy by being like-minded, having the same love, being of one accord, of one mind. Let nothing be done through selfish ambition or conceit, but in lowliness of mind let each esteem others better than himself."*

While there is much more cooperative effort today than there was twenty years ago, there are still dividing walls in the Body of Christ – between denominations, between Charismatics and Evangelicals, between local churches in the same city, between clergy and laity, between generations, between races, and between the genders. However, God's plan and purpose is to break down the dividing walls. Paul's words in Ephesians 2:11–18 reveal God's plan to reconcile Jews and Gentiles into one body and one man. However, this is the heart of the Father with regard to *every* place of separation and alienation in the Body of Christ. He is working to bring reconciliation and restoration, that in Christ we might be as one man:

> *"For He Himself is our peace, who has made both one, and has broken down the middle wall of separation ... so as to create in Himself one new man from the two, thus making peace, and*

> *that He might reconcile them both to God in one body through the cross, thereby putting to death the enmity."*
>
> (Ephesians 2:14–16)

The walls of separation that exist in the Church are given support posts in the form of the institutionalism that has crept in over the centuries. Institutionalism and authority-based models help to hold these walls in place. A friend recently gave me information from an article in the *Reader in Christian Education*. Some of the differences between institutionalized and Spirit-led Christianity were identified. Institutionalism leads to a focus on order, authority, government, rationality, hierarchy and officialdom. In contrast the Holy Spirit and revival lead to a focus on the things of the Spirit, freedom, spontaneity, heart issues, relationships and equality.[4]

Re-digging the ancient wells

I like what Michael Mitton shared in his book about Celtic Christianity. He contrasts the Roman and Celtic churches and points out a number of differences, which primarily arose out of the institutional nature and hierarchical structure of the Roman Church. He describes the Celtic leaders as being unworldly, immaterialistic, humble, caring shepherds of their flocks who said, "Do as I do", and hoped to be *followed*. In contrast, the Roman leaders said, "Do as I say", and expected to be *obeyed*. He describes them as worldly, materialistic, glorying in pomp, and as monarchs rather than shepherds of their dioceses.[5] As shown in Chapter 9, there is ample evidence to support that Celtic Christianity was the product of a purer form of Christianity than the Roman form. The Lord is calling us to put aside our institutional mentality and re-dig some ancient wells to tap into the pure stream of His Spirit. I don't think we will truly rediscover that stream until we are willing to set aside the traditions of man and our own ways of thinking.

When we are willing to divest ourselves of everything that is not from God, then we will finally see the Body begin to function the way God ordained it to function. We will begin to see the Church come into the measure of the fullness of the stature of Christ (Ephesians 4:13) as each joint or member supplies what God has given them to contribute to the whole. Interestingly enough, when Paul speaks of God giving gifts to *men* of pastors, teachers, prophets, apostles and evangelists to equip the saints for the work of the ministry in Ephesians 4:8–12, he actually speaks of gifts given to mankind, the Greek word *anthropos*. He gives both men and women these gifts that they might be equipped for the work of the ministry. All the saints are to be equipped for ministry – young, old, educated, uneducated, men, women, mature, and immature. The apostle doesn't make any distinction!

Dismantling the prison walls – setting women free

While every denomination or Christian group gives mental assent to the fact that the saints are to be equipped for ministry, Church practice reveals that so many restrictions and limitations have been placed upon God's people that they rarely *are* equipped for ministry. One well known prophetic minister recently declared that less than 10% of the Body of Christ know what their calling is, and fewer still are equipped or released to serve in this calling. With regards to women in particular, I see a number of reasons for this difference in theory and practice within the various Christian streams.

The first reason focuses on the man–woman alienation that began at the time of fall. Sin has created a barrier between the genders, fueled by fear and competition for control. I appreciate J. Julius Scott's honesty. In his paper, which looks at women in the Second Temple period of Judaism, he admits that women have often been put in a restricted position because "...the protection of male positions of dominance and power and the fear of losing them have and do play a part."[6] Dave Bilborough, one of the foremost songwriters and worship leaders in Britain today, has confessed, "In the recent past of the house church movement there was much emphasis on women submitting to men and men always being right. This was often sourced in insecurity..."[7] As mentioned earlier, the authority-based models which the Church has been operating under have contributed to keeping the barriers between men and women in place. Lorry Lutz shares some information developed by Linda Smith of Ontario Bible College and Seminary. In her seminars, Linda explains how the power-based model creates a tension between men and women. "Men then fear encouraging the 'power' of women and women resist the 'power' of men." She goes on to conclude that we need a paradigm that fosters servanthood, not dominance.[8]

I believe the second reason women and others have been so restricted in the Church has to do with our concepts of ministry and leadership. For many, ministry is something grand, and only for the privileged few. It is seen as something to attain, some lofty goal that can only be reached by meeting certain special requirements. But this kind of thinking is all skewed! Jesus defined ministry as serving. He didn't elevate it like we do as something glorious for the exalted few who "qualify". The kind of men He chose as His disciples should show us who qualifies! They were ordinary men, rough, with very few skills and many weaknesses. When Jesus defined His ministry in Mark 10:45, He used the word *diakoneo*, which means "to minister or to serve". Ministry equals servanthood or service in the original language of the New Testament. Further, according to Jesus, "leadership" also means servanthood, not exercising authority. He said in Mark 10:42–43 (emphasis added),

> *"You know that those who are considered rulers over the Gentiles lord it over them, and **their great ones exercise authority over them. Yet it shall not be so among you;** but whoever desires to become great among you shall be your servant. And whoever of you desires to be first shall be slave of all."*

We've adopted the secular concept of leadership somewhere along the way. For this reason, we are comfortable with women serving as ushers, but not with them "serving" the Church by leading. We are quite willing to allow the ladies to serve as Sunday School teachers or on the hospitality committee but we don't want them to "serve" from a pulpit by preaching. There is absolutely no difference, according to Jesus! *We* have created the categories and the limitations put upon women through our own humanistic systemization and human reasoning, all rooted in the pagan philosophy of the Greeks!

The third reason I see for the restrictions placed upon women in the Church is the result of our misunderstanding of what the

Scriptures teach. For so long, many of us have been taught things that were just not true to the heart of God or the original language of the Scriptures. It's a bit like evolution. The myths in both cases have been taught for so long as fact that everyone just *assumes* they are true! The Scriptures actually teach that women were created equal in power, authority, and dignity as God's ambassadors on the earth. They teach that women, like men, were redeemed from the curse of sin and the effects of the fall by the blood of Jesus. They teach that women are called to serve God and to minister by the leading and empowerment of the Holy Spirit.

The three issues discussed above have been interwoven together by unseen evil hands to hold women captive in the Church and build a wall of separation and imprisonment which has kept women feeling like second class citizens in the Body of Christ. The alienation between the genders and the false concepts of ministry and leadership are like bricks in the wall, with the theological justification as the mortar holding it all together. If we can chip out the mortar, by exposing the faulty theological arguments, then perhaps we can make room for the Spirit of God to come in and dismantle the prison walls.

A final consideration here is a *self-imposed* restriction placed upon women in the Church. Because of fear and intimidation, many women will not rise to answer the callings upon their lives, even when the liberty exists to do so. Michal Ann Goll offers a poignant personal account of her battle against intimidation in her book *Women On The Front Lines*. She urges us, "Don't let your fears stand in the way of your dreams! Take out the spike of intimidation and, like the Israelite woman Jael did to the Philistine Sisera in Judges 4, drive it into the enemy's head and kill the plans and schemes he has devised against you."[9] We will not find ourselves free to take our places in the body of Christ until we are willing to confront the fear and intimidation that hold us captive.

Answering the call – men and women

Making room for the Holy Spirit to dismantle the prison walls around God's women requires a number of things from all of us. We must come to the end of ourselves, being willing to trade

our wills for His. Honesty and humility are required on our part
so that we can confess our failures and our sin to Him. We must
submit to Him and invite Him to take control. We also need a
passionate desire for Him to change us, renew us, and fill us
again with all that He is! Making room for the Holy Spirit also
requires obedience when He leads one way and our training
leads us another. Our call to obedience means we are faced on a
moment by moment basis with the choice of whom we will
serve, the choice of life or death and the choice between
blessing or cursing.

We stand today on the brink of not just another reformation,
but a spiritual revolution. The call awaits us! Will we answer it?
Will we respond to the Spirit of God? Will we follow the cloud
of His Divine Presence or will we stay camped around our
particular watering hole in the wilderness, hoping it won't run
dry? My heartfelt prayer is that the Church will arise and shake
herself from the dust (Isaiah 52:1–2). We have the accumula-
tion of dirt from almost two thousand years weighing us down.
But we can be washed and cleansed by the fresh, life-giving
blood of the Lamb, if we will only come to Him and respond to
the voice of His Spirit who cries, "Arise!" As God led His people
from the bondage of Egypt to the blessing of the Promised Land,
so He endeavors today to bring us, His Bride, from bondage to
blessing. Precious saints, will we put our hands in His and allow
Him to lead us?

Chapter 16 notes

[1] Susan C. Hyatt, *In the Spirit We're Equal* (Hyatt Press, Dallas, 1998), p. 302.

[2] C. Peter Wagner, *Churchquake!* (Regal Books, a division of Gospel Light Publishing, Ventura, 1999), p. 6.

[3] Ibid., pp. 23–28.

[4] Finley B. Edge, "Experiential or Institutionalized Religion", *Reader in Christian Education*, Eugene S. Gibbs, Ed. (Baker, Grand Rapids, 1992), pp. 212–213.

[5] Michael Mitton, *Restoring the Woven Cord* (Darton, Longman and Todd, Ltd., London, 1995), p. 15.

6 J. Julius Scott, Jr., unpublished paper, Wheaton College Graduate School, "Women in Second Temple Judaism: Some Preliminary Observations".

7 Joan Martin, *Is Leadership Male?* (Nelson Word Publishing, Milton Keyes, England, 1996), p. 179.

8 Lorry Lutz, *Women As Risk-Takers for God* (World Evangelical Fellowship in assoc. with Paternoster Publishing, Carlisle, Cumbria, 1997), p. 257.

9 Michal Ann Goll, *Women On The Front Lines* (Destiny Image Publishers, Shippensburg, PA, 1999), p. 16.

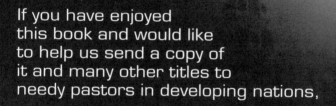

If you have enjoyed
this book and would like
to help us send a copy of
it and many other titles to
needy pastors in developing nations,

please write for further information,
or send your gift to:

Sovereign World Trust
PO Box 777
Tonbridge
Kent TN11 0ZS
United Kingdom

www.sovereignworldtrust.com